THE
LIVING
PAST
WESTERN HISTORIOGRAPHICAL TRADITIONS

THE LIVING PAST

WESTERN HISTORIOGRAPHICAL TRADITIONS

Alfred J. Andrea
Wolfe W. Schmokel

University of Vermont

John Wiley & Sons, Inc.
New York London Sydney Toronto

Library of Congress Cataloging in Publication Data

   1. World history—Addresses, essays, lectures.
2. Historiography—Addresses, essays, lectures.
I. Andrea, Alfred J., 1941–   II. Schmokel,
Wolfe W.

D21.3.L58   909   75-12680
ISBN 0-471-02914-9

Printed in the United States of America

10 9 8 7 6 5 4 3 2 1

To
Paul D. Evans
friend—colleague—historian

PREFACE

This anthology illustrates how different generations of Western man have perceived and written about the past. Its underlying assumption is that every age views the past in relation to its own attitudes, problems, and categories of thought.

During the last decade, teachers of history at every level have been challenged by students to make their courses relevant. Some students and educators have claimed that the study of history is of little interest or use, since it can never be made relevant (presumably to action that occurs here and now). History has been accused of offering nothing more than a grab bag of useless facts about dead people and events that are better forgotten. This kind of criticism indicates the serious purpose of the people who raise it, but it also betrays a common misunderstanding of the nature of historical study. History is inescapably relevant to any society that writes and teaches it because every society perceives the past in relationship to itself, and every historian is able to understand and interpret the past only within the context of his personal experiences. The fact that cultural environment conditions both a historian's choice of subject matter and the manner in which he treats it means that no historian is coldly objective (whatever that means) or presents the "facts" of history without impressing his personality upon them. But this does not mean that history is bunk and that all historical writing is equally biased and worthless. Although no historian can be objective, he can be honest and strive to uncover and perceive the truth insofar as he and his society see it. Moreover, a historian, whether he realizes it or not, asks questions of the past that illuminate the conditions and concerns of the present.

We have assembled a collection of chronologically arranged excerpts from the writings of many historians who express, in their accounts of the past, certain important trends in Western thought and experience. Hence, this anthology may serve to deepen the reader's understanding of the general intellectual and social development of Western civilization, as reflected in its changing perceptions of historical reality.

This book has another purpose: Historians have long been divided on the reasons for the study of history. While every historian explains the past to his contemporaries by presenting it in the terms of his own age, there are also certain general, almost timeless, attitudes and approaches to history that seem to recur in the works of historians of all ages. These themes, for instance, the tendency to present history as a moral guide and example, the predisposition to depict the past (and the present) as movement toward a fixed, metahistorical goal, and the striving for "objectivity," provide certain unifying elements to the writing of history throughout the ages of Western Civilization. In introducing readers to these elements in Western historiography, we hope that they will formulate their own answers to the question of the proper purpose and end of historical study.

We have not attempted to make this book an anthology on the philosophy of history. We have excluded from it writings that are primarily devoted to reflections on the nature of the discipline and the meaning of temporal human existence. What we present here are the actual products of historians, that is, specific accounts of past events. While these accounts, inevitably and implicitly, are informed by many different schools of philosophical opinion, this book does not do justice to the variety of philosophical thought addressed to the question "What is history?" (And thus, "What is the meaning of man's life?") Nevertheless, this volume will be useful as an ancillary text in philosophy of history courses, since it offers examples of the practical influence and concrete expression of the abstract ideas of philosophers.

Clearly, this book is not intended as a guide to historical methodology or to the stylistic elements of historical writing, although students will be able to learn from it something about the different methods of investigation and analysis employed by historians, and about the kinds of writing that have served as effective vehicles for the presentation of ideas about the past. Many of the historians included here, however, definitely should not be considered as models to be emulated by contemporary students, either as to method or style.

Finally, the book is not a survey of the "great" historians. If it were, the selections would be different ones. To be sure, a number of the authors whose works have been included qualify for the mantle of greatness. Others, however, do not by any standard. In making our selections we have been guided mainly by the desire to choose illustrations representative of a particular period's world view, values, and modes of perception and analysis.

The brief introductions to the chapters and to the individual selections link the texts and their authors to the general developments and intellectual climate of their times. Certainly, they cannot do justice to the complexity of the intellectual developments of several millennia. We trust, however, that our generalizations have not done violence to the historical past.

We thank Wayne Anderson and the staff of Wiley for their help in the development of this project, Carolyn Perry and Helen Riendeau for able clerical assistance, our patient wives for their good humor, and the following historians for their helpful suggestions:

Ilse N. Bulhof, University of Texas

Peter Reill, University of California, Los Angeles

G. A. Crump, Louisiana State University

C. Warren Hollister, University of California, Santa Barbara

Michael Ligget, Mount St. Mary's College

Allen W. Dirrim, California State University, Northridge

Robin Schlunk, University of Vermont

All errors of fact or interpretation are, of course, our sole responsibility.

Alfred J. Andrea
Wolfe W. Schmokel

CONTENTS

6. THE HIGH MIDDLE AGES

7. THE FOURTEENTH AND FIFTEENTH CENTURIES

8. THE CONFESSIONAL AGE

9. THE SEVENTEENTH CENTURY

14. THE TWENTIETH CENTURY

THE
LIVING
PAST

WESTERN HISTORIOGRAPHICAL TRADITIONS

1.

THE

HEBREWS

The ancient Near East was the cradle of Western civilization. Here a number of civilizations combined to produce many of the roots of Western society, one of which was historical consciousness. The following selections illustrate how a single ancient Near Eastern people, the Hebrews, created "an idea of history."

This achievement is especially impressive when we consider what a minor people they were. Numerically and politically they were fairly insignificant; chronologically their development as a civilization was relatively late. Yet, it was they and not their more impressive neighbors—the Mesopotamians, the Egyptians, the Persians—who created a consciousness of human history, thereby meriting the title, the first historians.

A historian is one who consciously perceives human existence to be an intelligible series of temporal events having an objective reality of its own, with patterns and trends that are capable and worthy of human comprehension and understanding. Many of the anonymous authors of the collection of sacred Jewish literature known as the *Old Testament* were historians according to this definition.

The other inhabitants of the ancient Near East were no less interested in comprehending the nature of human existence or in preserving records of their accomplishments. Yet, their thought was not historical; it was mythical. When considering human events, they did not think in terms of temporal cause or of trends of profane change. Myth was more than allegory; it was more than entertainment; it was certainly more than fantasy. It was the vehicle through which the vast majority of the people of the ancient Near East comprehended reality. Myth told how the gods created before all time the cosmological order, thereby establishing fixed, endlessly

1

recurrent patterns, of which man, his actions, and institutions were shadowy reflections. To put it another way, these mythmakers envisioned human time as cyclic but static. They saw a necessary harmony between man and the endless cycle of nature (which itself was divine and personal). Within this eternal circle there could be no clear distinction between past and present, between the natural and the supernatural; there certainly could be no proper or meaningful change. These myth centered people simply believed the human condition to be as it always had been and always would be, immersed totally in nature and governed by gods, whose wills and purposes were beyond human understanding; and human events had reality only in so far as they imitated or repeated arche-typal divine actions.

The Hebrews were in many respects like their neighbors. They arrived late on the Near Eastern scene, and when they finally settled down, they inhabited an area that served as the natural land bridge between the two dominant civilizations of Egypt and Mesopotamia. As one would naturally assume, they borrowed from their more advanced neighbors. They certainly shared much of the ancient Near East's mythic world view. Yet, the Hebrews remained a people apart and developed distinctive views, among which were a revolutionary concept of God and His relations with man and nature.

The God of the Hebrews became an absolutely transcendent God, who stood totally outside of nature. Because of this divine transcendence, human history now began to achieve an objective reality of its own. Yet, because of His transcendence, this God of the Hebrews also became a God of history. Human events—history—now were the stage on which the Will of God was realized and His Divine Plan worked out. Human events became part of a dynamic Linear History, and every human action and institution had a role to play in the unfolding of the Will of God. Human history now became a subject of preeminent interest and importance for those who served the God of the Hebrews.

However, if history was purposive, God's agent, man, was purposeful. His desires and purposes often ran counter to the Divine Plan. For the Hebrews, therefore, history became the story of the interplay between man and God. While history was moving forward toward God's inevitable and slowly unfolding ends, it often was a halting progress, as man's ambitions, passions, perversities, and intrinsic weaknesses delayed (but not defeated) the working out of the Divine Plan.

The excerpts contained in the three sections of this chapter illustrate the nature of the Hebrew historiographical vision and its evolution over a period of nine hundred years.

1.   EXODUS

Exodus relates the escape of the Hebrews from Egypt around 1200 B.C. and their years of slow migration into the land of Canaan, during which time they coalesced into a self-conscious people. Throughout most of this period they were led by a charismatic genius, Moses. So central was Moses to this event, for centuries he was believed to be the author of the first five books of the *Old Testament,* known collectively as the *Pentateuch.*

In fact, however, the authorship of the *Pentateuch* was very complex. These five books, of which *Exodus* is the second, appear to be products of at least four major literary-religious traditions.

The chapters of *Exodus* that appear below are basically an admixture of the two earliest and most important of these sources, which scholars have identified as J and E, because of their respective use of "Yahweh" (or "Jehovah") and "Elohim" for the name of God. J appears to have been a single genius, who around 950 B.C., during the reign of Solomon, pulled together and revised a number of disparate folk legends to create a Hebrew national epic. E was probably a priest who lived in Israel shortly before its conquest by Assyria in 722/721. Around 650 B.C., these two sources were joined into a single narrative by an unknown Judean editor, who took little care to eliminate contradictions and repetitions.

The two chapters below illustrate that for both J and E the line between myth and history, between the natural and the divine, was still shadowy at best. Direct divine intervention was a common belief in the ancient Near East and is inherent in any world view in which myths are the chief vehicle of truth.

In reading this passage the student should note the manner in which the independence of man vis-a-vis God is treated and how the concept of unique, unrepeatable "historical" events is emerging.

Chapter 3

Now Moses fed the sheep of Jethro his father in law, the priest of Madian: and he drove the flock to the inner parts of the desert, and came to the mountain of God, Horeb.

2 And the Lord appeared to him in a flame of fire out of the midst of a bush: and he saw that the bush was on fire and was not burnt....

4 And when the Lord saw that he went forward to see, he called to him out of the midst of the bush, and said: Moses, Moses. And he answered: Here I am.

5 And he said: Come not nigh hither, put off the shoes from thy feet: for the place whereon thou standest is holy ground.

6 And he said: I am the God of thy father, the God of Abraham, the God of Isaac, and the God of Jacob. Moses hid his face: for he durst not look at God.

7 And the Lord said to him: I have seen the affliction of my people in Egypt, and I have heard their cry because of the rigour of them that are over the works:

8 And knowing their sorrow, I am come down to deliver them out of the hands of the Egyptians, and to bring them out of that land into a good and spacious land, into a land that floweth with milk and honey, to the places of the Chanaanite, and Hethite, and Amorrhite, and Pherezite, and Hevite, and Jegusite.

9 For the cry of the children of Israel is come unto me: and I have seen their affliction, wherewith they are oppressed by the Egyptians.

10 But come, and I will send thee to Pharao, that thou mayst bring forth my people, the children of Israel out of Egypt.

11 And Moses said to God: Who am I that I should go to Pharao, and should bring forth the children of Israel out of Egypt?

12 And he said to him: I will be with thee: and this thou shalt have for a sign, that I have sent thee: When thou shalt have brought my people out of Egypt, thou shalt offer sacrifice to God upon this mountain.

13 Moses said to God: Lo, I shall go to the children of Israel, and say to them: The God of your fathers hath sent me to you. If they should say to me: What is his name? what shall I say to them?

14 God said to Moses: I AM WHO AM. He said: Thus shalt thou say to the children of Israel: HE WHO IS, hath sent me to you.

15 And God said again to Moses: Thus shalt thou say to the children of Israel: The Lord God of your fathers, the God of Abraham, the God of Isaac, and the God of Jacob, hath sent me to you: This is my name for ever, and this is my memorial unto all generations.

16 Go, gather together the ancients of Israel, and thou shalt say to them: The Lord God of your fathers, the God of Abraham, the God of Isaac, and the God of Jacob, hath appeared to me, saying. Visiting I have visited you: and I have seen all that hath befallen you in Egypt.

17 And I have said the word to bring you forth out of the affliction of Egypt, into the land of the Chanaanite, the Hethite, and the Amorrhite, and Pherezite, and Hevite, and Jebusite, to a land that floweth with milk and honey.

18 And they shall hear thy voice: and thou shalt go in, thou and the ancients of Israel, to the king of Egypt, and thou shalt say to him: The Lord God of the Hebrews hath called us: we will go three days' journey into the wilderness, to sacrifice unto the Lord our God.

19 But I know that the king of Egypt will not let you go, but by a mighty hand.

20 For I will stretch forth my hand, and will strike Egypt with all my wonders which I will do in the midst of them: after these he will let you go.

21 And I will give favour to this people, in the sight of the Egyptians: and when you go forth, you shall not depart empty:

22 But every woman shall ask of her neighbour, and of her that is in her house, vessels of silver and of gold, and raiment: and you shall put them on your sons and daughters, and shall spoil Egypt.

Chapter 4

Moses answered and said: They will not believe me, nor hear my voice, but they will say: The Lord hath not appeared to thee.

2 Then he said to him: What is that thou holdest in thy hand? He answered: A rod.

3 And the Lord said: Cast it down upon the ground. He cast it down, and it was turned into a serpent: so that Moses fled from it.

4 And the Lord said: Put out thy hand and take it by the tail. He put forth his hand, and took hold of it, and it was turned into a rod.

5 That they may believe, saith he, that the Lord God of their fathers, the God of Abraham, the God of Isaac, and the God of Jacob, hath appeared to thee.

6 And the Lord said again: Put thy hand into thy bosom. And when he had put it into *his* bosom, he brought it forth leprous as snow.

7 And he said: Put back thy hand into thy bosom. He put it back, and brought it out again, and it was like the other flesh.

8 If they will not believe thee, saith he, nor hear the voice of the former sign, they will believe the word of the latter sign.

9 But if they will not even believe these two signs, nor hear thy voice: take of the river water, and pour it out upon the dry land, and whatsoever thou drawest out of the river shall be turned into blood.

10 Moses said: I beseech thee, Lord, I am not eloquent from yesterday and the day before: and since thou hast spoken to thy servant, I have more impediment and slowness of tongue.

11 The Lord said to him: Who made man's mouth? or who made the dumb and the deaf, the seeing and the blind? did not I?

12 Go therefore, and I will be in thy mouth: and I will teach thee what thou shalt speak.

13 But he said: I beseech thee, Lord, send whom thou wilt send.

14 The Lord being angry at Moses, said: Aaron the Levite is thy brother, I know that he is eloquent: behold he cometh forth to meet thee, and seeing thee shall be glad at heart.

15 Speak to him, and put my words in his mouth: and I will be in thy mouth, and in his mouth, and will shew you what you must do.

16 He shall speak in thy stead to the people, and shall be thy mouth: but thou shalt be to him in those things that pertain to God.

17 And take this rod in thy hand, wherewith thou shalt do the signs.

18 Moses went his way, and returned to Jethro his father in law and said to him: I will go and return to my brethren into Egypt, that I may see if they be yet alive. And Jethro said to him: Go in peace.

19 And the Lord said to Moses, in Madian: Go, and return into Egypt: for they are all dead that sought thy life.

20 Moses therefore took his wife, and his sons, and set them upon an ass: and returned into Egypt, carrying the rod of God in his hand.

21 And the Lord said to him as he was returning into Egypt: See that thou do all the wonders before Pharao, which I have put in thy hand: I shall harden his heart, and he will not let the people go.

22 And thou shalt say to him: Thus saith the Lord: Israel is my son, my firstborn.

23 I have said to thee: Let my son go, that he may serve me, and thou wouldst not let him go: behold I will kill thy son, thy firstborn.

24 And when he was in his journey, in the inn, the Lord met him, and would have killed him.

25 Immediately Sephora took a very sharp stone, and circumcised the foreskin of her son, and touched his feet, and said: A bloody spouse art thou to me.

26 And he let him go after she had said: A bloody spouse are thou to me, because of the circumcision.

27 And the Lord said to Aaron: Go into the desert to meet Moses. And he went forth to meet him in the mountain of God, and kissed him.

28 And Moses told Aaron all the words of the Lord, by which he had sent him, and the signs that he had commanded.

29 And they came together, and they assembled all the ancients of the children of Israel.

30 And Aaron spoke all the words which the Lord had said to Moses: and he wrought the signs before the people,

31 And the people believed. And they heard that the Lord had visited the children of Israel: and that he had looked upon their affliction: and falling down they adored.

2. THE SECOND BOOK OF SAMUEL AND THE SECOND BOOK OF KINGS*

Around the middle of the eighth century B.C., a new element was introduced into the sacred literature of the Hebrews. This tradition was first expressed in *The Book of Deuteronomy* (the fifth book of the *Pentateuch*). Accordingly, biblical scholars designate it as the Deuteronomic tradition—or D for short.

Between *ca.* 750 and *ca.* 500 B.C., Deuteronomic authors revised extensively earlier versions of what we now know as *The Book of Joshua, The Book of Judges, I* and *II Samuel,* and *I Kings* and composed *The Second Book of Kings.* Collectively, these works trace the history of the Hebrews from their entry into Canaan (*ca.* 1200 B.C.) to the fall of Jerusalem and the beginning of the Babylonian Exile (587 B.C.). Running throughout these books is the basic theme of D—loving service to God (observance of the law; adherence to the covenant) results in temporal blessings, while disobedience brings swift and terrible punishment.

Such an outlook conveniently explained the dramatic fluctuations in Hebrew fortunes. The history of the Hebrews became a cycle of divine blessings and punishments within the larger framework of Yahweh's Linear History. This cycle was quite different, however, from the eternal cycles of mythology, since man exercised moral control over his earthly destiny.

The moral responsibility which D preached was both collective and individual. *I* and *II Kings* especially emphasized the theme that the Hebrews as a people were responsible for their misfortunes because of recurring infidelity to God. In similar fashion, individuals prospered or suffered in proportion to their obedient service to God. Service in both cases meant more than simple ritualism. It was ethical conduct pleasing to the Almighty.

Because individuals were now viewed as responsible moral agents, the historical works of the Deuteronomic school abound with vivid human portraits. The heroes and villains of these books are not stereotypes but complex and memorable human beings. Real people and genuine human actions became the focal point of Deuteronomic history.

*Some Roman Catholic editions of the *Bible* entitle *I* and *II Samuel* as *I* and *II Kings*. *I* and *II Kings* then become *III* and *IV Kings*.

These Deuteronomic historians certainly emphasized the central role of the Hebrews in human history and the special covenant that they had entered into with Yahweh. Yet their historical tradition tended to break away from the earlier ethnic provincialism of J and E. Deuteronomic authors explained Hebrew misfortunes as due to the Hebrews' all too eager attempts to assimilate with their Canaanite neighbors and to abandon their unique beliefs and role. However, they also viewed all humans as agents of God. The heathen Philistines, Assyrians, Babylonians, and others were used by this universal, now unique, and single God to chastise His disobedient people. In this limited manner, Deuteronomic historians wrote the first universal history.

The two excerpts below illustrate, in turn, the manner in which Deuteronomic historians wrote both biography and history on a larger scale. The first is the well known story of King David (ruled *ca.* 1005— *ca.* 1060 B.C.) and Bathsheba; the second is an account of the conquest of the Kingdom of Israel by the Assyrians in 772/721 B.C.

Chapter 11

And it came to pass at the return of the year, at the time when kings go forth to war, that David sent Joab and his servants with him, and all Israel, and they spoiled the children of Ammon, and besieged Rabba: but David remained in Jerusalem.

2 In the mean time it happened that David arose from his bed after noon, and walked upon the roof of the king's house: and he saw from the roof of his house a woman washing herself, over against him: and the woman was very beautiful.

3 And the king sent, and inquired who the woman was. And it was told him, that she was Bethsabee the daughter of Eliam, the wife of Urias the Hethite.

4 And David sent messengers, and took her, and she came in to him, and he slept with her: and presently she was purified from her uncleanness:

5 And she returned to her house having conceived. And she sent and told David, and said: I have conceived.

6 And David sent to Joab, saying: Send me Urias the Hethite. And Joab sent Urias to David.

7 And Urias came to David. And David asked how Joab did, and the people, and how the war was carried on.

8 And David said to Urias: Go into thy house, and wash thy feet. And

Urias went out from the king's house, and there went out after him a mess of meat from the king.

9 But Urias slept before the gate of the king's house, with the other servants of his lord, and went not down to his own house.

10 And it was told David by some that said: Urias went not to his house. And David said to Urias: Didst thou not come from thy journey? why didst thou not go down to thy house?

11 And Urias said to David: The ark of God and Israel and Juda dwell in tents, and my lord Joab and the servants of my lord abide upon the face of the earth: and shall I go into my house, to eat and to drink, and to sleep with my wife? By thy welfare and by the welfare of thy soul I will not do this thing.

12 Then David said to Urias: Tarry here to day, and to morrow I will send thee away. Urias tarried in Jerusalem that day and the next.

13 And David called him to eat and to drink before him, and he made him drunk: and he went out in the evening, and slept on his couch with the servants of his lord, and went not down into his house.

14 And when the morning was come, David wrote a letter to Joab: and sent it by the hand of Urias,

15 Writing in the letter: Set ye Urias in the front of the battle, where the fight is strongest: and leave ye him, that he may be wounded and die.

16 Wherefore as Joab was besieging the city, he put Urias in the place where he knew the bravest men were.

17 And the men coming out of the city, fought against Joab, and there fell some of the people of the servants of David, and Urias the Hethite was killed also.

18 Then Joab sent, and told David all things concerning the battle. . . .

26 And the wife of Urias heard that Urias her husband was dead, and she mourned for him.

27 And the mourning being over, David sent and brought her into his house, and she became his wife, and she bore him a son: and this thing which David had done, was displeasing to the Lord.

Chapter 12

And the Lord sent Nathan to David: and when he was come to him, he said to him: There were two men in one city, the one rich, and the other poor.

2 The rich man had exceeding many sheep and oxen.

3 But the poor man had nothing at all but one little ewe lamb, which he

had bought and nourished up, and which had grown up in his house together with his children, eating of his bread, and drinking of his cup, and sleeping in his bosom: and it was unto him as a daughter.

4 And when a certain stranger was come to the rich man, he spared to take of his own sheep and oxen, to make a feast for that stranger, who was come to him, but took the poor man's ewe, and dressed it for the man that was come to him.

5 And David's anger being exceedingly kindled against that man, he said to Nathan: As the Lord liveth, the man that hath done this is a child of death.

6 He shall restore the ewe fourfold, because he did this thing, and had no pity.

7 And Nathan said to David: Thou art the man. Thus saith the Lord the God of Israel: I anointed thee king over Israel, and I delivered thee from the hand of Saul,

8 And gave thee thy master's house and thy master's wives into thy bosom, and gave thee the house of Israel and Juda: and if these things be little, I shall add far greater things unto thee.

9 Why therefore hast thou despised the word of the Lord, to do evil in my sight? Thou hast killed Urias the Hethite with the sword, and hast taken his wife to be thy wife, and hast slain him with the sword of the children of Ammon.

10 Therefore the sword shall never depart from thy house, because thou hast despised me, and hast taken the wife of Urias the Hethite to be thy wife.

11 Thus saith the Lord: Behold, I will raise up evil against thee out of thy own house, and I will take thy wives before thy eyes and give them to thy neighbour, and he shall lie with thy wives in the sight of this sun.

12 For thou didst it secretly: but I will do this thing in the sight of all Israel, and in the sight of the sun.

13 And David said to Nathan: I have sinned against the Lord. And Nathan said to David: The Lord also hath taken away thy sin: thou shalt not die.

14 Nevertheless, because thou hast given occasion to the enemies of the Lord to blaspheme, for this thing, the child that is born to thee, shall surely die.

15 And Nathan returned to his house. The Lord also struck the child which the wife of Urias had borne to David, and his life was despaired of.

16 And David besought the Lord for the child: and David kept a fast, and going in by himself lay upon the ground.

17 And the ancients of his house came, to make him rise from the ground: but he would not, neither did he eat meat with them.

18 And it came to pass on the seventh day that the child died: and the ser-

vants of David feared to tell him, that the child was dead. For they said: Behold when the child was yet alive, we spoke to him, and he would not hearken to our voice: how much more will he afflict himself if we tell him that the child is dead?

19 But when David saw his servants whispering, he understood that the child was dead: and he said to his servants: Is the child dead? They answered him: He is dead.

20 Then David arose from the ground, and washed and anointed himself: and when he had changed his apparel, he went into the house of the Lord: and worshipped, and then he came into his own house, and he called for bread, and ate.

21 And his servants said to him: What thing is this that thou hast done? thou didst fast and weep for the child, while it was alive, but when the child was dead, thou didst rise up, and eat bread.

22 And he said: While the child was yet alive, I fasted and wept for him: for I said: Who knoweth whether the Lord may not give him to me, and the child may live?

23 But now that he is dead, why should I fast? Shall I be able to bring him back any more? I shall go to him rather: but he shall not return to me.

24 And David comforted Bethsabee his wife, and went in unto her, and slept with her: and she bore a son, and he called his name Solomon, and the Lord loved him.

25 And he sent by the hand of Nathan the prophet, and called his name, Amiable to the Lord, because the Lord loved him.

Chapter 17

In the twelfth year of Achaz king of Juda, Osee the son of Ela reigned in Samaria over Israel nine years.

2 And he did evil before the Lord: but not as the kings of Israel that had been before him.

3 Against him came up Salmanasar king of the Assyrians, and Osee became his servant, and paid him tribute.

4 And when the king of the Assyrians found that Osee endeavouring to rebel had sent messengers to Sua the king of Egypt, that he might not pay tribute to the king of the Assyrians, as he had done every year, he besieged him, bound him, and cast him into prison.

5 And he went through all the land: and going up to Samaria, he besieged it three years.

6 And in the ninth year of Osee, the king of the Assyrians took Samaria, and carried Israel away to Assyria: and he placed them in Hala and Habor by the river of Gozan, in the cities of the Medes.

7 For so it was that the children of Israel had sinned against the Lord their God, who brought them out of the land of Egypt, from under the hand of Pharao king of Egypt, and they worshipped strange gods.

8 And they walked according to the way of the nations which the Lord had destroyed in the sight of the children of Israel and of the kings of Israel: because they had done in like manner.

9 And the children of Israel offended the Lord their God with things that were not right: and built them high places in all their cities from the tower of the watchmen to the fenced city.

10 And they made them statues and groves on every high hill, and under every shady tree:

11 And they burnt incense there upon altars after the manner of the nations which the Lord had removed from their face: and they did wicked things, provoking the Lord.

12 And they worshipped abominations, concerning which the Lord had commanded them that they should not do this thing.

13 And the Lord testified to them in Israel and in Juda by the hand of all the prophets and seers, saying: Return from your wicked ways, and keep my precepts, and ceremonies, according to all the law which I commanded your fathers: and as I have sent to you in the hand of my servants the prophets.

14 And they hearkened not, but hardened their necks like to the neck of their fathers, who would not obey the Lord their God.

15 And they rejected his ordinances and the covenant that he made with their fathers, and the testimonies which he testified against them: and they followed vanities, and acted vainly: and they followed the nations that were round about them, concerning which the Lord had commanded them that they should not do as they did.

16 And they forsook all the precepts of the Lord their God: and made to themselves two molten calves, and groves, and adored all the host of heaven: and they served Baal.

17 And consecrated their sons, and their daughters through fire: and they gave themselves to divinations, and soothsayings: and they delivered themselves up to do evil before the Lord, to provoke him.

18 And the Lord was very angry with Israel, and removed them from his sight, and there remained only the tribe of Juda.

19 But neither did Juda itself keep the commandments of the Lord their God: but they walked in the errors of Israel, which they had wrought.

20 And the Lord cast off all the seed of Israel, and afflicted them and delivered them into the hand of spoilers, till he cast them away from his face:

21 Even from that time, when Israel was rent from the house of David, and made Jeroboam son of Nabat their king: for Jeroboam separated Israel from the Lord, and made them commit a great sin.

22 And the children of Israel walked in all the sins of Jeroboam, which he had done: and they departed not from them,

23 Till the Lord removed Israel from his face, as he had spoken in the hand of all his servants the prophets: and Israel was carried away out of their land to Assyria, unto this day.

3. THE FIRST BOOK OF MACCABEES*

A thousand years after their flight from Egypt, the Hebrews (or now, more correctly, Jews) were again struggling to free themselves from foreign domination. This time they were captives of heirs of Alexander the Great. Alexander had conquered the Persian Empire, including Palestine, between 333 and 330 B.C. Following his death in 323, his Macedonian generals fought among themselves for portions of the empire and established several successor kingdoms. Palestine first passed under the control of the Ptolemaic kings of Egypt, from whom the Jews adopted many new Greco-Oriental (Hellenistic)* customs and modes of thought. In 200 B.C. the Seleucid kings of Syria gained control of Jerusalem and its surrounding territories. A quarter of a century later, Antiochus IV succeeded to the Seleucid throne and began a cultural-political attack upon what he considered to be narrowly provincial, therefore potentially dangerous, Jewish practices, that went counter to the cosmopolitan traditions and realities of the Hellenistic world. Although many Hellenized Jews assisted or acceded to Antiochus' policies, a significant number of patriots resisted, fighting what seemed to them to be heathen blasphemies.

This fight for Jewish independence and cultural-religious integrity was led successfully by the Hasmonean family, particularly Judas Maccabaeus and his brothers. *The First Book of Maccabees* narrates the patriotic adventures of Judas and his kin from 175 to 135 B.C. Its anonymous author probably composed the history around 100 B.C.

The author was an avid defender of Jewish cultural and religious traditions. Yet his history betrays the strong imprint of Hellenistic civilization upon even the most conservative elements of second-century B.C. Judaism. Although he wrote religious history, he did so with a secular orientation. There are no miracles in this work; the God of the Jews did not intervene directly and dramatically to bring victory to His people. The victories enjoyed by the Maccabaeans were due to their own human prowess; Jewish defeats were due to ineptitude, stupidity, and an inability to master the art of war, not to divine displeasure. Indeed, God is

---

The First Book of Maccabees is not accorded biblical status by Jews and Protestants. Both place it in a special category of *Apocrypha*—books of great worth, interest, and authority but not divinely inspired. The Catholic Church, however, has officially numbered it among the books of the *Old Testament* since the fifteenth century.

*See Chapter 2, pp. 44-48.

not the hero of this history; Judas Maccabaeus and his family are its central characters. Certainly, these Jewish patriots prayed for divine assistance and ascribed their victories to the Almighty. But the author made it clear that the events that he narrated were governed by those natural laws which determine the outcome of all human actions. This is, on one level, a fairly sophisticated view of Divine Providence, but it is, even more so, historical consciousness within the Greek tradition.

Indeed, by the highest standards of Greek historical scholarship, this is good history. There are many errors, especially where the author dealt with distant events and people. But he consciously attempted to record factual history and made the effort to research and use a number of diverse written and oral sources. The treaty between the Romans and the Jews, which is recorded in chapter eight, is typical of the author's careful use and citation of those official records which were available to him.

That very treaty was a curious affair. For centuries Israel's prophets and other religious leaders had warned God's Chosen People of the dangers which lay in its "whoring after" the Gentiles (see *Ezechial*, 23). Yet, this history attempted to place that treaty and the Romans in the most favorable light. It is no exaggeration to say that the author, although consciously traditional and conservative, was first and foremost a Jewish patriot. He did not abandon the Hebrew concept of divinely directed Linear History. He simply believed the goal of history to be the exaltation of a Jewish state.

Chapter 1

Now it came to pass, after that Alexander the son of Philip the Macedonian, who first reigned in Greece, coming out of the land of Cethim, had overthrown Darius king of the Persians and Medes:

2 He fought many battles, and took the strong holds of all, and slew the kings of the earth:

3 And he went through even to the ends of the earth, and took the spoils of many nations: and the earth was quiet before him.

4 And he gathered a power, and a very strong army: and his heart was exalted and lifted up.

5 And he subdued countries of nations and princes: and they became tributaries to him.

6 And after these things, he fell down upon his bed, and knew that he should die.

7 And he called his servants the nobles that were brought up with him from his youth: and he divided his kingdom among them, while he was yet alive.

8 And Alexander reigned twelve years and he died.

9 And his servants made themselves kings every one in his place:

10 And they all put crowns upon themselves after his death, and their sons after them many years, and evils were multiplied in the earth.

11 And there came out of them a wicked root, Antiochus the Illustrious, the son of king Antiochus, who had been a hostage at Rome: and he reigned in the hundred and thirty-seventh year of the kingdom of the Greeks.

12 In those days there went out of Israel wicked men, and they persuaded many, saying: Let us go, and make a covenant with the heathens that are round about us: for since we departed from them, many evils have befallen us.

13 And the word seemed good in their eyes.

14 And some of the people determined to do this, and went to the king: and he gave them license to do after the ordinances of the heathens. . . .

16 And they . . . departed from the holy covenant, and joined themselves to the heathens, and were sold to do evil.

17 And the kingdom was established before Antiochus, . . .

22 And he went up to Jerusalem with a great multitude.

23 And he proudly entered into the sanctuary, . . .

24 And he took the silver and gold, and the precious vessels: and he took the hidden treasures which he found: and when he had taken all away he departed into his own country.

25 And he made a great slaughter of men, and spoke very proudly.

26 And there was great mourning in Israel, and in every place where they were: . . .

29 And the land was moved for the inhabitants thereof, and all the house of Jacob was covered with confusion.

30 And after two full years the king sent the chief collector of his tributes to the cities of Juda, and he came to Jerusalem with a great multitude.

31 And he spoke to them peaceable words in deceit: and they believed him.

32 And he fell upon the city suddenly, and struck it with a great slaughter, and destroyed much people in Israel.

33 And he took the spoils of the city, and burnt it with fire, and threw down the houses thereof, and the walls thereof round about:

34 And they took the women captive, and the children, and the cattle they possessed.

35 And they built the city of David with a great and strong wall, and with strong towers, and made it a fortress for them:

36 And they placed there a sinful nation, wicked men, and they fortified themselves therein: and they stored up armour, and victuals, and gathered together the spoils of Jerusalem. . . .

39 And they shed innocent blood round about the sanctuary, and defiled the holy place.

40 And the inhabitants of Jerusalem fled away by reason of them, and the city was made the habitation of strangers, and she became a stranger to her own seed, and her children forsook her.

41 Her sanctuary was desolate like a wilderness, her festival days were turned into mourning, her sabbaths into reproach, her honours were brought to nothing.

42 Her dishonour was increased according to her glory, and her excellency was turned into mourning.

43 And king Antiochus wrote to all his kingdom, that all the people should be one: and every one should leave his own law.

44 And all nations consented according to the word of king Antiochus.

45 And many of Israel consented to his service, and they sacrificed to idols, and profaned the sabbath.

46 And the king sent letters by the hands of messengers to Jerusalem, and to all the cities of Juda: that they should follow the law of the nations of the earth,

47 And should forbid holocausts and sacrifices, and atonements to be made in the temple of God.

48 And should prohibit the sabbath, and the festival days, to be celebrated.

49 And he commanded the holy places to be profaned, and the holy people of Israel.

50 And he commanded altars to be built, and temples, and idols, and swine's flesh to be immolated, and unclean beasts.

51 And that they should leave their children uncircumcised, and let their souls be defiled with all uncleannesses, and abominations, to the end that they should forget the law, and should change all the justifications of God.

52 And that whosoever would not do according to the word of king Antiochus should be put to death. . . .

65 And many of the people of Israel determined with themselves, that they would not eat unclean things: and they chose rather to die than to be defiled with unclean meats.

66 And they would not break the holy law of God, and they were put to death:

67 And there was very great wrath upon the people.

Chapter 3

Then . . . Judas called Machabeus, rose up. . . .

2 And all his brethren helped him, and all they that had joined themselves to his father, and they fought with cheerfulness the battle of Israel.

3 And he got his people great honour, and put on a breastplate as a giant, and girt his warlike armour about him in battles, and protected the camp with his sword.

4 In his acts he was like a lion, and like a lion's whelp roaring for his prey.

5 And he pursued the wicked and sought them out, and them that troubled his people he burnt with fire:

6 And his enemies were driven away for fear of him, and all the workers of iniquity were troubled: and salvation prospered in his hand.

7 And he grieved many kings, and made Jacob glad with his works, and his memory is blessed for ever.

8 And he went through the cities of Juda, and destroyed the wicked out of them, and turned away wrath from Israel.

9 And he was renowned even to the utmost part of the earth, and he gathered them that were perishing. . . .

Chapter 5

Now it came to pass, when the nations round about heard that the altar and the sanctuary were built up as before, that they were exceeding angry.

2 And they thought to destroy the generation of Jacob that were among them, and they began to kill some of the people, and to persecute them. . . .

9 And the Gentiles that were in Galaad, assembled themselves together against the Israelites that were in their quarters to destroy them: and they fled into the fortress of Datheman.

10 And they sent letters to Judas and his brethren, saying: The heathens that are round about are gathered together against us, to destroy us. . . .

12 Now therefore come, and deliver us out of their hands, for many of us are slain. . . .

16 Now when Judas and the people heard these words, a great assembly met together to consider what they should do for their brethren that were in trouble, and were assaulted by them.

17 And Judas said to Simon his brother: Choose thee men, and go, and deliver thy brethren in Galilee: and I, and my brother Jonathan will go into the country of Galaad.

18 And he left Joseph the son of Zacharias, and Azarias captains of the people with the remnant of the army in Judea to keep it:

19 And he commanded them, saying: Take ye the charge of this people: but make no war against the heathens, till we return.

20 Now three thousand men were allotted to Simon, to go into Galilee: and eight thousand to Judas to go into the land of Galaad.

21 And Simon went into Galilee, and fought many battles with the heathens: and the heathens were discomfited before his face, and he pursued them even to the gate of Ptolemais.

22 And there fell of the heathens almost three thousand men, and he took the spoils of them. . . .

56 Joseph the son of Zacharias, and Azarias captain of the soldiers, heard of the good success, and the battles that were fought.

57 And he said: Let us also get us a name, and let us go fight against the Gentiles that are round about us.

58 And he gave charge to them that were in his army, and they went towards Jamnia.

59 And Gorgias and his men went out of the city, to give them battle.

60 And Joseph and Azarias were put to flight, and were pursued unto the borders of Judea: and there fell, on that day, of the people of Israel about two thousand men, and there was a great overthrow of the people:

61 Because they did not hearken to Judas, and his brethren, thinking that they should do manfully.

62 But they were not of the seed of those men by whom salvation was brought to Israel.

63 And the men of Juda were magnified exceedingly in the sight of all Israel, and of all the nations where their name was heard.

Chapter 8

Now Judas heard of the fame of the Romans, that they are powerful and strong, and willingly agree to all things that are requested of them: and that whosoever have come to them, they have made amity with them, and that they are mighty in power.

2 And they heard of their battles, and their noble acts, which they had done in Galatia, how they had conquered them, and brought them under tribute. . . .

17 So Judas chose Eupolemus the son of John, the son of Jacob, and Jason the son of Eleazar, and he sent them to Rome to make a league of amity and confederacy with them.

18 And that they might take off from them the yoke of the Grecians, for they saw that they oppressed the kingdom of Israel with servitude.

19 And they went to Rome, a very long journey, and they entered into the senate house, and said:

20 Judas Machabeus, and his brethren, and the people of the Jews have sent us to you, to make alliance and peace with you, and that we may be registered your confederates and friends.

21 And the proposal was pleasing in their sight.

22 And this is the copy of the writing that they wrote back again, graven in tables of brass, and sent to Jerusalem, that it might be with them there for a memorial of the peace and alliance.

23 GOOD SUCCESS BE TO THE ROMANS, and to the people of the Jews, by sea and by land for ever: and far be the sword and enemy from them.

24 But if there come first any war upon the Romans, or any of their confederates, in all their dominions:

25 The nation of the Jews shall help them according as the time shall direct with all their heart:

26 Neither shall they give them, whilst they are fighting, or furnish them with wheat, or arms, or money, or ships, as it hath seemed good to the Romans: and they shall obey their orders, without taking any thing of them.

27 In like manner also if war shall come first upon the nation of the Jews, the Romans shall help them with all their heart, according as the time shall permit them.

28 And there shall not be given to them that come to their aid, either wheat, or arms, or money, or ships, as it hath seemed good to the Romans: and they shall observe their orders without deceit.

29 According to these articles did the Romans covenant with the people of the Jews.

30 And if after this one party or the other shall have a mind to add to these articles, or take away any thing, they may do it at their pleasure: and whatsoever they shall add, or take away, shall be ratified.

31 Moreover concerning the evils that Demetrius the king hath done against them, we have written to him, saying: Why hast thou made thy yoke heavy upon our friends, and allies, the Jews?

32 If therefore they come again to us complaining of thee, we will do them justice, and will make war against thee by sea and land.

SOURCE NOTES

1. From *The Holy Bible, Exodus,* 3 and 4. Douay translation (1609).
2. From *The Holy Bible, II Samuel,* 11 and 12; *II Kings,* 17, *passim.* Douay translation (1609).
3. From *The Holy Bible, I Maccabees,* 1, 3, 5, and 8, *passim.* Douay translation (1609).

2.

THE GREEKS

Early in the sixth century B.C. a small group of Greek intellectuals residing on the western shores of Asia Minor created a new mode of thought— rational speculation about the underlying natural forces governing the universe. These thinkers became the world's first known natural scientists and philosophers, as they attempted to discover through rational processes the material bases of physical existence.

This new Greek rationalism manifested itself in several forms. Some philosophers theorized magnificently and boldly, often with little supportive concrete evidence, on the physical nature of the cosmos. Others, notably geographers and physicians, attempted to investigate the world through close empirical observation.

As with everything else, the Greeks gave a generic name to this whole movement of rational investigation. They called it "history" (*historia*—knowledge acquired by inquiry). Originally, the historian was any truthseeker who utilized any form of rational inquiry. It was not until at least the middle of the second century B.C. that the title "historian" applied more or less exclusively to the researchers who wrote prose narratives of the human past.

We would be in error if we pictured these early rationalists as men who destroyed all mythic thought. Most Greeks lived, worshipped, and thought in mythical patterns. Rationalism was the province of a small intellectual elite, and even Greek rationalism had its mythology. This rational mythmaking was quite evident in the works of those Greeks who wrote about the human past. Although they sought natural causes for human events and attempted to understand what motivated man and his society, their analysis of history was formed by the prevailing Greek view of human life and destiny.

Paradoxically, the Greeks glorified man and took a lusty delight in life, but found human existence to be ultimately meaningless. They lacked the concept of a transcendental Order that imparted meaning to human life by using it for a Purpose. Rather, the Greeks accepted a cyclical view of natural eternal time and saw man as a slave to timeless fate. To be sure, they attributed free will to man and granted him a limited causal role in effecting his destiny. They believed that a few exceptional men could achieve excellence in this life and rise, thereby, above the masses. They also accepted an ethic that taught that the proud, immoderate person or city courted inevitable humbling punishment. Still, in the last analysis, the Greeks believed that man was not the final director of his natural life, nor did he share in any supernatural destiny. Human existence was a cosmic joke. But it was worthy of study because it was all that man had. Man, therefore, became the center of history.

We have seen how the Hebrews created a concept of linear, purposive, and progressive history—one of the two distinguishing features of the West's historical consciousness. The Greeks provided the second distinctive element—rational inquiry into essentially human, not divine, actions. We might say that the Hebrews historicized myth, while the Greeks rationalized and humanized it.

4. HERODOTUS: THE HISTORIES

Herodotus of Halicarnassus (484?-*ca.* 424 B.C.), whom Cicero apostrophized as the "Father of History," was born in Asia Minor, the original home of Greek rationalism. A man of universal curiosity, he traveled extensively throughout the Mediterranean world—from Babylon to Italy, from the Crimea to Egypt—collecting stories and viewing the wonders of his age. Around the middle of the century he migrated to Athens, the center of fifth century Hellenic Greek civilization; here he was admitted to the brilliant circle of Periclean intellectuals and artists, of whom the tragic playwright Sophocles, author of *Oedipus the King,* became an especially close friend. Here also he composed large parts of his *Histories* and read them to admiring audiences.

These public readings reveal the transitional importance of the *Histories*. Herodotus, nephew of one of his age's most prominent epic poets, chose to write prose—the first known work of literary prose in Greek—thereby breaking out of the tradition of Homeric poetry. Yet his work contained many of epic poetry's qualities—qualities that would remain integral elements of subsequent Greco-Roman historical writing. The most notable of these was the assumption that the historian was an artist who proclaimed the laws of right and wrong and glorified for all time the heroic deeds of men. However, Herodotus' technique was essentially rational and his concern historical: To uncover and preserve the *truth* about noteworthy human affairs.

Rational inquiry or "history" meant for Herodotus encyclopedic investigation of all that was interesting and open to research. Folklore, customs, and geography fascinated him and provided Herodotus much material for exposition and study. His approach to knowledge belonged to an age in which rational investigation was still an exciting new tool, and academic disciplines with their narrow boundaries had not yet been created.

One's first impression of his work is confusion amidst richness of detail. It appears to be a vast and formless collection of unconnected stories told by a garrulous and, at times, gullible traveler. Yet, for all of its apparent rambling, it is a magnificently told story of the conflicts between the Greeks and the Persians. More than a chronicle, it was an attempt to analyze the causes of those conflicts and the reasons behind the eventual Persian defeat. His answer became the underlying theme of the

Histories—the state of human affairs is precarious at best and inevitable disaster awaits prideful man.

Herodotus' message had a special, obvious relevance for his Athenian audience. By the mid-fifth century, Athens had become a proud imperial power, whose aggressive policies were unsettling the Hellenic balance of power and threatening eventual conflict in the Greek world. But then, as now, action rarely conformed to perception.

The following excerpts (from Books III and VII) illustrate Herodotus' historical abilities at their best, as well as his anecdotal manner of presentation. The reader should note how Herodotus' view of the moral underpinnings of human existence allow him to balance in his mind two apparently contradictory attitudes: A belief in the precarious, ultimately meaningless (in any absolute sense) state of human affairs and an exaltation of man the hero and his central role in earthly deeds.

While Cambyses was invading Egypt, the Lacedæmonians made an expedition against Samos and Polycrates, the son of Æaces, who had made an insurrection and seized on Samos. At first, having divided the state into three parts, he shared it with his brothers Pantagnatos and Syloson; but afterward, having put one of them to death, and expelled Syloson, the younger, he held the whole of Samos; and holding it, made a treaty of friendship with Amasis, King of Egypt, sending presents and receiving others from him in return. In a very short time the power of Polycrates increased, and was noised abroad throughout Ionia and the rest of Greece; for wherever he turned his arms everything turned out prosperously. He had a hundred fifty-oared galleys, and a thousand archers. And he plundered all without distinction; for he said that he gratified a friend more by restoring what he had seized than by taking nothing at all. He accordingly took many of the islands, and many cities on the continent; he moreover overcame in a sea-fight, and took prisoners, the Lesbians, who came to assist the Milesians with all their forces: these, being put in chains, dug the whole trench that surrounds the walls of Samos. Somehow the exceeding good fortune of Polycrates did not escape the notice of Amasis, but was the cause of uneasiness to him; and when his successes continued to increase, having written a letter in the following terms, he dispatched it to Samos: "Amasis to Polycrates says thus: It is pleasant to hear of the successes of a friend and ally. But your too great good fortune does not please me, knowing, as I do, that the divinity is jealous. As for me, I would rather choose that both I and those for whom I am solicitous should be partly successful in our undertakings, and partly suffer reverses; and so pass life, meeting with vicissitudes of fortune, than being prosperous in all things. For I can not remember that I ever heard of any man who, having been constantly successful, did not at last utterly perish. Be advised therefore by me, and act thus with regard to your good fortune. Having considered what you can find that you value most, and the loss of which would most pain your soul, this cast away, that it may never more be seen of man: and if after this successes are not mingled interchangeably with reverses, again have recourse to the remedy I have suggested." Polycrates, having read this letter, and conceived that Amasis had given him good advice, inquired of himself by the loss of which of his valuables he should most afflict his soul; and on inquiry, he discovered the following: He had a seal which he wore, set in gold, made of an emerald, and it was the workmanship of Theodorus, the son of Telecles, a Samian; when therefore he had determined to cast this away, he did as follows: Having manned a fifty-oared galley, he went on board it, and then ordered to put out to sea; and when he was a considerable distance from the island, he took off the seal, and in the sight of all on board, threw it into the sea. This done, he sailed back again; and having reached his palace, he mourned it as a great misfortune. But on the fifth or sixth day after this the following circumstance occurred: A fisherman, having caught a large and beautiful fish, thought it a present worthy to be given to Polycrates; he accordingly carried it to the gates, and said that he wished to be admitted to the presence of Polycrates; and when this was granted, he presented the fish, and said: "O king, having caught this, I did not think it right to take it to market, although I get my living by hard labour; but it seemed to me worthy of you and your empire; I bring it, therefore, and present it to you." He, pleased with these words, replied, "You have done well, and I give you double thanks for your speech and your present, and I invite you to supper." The fisherman, thinking a great deal of this, went away to his own home; but the servants, opening the fish, found the seal of Polycrates in its belly; and as soon as they had seen it, and taken it out, they carried it with great joy to Polycrates, and as they gave him the seal they acquainted him in what manner it had been found. But when it occurred to him that the event was superhuman, he wrote an account of what he had done, and of what had happened, and having written, he despatched the account to Egypt. But Amasis, having read the letter that came from Polycrates, felt persuaded that it was impossible for man to rescue man from the fate that awaited him, and that Polycrates would not come to a good end, since he was fortunate in everything, and even found what he had thrown away; having therefore sent a herald to Samos, he said that he must renounce his friendship. He did this for the following reason, lest if some dreadful and great calamity befell Polycrates, he might himself be grieved for him, as for a friend. . . .

Near about the time of Cambyses's illness the following events took place: Orœtes, a Persian, had been appointed governor of Sardis by Cyrus; this man conceived an impious project; for without having sustained any injury, or heard a hasty word from Polycrates the Samian, and without having seen him before, he conceived the design of seizing him and putting him to death; as most people say, for some such cause as this. Orœtes and another Persian, whose name was Mitrobates, governor of the district of Dascylium, were sitting together at the palace gates, and fell into a dispute. As they were quarrelling about valour, Mitrobates said to Orœtes tauntingly: "Are you to be reckoned a brave man, who have not yet acquired for the king the island of Samos, that lies near your government, and is so easy to be subdued? which one of its own inhabitants, having made an insurrection with fifteen armed men, obtained possession of, and now reigns over?" Some say that he, having heard this, and being stung with the reproach, conceived a desire, not so much to revenge himself on the man who said it, as of utterly destroying Polycrates, on whose account he had been reproached. A fewer number say that Orœtes sent a herald to Samos to make some demand which is not mentioned, and that Polycrates happened to be reclining in the men's apartment, and that Anacreon of Teos was with him; and somehow (whether designedly disregarding the business of Orœtes, or by chance it so happened), when the herald of Orœtes came forward and delivered his message, Polycrates, as his face chanced to be turned toward the wall, neither turned about, nor made any answer. These twofold causes are assigned for the death of Polycrates; every man may give credit to whichever he pleases. However, Orœtes, who resided in Magnesia, situated on the river Mæander, being acquainted with the intentions of Polycrates, sent Myrsus, a Lydian, son of Gyges, with a message to Samos; for Polycrates is the first of the Grecians of whom we know who formed a design to make himself master of the sea, except Minos the Cnossian, or any other, who before his time obtained the empire of the sea; but within what is called the historical age, Polycrates is the first who had entertained great expectations of ruling Ionia and the islands. Orœtes, therefore, having ascertained that he had formed this design, sent a message to the following effect: "Orœtes to Polycrates says as follows: I understand that you are planning vast enterprises, and that you have not money answerable to your projects. Now, if you will do as I advise, you will promote your own success, and preserve me; for King Cambyses meditates my death, and of this I have certain information. Now, do you convey me and my wealth out of the country, and take part of it, and suffer me to enjoy the rest: by means of the wealth, you will become master of all Greece. If you doubt what I say concerning my riches, send to me the most trusty of your servants, to whom I will show them." Polycrates, having heard this, was

delighted, and accepted the offer; and as he was very eager for wealth, he first
sent Mæandrius, son of Mæandrius, to view it, a citizen who was his secretary:
he not long after dedicated to the Temple of Juno all the ornamental furniture
from the men's apartment of Polycrates, which was indeed magnificent. Orœtes,
having learned that an inspector might be expected, did as follows: having filled
eight chests with stones, except a very small space round the brim, he put gold on
the surface of the stones, and having made the chests fast with cords, he kept
them in readiness. But Mæandrius, having come and inspected the chests, took
back a report to Polycrates. He, though earnestly dissuaded by the oracles and by
his friends, resolved to go in person; and moreover, though his daughter had seen
in a dream this vision: she imagined she saw her father elevated in the air, washed
by Jupiter, and anointed by the sun. Having seen this vision, she endeavoured by
all possible means to divert Polycrates from going from home to Orœtes; and as
he was going on board a fifty-oared galley, she persisted in uttering words of bad
omen. But he threatened her, if he should return safe, that she should long
continue unmarried; and she prayed that so it might be brought to pass; for she
chose to continue a longer time unmarried than be deprived of her father. Thus
Polycrates, disregarding all advice, set sail to visit Orœtes, taking with him
many others of his friends, and among them Democedes, son of Calliphon, a
Crotonian, who was a physician, and the most skilful practitioner of his time.
But Polycrates, on his arrival at Magnesia, was put to death in a horrid manner,
unworthy of himself and his lofty thoughts: for, with the exception of those who
have been tyrants of Syracuse, not one of all the Grecian tyrants deserves to be
compared with Polycrates for magnificence. But Orœtes, having put him to
death in a manner not to be described, caused him to be crucified: of those that
accompanied Polycrates, as many as were Samians, he dismissed, bidding them
to feel thankful to him for their liberty; but as many as were strangers and
servants he detained and treated as slaves. Thus Polycrates, being crucified,
fulfilled the vision of his daughter in every particular: for he was washed by
Jupiter, when it rained, and was anointed by the sun, himself emitting moisture
from his body. Thus the constant good fortune of Polycrates ended as Amasis,
King of Egypt, had foretold.

[Xerxes] . . . remained several days about Pieria, for a third division of his
army was employed in felling the trees on the Macedonian range, that the whole
army might pass in that direction to the Perrhæbi. In the meantime the heralds,
who had been sent to Greece to demand earth*, returned to Xerxes; some empty,

*A symbol of submission to the King of Persia.

and others bringing earth and water. Of those who gave them were the following: the Thessalians, the Dolopes, the Enienes, the Perrhæbi, the Locrians, the Magnetes, the Melians, the Achæans of Pthiotis, and the Thebans, and all the rest of the Bœotians, except the Thespians and Platæans. Against these the Greeks who engaged in war with the barbarians made a solemn oath. The oath ran as follows: "Whatever Greeks have given themselves up to the Persian, without compulsion, so soon as their affairs are restored to order, these shall be compelled to pay a tithe to the god at Delphi." Such was the oath taken by the Greeks. To Athens and Sparta he did not send heralds to demand earth, for the following reasons: On a former occasion when Darius sent for the same purpose, the former having thrown those who made the demand into the barathrum, and the latter into a well, bade them carry earth and water to the king from those places. For that reason Xerxes did not send persons to make the demand. What calamity befell the Athenians in consequence of their having treated the heralds in this manner, I can not say, except that their territory and city were ravaged; but I do not think that happened in consequence of that crime. On the Lacedæmonians, however, the anger of Talthybius, Agamemnon's herald, alighted. For Talthybius has a temple in Sparta; and there are descendants of Talthybius, called Talthybiadæ, to whom all embassies from Sparta are given as a privilege. After these events the Spartans were unable, when they sacrificed, to get favourable omens; and this continued for a long time. The Lacedæmonians being grieved, and considering it a great calamity, and having frequently held assemblies, and at length made inquiry by public proclamation, whether any Lacedæmonian was willing to die for Sparta, Sperthies, son of Aneristus, and Bulis, son of Nicolaus, both Spartans of distinguished birth, and eminent for their wealth, voluntarily offered to give satisfaction to Xerxes for the heralds of Darius who had perished at Sparta. Accordingly, the Spartans sent them to the Medes, for the purpose of being put to death. And both the courage of these men deserves admiration, and also the following words on this occasion. For on their way to Susa they came to Hydarnes; but Hydarnes was a Persian by birth, and governor of the maritime people in Asia; he having offered them hospitality, entertained them, and while he was entertaining them he questioned them as follows, saying: "Men of Lacedæmon, why do you refuse to be friendly with the king? For you may see how well the king shows how to honour brave men, by looking at me and my condition. So also, if you would surrender yourselves to the king, for you are deemed by him to be brave men, each of you would obtain a government in some part of Greece, at the hands of the king." To this they answered as follows: "Hydarnes, the advice you hold out to us is not impartial; for you advise us, having tried the one state, but being inexperienced in the other: what it is to be a slave you know perfectly well, but you have never tried liberty, whether it is sweet or not. For if you had tried it you would advise us to fight for it, not with spears, but even with hatchets.'' Thus they answered Hydarnes. Afterward, when they went up to Susa, and were come into the king's presence, in the first place, when the guards commanded and endeavoured to compel them to prostrate themselves and worship the king, they said they would by no means do so, although they were thrust by them on their heads; for that it was not their custom to worship a man, nor had they come for that purpose. When they had fought off this, and on their addressing Xerxes in words to the following effect, ''King of the Medes, the Lacedæmonians have sent us in return for the heralds who were killed at Sparta, to make satisfaction for them''; on their saying this, Xerxes answered with magnanimity that he would not be like the Lacedæmonians, for that they had violated the law of all nations by murdering his heralds; but he would not do the very thing which he blamed in them; nor by killing them in return, would relieve the Lacedæmonians from guilt. Thus the wrath of Talthybius, when the Spartans acted in this manner, ceased for the time, although Sperthies and Bulis returned to Sparta. But some time afterward it was again aroused, during the war between the Peloponnesians and Athenians, as the Lacedæmonians say; and this appears to me to have happened in a most extraordinary manner: for that the wrath of Talthybius alighted on the messengers, and did not cease until it was satisfied, justice allowed; but that it should fall on the sons of the men who went up to the king on account of that wrath, on Nicolaus, son of Bulis, and on Aneristus, son of Sperthies, who, sailing in a merchant vessel fully manned, captured some fisherman from Tiryns, makes it clear to me that the occurrence was extraordinary in consequence of that wrath. For they, being sent by the Lacedæmonians as ambassadors to Asia, and being betrayed by Sitalces, son of Teres, King of the Thracians, and by Nymphodorus, son of Pytheas of Abdera, were taken near Bisanthe on the Hellespont, and being carried to Attica, were put to death by the Athenians; and with them Aristeas, son of Adimantus, a Corinthian. These things, however, happened many years after the expedition of the king.

But I return to my former subject. This expedition of the king was nominally directed against Athens, but was really sent against all Greece. The Greeks, however, though they had heard of it long beforehand, were not all affected alike. For those who had given earth and water to the Persians felt confident that they should suffer no harm from the barbarians; but those who had refused to give them were in great consternation, since the ships in Greece were not sufficient in number to resist the invader, and many were unwilling to engage in the war, and were much inclined to side with the Medes. And here I feel constrained by necessity to declare my opinion, although it may excite the envy of most men; however, I will not refrain from expressing how the truth appears to me to be. If the Athenians, terrified with the impending danger, had abandoned their country; or not having abandoned it, but remaining in it, had given themselves up to Xerxes, no other people would have attempted to resist the king at sea. If, then, no one had opposed Xerxes by sea, the following things must have occurred on land: Although many lines of walls had been built by the Peloponnesians across the isthmus, yet the Lacedæmonians, being abandoned by the allies (not willing, but by necessity, they being taken by the barbarians city by city), would have been left alone; and being left alone, after having displayed noble deeds, would have died nobly. They would either have suffered thus, or before that, seeing the rest of the Greeks siding with the Medes, would have made terms with Xerxes; and so, in either case, Greece would have become subject to the Persians; for I am unable to discover what would have been the advantage of the walls built across the isthmus if the king had been master of the sea. Any one, therefore, who should say that the Athenians were the saviours of Greece would not deviate from the truth; for to whichever side they turned, that must have preponderated. But having chosen that Greece should continue free, they were the people who roused the rest of the Greeks who did not side with the Medes, and who, next to the gods, repulsed the king. Neither did alarming oracles that came from Delphi, and inspired them with terror, induce them to abandon Greece; but, standing their ground, they had courage to await the invader of their country.

5.   THUCYDIDES: HISTORY OF THE PELOPONNESIAN WAR

In 431 B.C. hostilities broke out between Athens and Sparta. This conflict, known as the Peloponnesian War, was the single greatest catastrophe to befall Hellenic Greek society. When the war finally ended in 404 B.C., Athens lay prostrate and the Golden Age of Hellas was a memory. Early in the war, an Athenian general, Thucydides (*ca.* 460-*ca.* 400 B.C.), fell into disgrace and was exiled for the remainder of the conflict. A curious and observant student of political affairs, Thucydides had studied the war from its earliest days. His enforced retirement now allowed him the time and freedom to collect information from all sides, to analyze that data, and to record his conclusions. Sometime during the course of the war, he probably began to compose, polish, and repolish what he envisioned as the definitive history of that conflict. At the war's end he returned to Athens, only to die a short while later, leaving his *History* unfinished. Yet, even in its incomplete state it is a masterpiece of impressive scope and artistry.

Thucydides began his *History* by boldly stating that he would write only about the immediate past. He believed the historical present to be the only period of history one could analyze with any certainty, because its facts alone are reasonably verifiable. His passion for establishing the truth of all he reported followed from the purposes for which his work was intended and the methods of analysis he employed.

A wealthy gentleman of superior intelligence, Thucydides had enjoyed all the educational benefits that fifth century Athens offered her citizens. Three of the many formative influences on his life were sophistic philosphy, the public tragic theater, and the new science of medicine. Of these, sophism was the most important factor in Athenian intellectual development, especially after 427 B.C.

The fifth century sophists were itinerant teachers. Unlike the earliest Greek philosophers, they did not seek after the first principles of the universe, but developed and taught such practical civic skills as the art of public discourse and the empirical study of moral philosophy. Known for their iconoclastic questioning of traditional beliefs and their close investigation of all natural and social phenomena, the sophists profoundly influenced the development of Greek science and the arts, including medicine and the theater.

Fifth century Greek tragic drama was dominated in turn by three playwrights: Aeschylus (525-456 B.C.); Sophocles (495-406 B.C.); and Euripides (480-406 B.C.). Both Aeschylus and Sophocles were pious, conservative artists, who reflected the values of the early fifth century. For them mankind was meaningless without the gods; it was pride that turned one from the gods and hurtled one toward inevitable disaster. Euripides was no less the moralist and also believed that disastrous retribution awaited the immoderate person. But, influenced by the sophists, he was a free-thinker, less sure of the gods and more concerned with investigating the purely natural—especially the violence of human passions. According to an oft-quoted dictum, he portrayed humans, "not as they ought to be, but as they are." Euripides' dramas reflected and helped form the skepticism of the New Breed—an educated elite that, with the onslaught of a fratricidal war and pestilence, tended to become more critical of the deistic principles of an earlier, spiritually more homogeneous, generation. Herodotus had been at home in the theater of Aeschylus and Sophocles; Thucydides found a kindred spirit in Euripides. It was no accident that in his deeply moralistic *History* the gods played no part.

Hippocratic medicine also stressed the purely natural, denying the supernatural origins of disease. Its method stressed the collection of case histories: Close observation and minute recording of the physical manifestations of different diseases, in order that the medical community could learn through accumulated experience. From about 450 to about 430, during Thucydides' formative years, the physican Hippocrates taught in Athens. The young aristocrat was undoubtedly one of his students.

With this background, Thucydides set out to discover and record the physical and moral causes of his city's tragic failure. He believed he could establish a clinically accurate case study of the war that would serve as both a moral example of the mortal effects of war on a society's soul and as the prognostic basis from which future generations could graph the general course that the "diseases" of similar wars would take. Because of its scientific accuracy and its noble humanistic purposes, he believed his *History* would be, in his words, "an everlasting possession."

In the selection below, Thucydides records his version of Pericles' Funeral Oration of 431 and describes the plague of 430. These two passages have been chosen to illustrate how Thucydides, working within the framework of the three intellectual currents mentioned above, presented, like his older contemporary Herodotus, the characteristically Hellenic message of the glory yet vain precariousness of man and his mortal accomplishments (in this case Athens, a city of laws and "the school of Hellas"). Yet, while the message was the same, the mode of presentation and analysis differed strikingly.

During the same winter, in accordance with an old national custom, the funeral of those who first fell in this war was celebrated by the Athenians at the public charge . . . . Over those who were the first buried Pericles was chosen to speak. At the fitting moment he advanced from the sepulchre to a lofty stage, which had been erected in order that he might be heard as far as possible by the multitude, and spoke as follows:

(Funeral Speech)

"Most of those who have spoken here before me have commended the lawgiver who added this oration to our other funeral customs; it seemed to them a worthy thing that such an honour should be given at their burial to the dead who have fallen on the field of battle. But I should have preferred that, when men's deeds have been brave, they should be honoured in deed only, and with such an honour as this public funeral, which you are now witnessing. Then the reputation of many would not have been imperilled on the eloquence or want of eloquence of one, and their virtues believed or not as he spoke well or ill. For it is difficult to say neither too little nor too much; and even moderation is apt not to give the impression of truthfulness. The friend of the dead who knows the facts is likely to think that the words of the speaker fall short of his knowledge and of his wishes; another who is not so well informed, when he hears of anything which surpasses his own powers, will be envious and will suspect exaggeration. Mankind are tolerant of the praises of others so long as each hearer thinks that he can do as well or nearly as well himself, but, when the speaker rises above him, jealousy is aroused and he begins to be incredulous. However, since our ancestors have set the seal of their approval upon the practice, I must obey, and to the utmost of my power shall endeavour to satisfy the wishes and beliefs of all who hear me.

"I will speak first of our ancestors, for it is right and becoming that now, when we are lamenting the dead, a tribute should be paid to their memory. There has never been a time when they did not inhabit this land, which by their valour they have handed down from generation to generation, and we have received from them a free state. But if they were worthy of praise, still more were our fathers, who added to their inheritance, and after many a struggle transmitted to us their sons this great empire. And we ourselves assembled here to-day, who are still most of us in the vigour of life, have chiefly done the work of improvement, and have richly endowed our city with all things, so that she is sufficient for herself both in peace and war. Of the military exploits by which our various possessions were acquired, or of the energy with which we or our fathers drove back the tide of war, Hellenic or Barbarian, I will not speak; for the tale would be long and is familiar to you. But before I praise the dead, I should like to point out by what principles of action we rose to power, and under what institutions and through what manner of life our empire became great. For I conceive that such thoughts are not unsuited to the occasion, and that this numerous assembly of citizens and strangers may profitably listen to them.

"Our form of government does not enter into rivalry with the institutions of others. We do not copy our neighbours, but are an example to them. It is true that we are called a democracy, for the administration is in the hands of the many and not of the few. But while the law secures equal justice to all alike in their private disputes, the claim of excellence is also recognised; and when a citizen is in any way distinguished, he is preferred to the public service, not as a matter of privilege, but as the reward of merit. Neither is poverty a bar, but a man may benefit his country whatever be the obscurity of his condition. There is no exclusiveness in our public life, and in our private intercourse we are not suspicious of one another, nor angry with our neighbour if he does what he likes; we do not put on sour looks at him which, though harmless, are not pleasant. While we are thus unconstrained in our private intercourse, a spirit of reverence pervades our public acts; we are prevented from doing wrong by respect for authority and for the laws, having an especial regard to those which are ordained for the protection of the injured as well as to those unwritten laws which bring upon the transgressor of them the reprobation of the general sentiment.

"And we have not forgotten to provide for our weary spirits many relaxations from toil; we have regular games and sacrifices throughout the year; at home the style of our life is refined; and the delight which we daily feel in all these things helps to banish melancholy. Because of the greatness of our city the fruits of the whole earth flow in upon us; so that we enjoy the goods of other countries as freely as of our own.

"Then, again, our military training is in many respects superior to that of our adversaries. Our city is thrown open to the world, and we never expel a foreigner or prevent him from seeing or learning anything of which the secret if revealed to an enemy might profit him. We rely not upon management or trickery, but upon our own hearts and hands. And in the matter of education, whereas they from early youth are always undergoing laborious exercises which are to make them brave, we live at ease, and yet are equally ready to face the perils which they face . . . .

"If then we prefer to meet danger with a light heart but without laborious training, and with a courage which is gained by habit and not enforced by law, are we not greatly the gainers? Since we do not anticipate the pain, although, when the hour comes, we can be as brave as those who never allow themselves to rest; and thus too our city is equally admirable in peace and in war. For we are lovers of the beautiful, yet simple in our tastes, and we cultivate the mind without loss of manliness. Wealth we employ, not for talk and ostentation, but when there is a real use for it. To avow poverty with us is no disgrace; the true disgrace is in doing nothing to avoid it. An Athenian citizen does not neglect the state because he takes care of his own household; and even those of us who are engaged in business have a very fair idea of politics. We alone regard a man who takes no interest in public affairs, not as a harmless, but as a useless character; and if few of us are originators, we are all sound judges of a policy. The great impediment to action is, in our opinion, not discussion, but the want of that knowledge which is gained by discussion preparatory to action. For we have a peculiar power of thinking before we act and of acting too, whereas other men are courageous from ignorance but hesitate upon reflection. And they are surely to be esteemed the bravest spirits who, having the clearest sense both of the pains and pleasures of life, do not on that account shrink from danger. . . . To sum up: I say that Athens is the school of Hellas, and that the individual Athenian in his own person seems to have the power of adapting himself to the most varied forms of action with the utmost versatility and grace. This is no passing and idle word, but truth and fact; and the assertion is verified by the position to which these qualities have raised the state. For in the hour of trial Athens alone among her contemporaries is superior to the report of her. No enemy who comes against her is indignant at the reverses which he sustains at the hands of such a city; no subject complains that his masters are unworthy of him. And we shall assuredly not be without witnesses; there are mighty monuments of our power which will make us the wonder of this and of succeeding ages; we shall not need the praises of Homer or of any other panegyrist whose poetry may please for the moment, although his representation of the facts will not bear the light of day. For we have compelled every land and every sea to open a path for our valour, and have everywhere planted eternal memorials of our friendship and of our enmity. Such is the city for whose sake these men nobly fought and died; they could not bear the thought that she might be taken from them; and every one of us who survive should gladly toil on her behalf.

"I have dwelt upon the greatness of Athens because I want to show you that we are contending for a higher prize than those who enjoy none of these privileges, and to establish by manifest proof the merit of these men whom I am now commemorating. Their loftiest praise has been already spoken. For in magnifying the city I have magnified them, and men like them whose virtues made her glorious . . . ."

Such was the order of the funeral celebrated in this winter, with the end of which ended the first year of the Peloponnesian War. As soon as summer returned, the Peloponnesian army, comprising as before two-thirds of the force of each confederate state, under the command of the Lacedæmonian king Archidamus, the son of Zeuxidamus, invaded Attica, where they established themselves and ravaged the country. They had not been there many days when the plague broke out at Athens for the first time. A similar disorder is said to have previously smitten many places, particularly Lemnos, but there is no record of such a pestilence occurring elsewhere, or of so great a destruction of human life. For a while physicians, in ignorance of the nature of the disease, sought to apply remedies; but it was in vain, and they themselves were among the first victims, because they oftenest came into contact with it. No human art was of any avail, and as to supplications in temples, enquiries of oracles, and the like, they were utterly useless, and at last men were overpowered by the calamity and gave them all up.

The disease is said to have begun south of Egypt in Aethiopia; thence it descended into Egypt and Libya, and after spreading over the greater part of the Persian empire, suddenly fell upon Athens. It first attacked the inhabitants of the Piraeus, and it was supposed that the Peloponnesians had poisoned the cisterns, no conduits having as yet been made there. It afterwards reached the upper city, and then the mortality became far greater. As to its probable origin or the causes which might or could have produced such a disturbance of nature, every man, whether a physician or not, will give his own opinion. But I shall describe its actual course, and the symptoms by which any one who knows them beforehand may recognise the disorder should it ever reappear. For I was myself attacked, and witnessed the sufferings of others.

The season was admitted to have been remarkably free from ordinary sickness; and if anybody was already ill of any other disease, it was absorbed in this. Many who were in perfect health, all in a moment, and without any apparent reason, were seized with violent heats in the head and with redness and inflammation of the eyes. Internally the throat and the tongue were quickly suffused with blood, and the breath became unnatural and fetid. There followed sneezing and hoarseness; in a short time the disorder, accompanied by a violent cough, reached the chest; then fastening lower down, it would move the stomach and bring on all the vomits of bile to which physicans have ever given names; and they were very distressing. An ineffectual retching producing violent convulsions attacked most of the sufferers; some as soon as the previous symptoms had abated, others not until long afterwards. The body externally was not so very hot to the touch, nor yet pale; it was of a livid colour inclining to red, and breaking out in pustules and ulcers. But the internal fever was intense; the sufferers could not bear to have on them even the finest linen garment; they insisted on being naked, and there was nothing which they longed for more eagerly than to throw themselves into cold water. And many of those who had no one to look after them actually plunged into the cisterns, for they were tormented by unceasing thirst, which was not in the least assuaged whether they drank little or much. They could not sleep; a restlessness which was intolerable never left them. While the disease was at its height the body, instead of wasting away, held out amid these sufferings in a marvellous manner, and either they died on the seventh or ninth day, not of weakness, for their strength was not exhausted, but of internal fever, which was the end of most; or, if they survived, then the disease descended into the bowels and there produced violent ulceration; severe diarrhoea at the same time set in, and at a later stage caused exhaustion, which finally with few exceptions carried them off. For the disorder which had originally settled in the head passed gradually through the whole body, and, if a person got over the worst, would often seize the extremities and leave its mark, attacking the privy parts and the fingers and the toes, and some escaped with the loss of these, some with the loss of their eyes. Some again had no sooner recovered than they were seized with a forgetfulness of all things and knew neither themselves nor their friends.

The malady took a form not to be described, and the fury with which it fastened upon each sufferer was too much for human nature to endure. There was one circumstance in particular which distinguished it from ordinary diseases. The birds and animals which feed on human flesh, although so many bodies were lying unburied, either never came near them, or died if they touched them. This was proved by a remarkable disappearance of the birds of prey, who were not to be seen either about the bodies or anywhere else; while in the case of the dogs the fact was even more obvious, because they live with man.

Such was the general nature of the disease: I omit many strange peculiarities which characterized individual cases. None of the ordinary sicknesses attacked any one while it lasted, or, if they did, they ended in the plague. Some of the sufferers died from want of care, others equally who were receiving the greatest attention. No single remedy could be deemed a specific; for that which did good to one did harm to another. No constitution was of itself strong enough to resist or weak enough to escape the attacks; the disease carried off all alike and defied every mode of treatment. Most appalling was the despondency which seized upon any one who felt himself sickening; for he instantly abandoned his mind to despair and, instead of holding out, absolutely threw away his chance of life. Appalling too was the rapidity with which men caught the infection; dying like sheep if they attended on one another; and this was the principal cause of mortality. When they were afraid to visit one another, the sufferers died in their solitude, so that many houses were empty because there had been no one left to take care of the sick; or if they ventured they perished, especially those who aspired to heroism. For they went to see their friends without thought of themselves and were ashamed to leave them, even at a time when the very relations of the dying were at last growing weary and ceased to make lamentations, overwhelmed by the vastness of the calamity. But whatever instances there may have been of such devotion, more often the sick and the dying were tended by the pitying care of those who had recovered, because they knew the course of the disease and were themselves free from apprehension. For no one was ever attacked a second time, or not with a fatal result. All men congratulated them, and they themselves, in the excess of their joy at the moment, had an innocent fancy that they could not die of any other sickness.

The crowding of the people out of the country into the city aggravated the misery; and the newly-arrived suffered most. For, having no houses of their own, but inhabiting in the height of summer stifling huts, the mortality among them was dreadful, and they perished in wild disorder. The dead lay as they had died, one upon another, while others hardly alive wallowed in the streets and crawled about every fountain craving for water. The temples in which they lodged were full of the corpses of those who died in them; for the violence of the calamity was such that men, not knowing where to turn, grew reckless of all law, human and divine. The customs which had hitherto been observed at funerals were universally violated, and they buried their dead each one as best he could. Many, having no proper appliances, because the deaths in their household had been so frequent, made no scruple of using the burial-place of others. When one man had raised a funeral pile, others would come, and throwing on their dead first, set fire to it; or when some other corpse was already burning, before they could be stopped would throw their own dead upon it and depart.

There were other and worse forms of lawlessness which the plague introduced at Athens. Men who had hitherto concealed their indulgence in plea-sure now grew bolder. For, seeing the sudden change,—how the rich died in a moment, and those who had nothing immediately inherited their property,—they reflected that life and riches were alike transitory, and they resolved to enjoy themselves while they could, and to think only of pleasure. Who would be willing to sacrifice himself to the law of honour when he knew not whether he would ever live to be held in honour? The pleasure of the moment and any sort of thing which conduced to it took the place both of honour and of expediency. No fear of God or law of man deterred a criminal. Those who saw all perishing alike, thought that the worship or neglect of the Gods made no difference. For offences against human law no punishment was to be feared; no one would live long enough to be called to account. Already a far heavier sentence had been passed and was hanging over a man's head; before that fell, why should he not take a little pleasure?

Such was the grievous calamity which now afflicted the Athenians; within the walls their people were dying, and without, their country was being ravaged. In their troubles they naturally called to mind a verse which the elder men among them declared to have been current long ago:

"A Dorian war will come and a plague with it."

There was a dispute about the precise expression; some saying that *limos*, a famine, and not *loimos*, a plague, was the original word. Nevertheless, as might have been expected, for men's memories reflected their sufferings, the argument in favour of *loimos* prevailed at the time. But if ever in future years another Dorian war arises which happens to be accompanied by a famine, they will probably repeat the verse in the other form. The answer of the oracle to the Lacedaemonians when the God was asked 'whether they should go to war or not,' and he replied 'that if they fought with all their might, they would conquer, and that he himself would take their part,' was not forgotten by those who had heard of it, and they quite imagined that they were witnessing the fulfilment of his words. The disease certainly did set in immediately after the invasion of the Peloponnesians, and did not spread into Peloponnesus in any degree worth speaking of, while Athens felt its ravages most severely, and next to Athens the places which were most populous. Such was the history of the plague.

6. PLUTARCH: PARALLEL LIVES

Two generations after Thucydides' death Hellenic civilization had passed away. In the aftermath of Alexander the Great's conquest of the Near East, an international Mediterranean culture emerged. This civilization, often entitled the Hellenistic World, was basically an amalgam of Greek and Near Eastern elements that eventually spread from Spain to India. It proved to be the last and greatest synthesis of ancient cultures, flourishing from the fourth century B.C. to the fourth century of the Christian Era, and in time encompassing a number of new people in the Western regions. The most notable of these were the Romans, who ultimately became masters of the Hellenistic world and carriers of its civilization to such distant lands as Gaul and England.

The Hellenic Greek had made his local city-state his world; Hellenistic man had the world as his city. This widening of intellectual horizons, and its resultant meshing of disparate cultures, spurred new modes of artistic and intellectual perception. Two of these were the concurrent emphases on universal humanity and the individual.

During this period historical writing generally fell from the position of scientific and artistic preeminence to which Thucydides had raised it and became an ancillary branch of the new art of rhetoric. Most Hellenistic historians, catering to the tastes of a new, greatly expanded reading public, strove more for dramatic effect than truth or understanding. All too often their moralizing was insipid at its best, saccharine at its worst, and many did not scruple from creating "historical" incidents and speeches of the most florid and artificially theatrical sort. It was the rare historian who did not engage in these excesses.

Ironically, one of the better historians of this age disclaimed the historian's mantle. This was Plutarch (*ca.* 47 A.D.-*ca.* 120). Not wholly enslaved to rhetoric, he nevertheless employed many of the devices made infamous by Hellenistic soap-opera historians. Yet, on the whole, Plutarch rose above romantic fiction and wrote history.

In his *Parallel Lives* Plutarch compared pairs of like statesmen—one a Greek, the other a Roman—selectively concentrating upon those actions and words that best illustrated each subject's character. His avowed purpose was to provide his readers with moral examples through which they could fashion their lives for the better. He was, by his own admission, a teacher of practical ethics.

Yet, while he was not an original researcher, deriving virtually all his information from the histories of other men, he was a historian. He did not write fiction, not even historical fiction. He expected his readers to accept the historical accuracy of what he reported; he assumed that the validity of each moral message depended on the truthfulness of the data he selected for analysis. In this probing of the souls of historic persons, Plutarch wrote, indeed created, a special branch of history— psychological biography.

As a teacher of the Good Life, Plutarch did not divorce ethics from religion. He lived during one of the most intensely religious periods of Western history. In this age of uncertainty, Plutarch, priest of the Apollo at Delphi, joined with the majority of his contemporaries in accepting the immediacy of the Divine and in probing the spiritual underpinnings of life.

Plutarch spent most of his long life in his homeland in central Greece, yet he traveled widely, visiting Rome several times. Here he won wide acclaim for his lectures on moral philosophy and gained the friendship of many influential Romans. He admired Latin civilization enough to acquire Roman citizenship, but he remained always a Greek—proud of his heritage and owing first allegiance to his beloved native city, Chaeronea.

Our selection is taken from Plutarch's biography of Alexander the Great.

IT being my purpose to write the lives of Alexander the king, and of Cæsar, by whom Pompey was destroyed, the multitude of their great actions affords so large a field that I were to blame if I should not by way of apology forewarn my reader that I have chosen rather to epitomise the most celebrated parts of their story, than to insist at large on every particular circumstance of it. It must be borne in mind that my design is not to write histories, but lives. And the most glorious exploits do not always furnish us with the clearest discoveries of virtue or vice in men; sometimes a matter of less moment, an expression or a jest, informs us better of their characters and inclinations, than the most famous sieges, the greatest armaments, or the bloodiest battles whatsoever. Therefore as portrait-painters are more exact in the lines and features of the face, in which the character is seen, than in the other parts of the body, so I must be allowed to give my more particular attention to the marks and indications of the souls of men, and while I endeavour by these to portray their lives, may be free to leave more weighty matters and great battles to be treated of by others. . . .

As he was upon his way to Babylon, Nearchus, who had sailed back out of the ocean up the mouth of the river Euphrates, came to tell him he had met with some Chaldæan diviners, who had warned him against Alexander's going thither. Alexander, however, took no thought of it, and went on, and when he came near the walls of the place, he saw a great many crows fighting with one another, some of whom fell down just by him. After this, being privately informed that Apollodorus, the governor of Babylon, had sacrificed, to know what would become of him, he sent for Pythagoras, the soothsayer, and on his admitting the thing, asked him in what condition he found the victim; and when he told him the liver was defective in its lobe, "A great presage indeed!" said Alexander. However, he offered Pythagoras no injury, but was sorry that he had neglected Nearchus's advice, and stayed for the most part outside the town, removing his tent from place to place, and sailing up and down the Euphrates. Besides this, he was disturbed by many other prodigies. A tame ass fell upon the biggest and handsomest lion that he kept, and killed him by a kick. And one day after he had undressed himself to be anointed, and was playing at ball, just as they were going to bring his clothes again, the young men who played with him perceived a man clad in the king's robes with a diadem upon his head, sitting silently upon his throne. They asked him who he was, to which he gave no answer a good while, till at last, coming to himself, he told them his name was Dionysius, that he was of Messenia, that for some crime of which he was accused he was brought thither from the seaside, and had been kept long in prison, that Serapis appeared to him, had freed him from his chains, conducted him to that place, and commanded him to put on the king's robe and diadem, and to sit where they found him, and to say nothing. Alexander, when he heard this, by the direction of his soothsayers, put the fellow to death, but he lost his spirits, and grew diffident of the protection and assistance of the gods, and suspicious of his friends. His greatest apprehension was of Antipater and his sons, one of whom, Iolaus, was his chief cupbearer; and Cassander, who had lately arrived, and had been bred up in Greek manners, the first time he saw some of the barbarians adore the king could not forbear laughing at it aloud, which so incensed Alexander that he took him by the hair with both hands and dashed his head against the wall. Another time, Cassander would have said something in defence of Antipater to those who accused him, but Alexander interrupting him, said, "What is it you say? Do you think people, if they had received no injury, would come such a journey only to calumninate your father?"

To which when Cassander replied, that their coming so far from the evidence was a great proof of the falseness of their charges, Alexander smiled, and said those were some of Aristotle's sophisms, which would serve equally on both sides; and added, that both he and his father should be severely punished, if they were found guilty of the least injustice towards those who complained. All which made such a deep impression of terror in Cassander's mind that, long after, when he was King of Macedonia and master of Greece, as he was walking up and down at Delphi, and looking at the statues, at the sight of that of Alexander he was suddenly struck with alarm, and shook all over, his eyes rolled, his head grew dizzy, and it was long before he recovered himself.

When once Alexander had given way to fears of supernatural influence, his mind grew so disturbed and so easily alarmed that, if the least unusual or extraordinary thing happened, he thought it a prodigy or a presage, and his court was thronged with diviners and priests whose business was to sacrifice and purify and foretell the future. So miserable a thing is incredulity and contempt of divine power on the one hand, and so miserable, also, superstition on the other, which like water, where the level has been lowered, flowing in and never stopping, fills the mind with slavish fears and follies, as now in Alexander's case. But upon some answers which were brought him from the oracle concerning Hephæstion, he laid aside his sorrow, and fell again to sacrificing and drinking; and having given Nearchus a splendid entertainment, after he had bathed, as was his custom, just as he was going to bed, at Medius's request he went to supper with him. Here he drank all the next day, and was attacked with a fever, which seized him, not as some write, after he had drunk of the bowl of Hercules, nor was he taken with any sudden pain in his back, as if he had been struck with a lance, for these are the inventions of some authors who thought it their duty to make the last scene of so great an action as tragical and moving as they could. Aristobulus tells us, that in the rage of his fever and a violent thirst, he took a draught of wine, upon which he fell into delirium, and died on the thirtieth day of the month Dæsius.

But the journals give the following record. On the eighteenth day of the month he slept in the bathing-room on account of his fever. The next day he bathed and removed into his chamber, and spent his time in playing at dice with Medius. In the evening he bathed and sacrificed, and ate freely, and had the fever on him through the night. On the twentieth, after the usual sacrifices and bathing, he lay in the bathing-room and heard Nearchus's narrative of his voyage, and the observations he had made in the great sea. The twenty-first he passed in the same manner, his fever still increasing, and suffered much during the night. The next day the fever was very violent, and he had himself removed and his bed set by the great bath, and discoursed with his principal officers about finding fit men to fill up the vacant places in the army. On the twenty-fourth he was much worse, and was carried out of his bed to assist at the sacrifices, and gave order that the general officers should wait within the court, whilst the inferior officers kept watch without doors. On the twenty-fifth he was removed to his palace on the other side the river, where he slept a little, but his fever did not abate, and when the generals came into his chamber, he was speechless and continued so the following day. The Macedonians, therefore, supposing he was dead, came with great clamours to the gates, and menaced his friends so that they were forced to admit them, and let them all pass through unarmed by his bedside. The same day Python and Seleucus were despatched to the temple of Serapis to inquire if they should bring Alexander thither, and were answered by the god that they should not remove him. On the twenty-eighth, in the evening, he died. This account is most of it word for word as it is written in the diary.

At the time, nobody had any suspicion of his being poisoned, but upon some information given six years after, they say Olympias put many to death, and scattered the ashes of Iolaus, then dead, as if he had given it him. But those who affirm that Aristotle counselled Antipater to do it, and that by his means the poison was brought, adduced one Hagnothemis as their authority, who, they say, heard King Antigonus speak of it, and tell us that the poison was water, deadly cold as ice, distilled from a rock in the district of Nonacris, which they gathered like a thin dew, and kept in an ass's hoof; for it was so very cold and penetrating that no other vessel would hold it. However, most are of opinion that all this is a mere made-up story, no slight evidence of which is, that during the dissensions among the commanders, which lasted several days, the body continued clear and fresh, without any sign of such taint or corruption, though it lay neglected in a close sultry place.

Roxana, who was now with child, and upon that account much honoured by the Macedonians, being jealous of Statira, sent for her by a counterfeit letter, as if Alexander had been still alive; and when she had her in her power, killed her and her sister, and threw their bodies into a well, which they filled up with earth, not without the privity and assistance of Perdiccas, who in the time immediately following the king's death, under cover of the name of Arrhidæus, whom he carried about him as a sort of guard to his person, exercised the chief authority. Arrhidæus, who was Philip's son by an obscure woman of the name of Philinna, was himself of weak intellect, not that he had been originally deficient either in body or mind, on the contrary, in his childhood, he had showed a happy and promising character enough. But a diseased habit of body, caused by drugs which Olympias gave him, had ruined, not only his health, but his understanding.

SOURCE NOTES

1. From *The Histories of Herodotus,* translated by Henry Cary (New York: D. Appleton and Company, 1904), pp. 168-170, 198-200, and 406-409.
2. From *Thucydides Translated into English* by B. Jowett (Oxford: Clarendon Press, 1881), I, pp. 115-129.
3. From Plutarch, *The Lives of the Noble Grecians and Romans,* translated by John Dryden and revised by Arthur Hugh Clough (original edition, 1864, reprinted in New York: Random House [n.d.]), pp. 801, and 852-854.

3.
CLASSICAL
ROME

The predominant cultural influence on Rome was Greek, but it would be wrong for us to see Roman society as simply a pale shadow of Greek civilization. We would unjustly slight the native Roman genius if we overlooked the manner in which this Latin people developed remarkably distinctive institutions and outlooks that helped Rome become master of the Hellenistic world. Yet, in its mastery it also became a student.

Horace, a Latin poet of the first century B.C., wrote, "Captive Greece overcame the uncouth conqueror and introduced the arts into rustic Latium." One of those arts was history. It was no accident that the first Roman historian, Quintus Fabius Pictor (*ca.* 254-*ca.* 216 B.C.), wrote in Greek, and the best history of Rome produced in ancient times was written by a Greek (in Greek), Polybius (*ca.* 198-*ca.* 117 B.C.).

In time, Romans began recording their own history in their own tongue, although never were their numbers large. The father of Latin historiography was Cato the Censor (234-149 B.C.), who wrote a history of Rome down to his own day. Cato, known to history as the most Roman of the Romans, hated everything Hellenistic (although even he learned Greek in his old age). Yet, the surviving fragments of his history reveal a mind steeped in Hellenism, despite itself; he could not help writing history in the Greek style. Indeed, the entire Roman historiographical tradition, while inevitably shaped by Latin ethnic culture and the Roman character, largely followed Greek models, particularly those of the Hellenistic Age: History was approached mainly as literature and moral philosophy.

At their best, several Latin historians were able to rise above the excesses of rhetorical history. Yet, even these exceptions labored under the burden of the inherited Hellenistic tradition. Still, the history they wrote was Roman, the tongue they employed was Latin, and the values they magnified—reverence for the old domestic virtues, respect for law and order, and unselfish devotion to the *res publica*—were decidedly Roman. Furthermore, in one important respect, certain Roman historians departed from their Greek models.

The Greek historiographical vision had been shaped largely by the apparent circularity of fortune enjoyed by Greek cities and individuals: The more things changed, the more they remained the same. Therefore, human life seemed to run according to more or less constant laws of cyclical change.

By the mid-second century B.C., Romans confronted different phenomena. This once minor Latin city had risen to mastery over the Mediterranean. Moreover, when Republican Rome became an imperial power (almost in a fit of absent-mindedness), many of its institutions inevitably had to change, and Roman society lay open to strange, new foreign influences. The Romans, ever a conservative people, were confused and frightened by these changes.

During the last century of the Republic the stresses of empire threatened to tear apart the political and social fabric of Roman civilization. In the latter stages of this troubled age and shortly following, two of Rome's greatest native historians, Caius Crispus Sallustius (Sallust) and Titus Livius (Livy), applied their talents to studies of the meaning of Roman history. Their approaches were different, their conclusions similar.

Both historians perceived Rome's past to have been a steady evolution into greatness. But if the Roman story was progressive, it was also regressive. An integral element of their linear analysis of Roman history was the concomitant belief that Roman virtue had declined as a result of this development: Rome had risen to its heights because of the virtues of its early heroes, but their very successes had laid the basis for the corruption of their heirs—the contemporaries of Sallust and Livy.

In practical Roman fashion, both men were avowedly fulfilling political and social roles: To rekindle patriotic zeal in the hearts of their countrymen and to shame their decadent contemporaries into wishing to rival their forebears. Such ends have continued to motivate the writing of history, particularly national histories, even into our own day.

7. SALLUST: THE CONSPIRACY OF CATILINE

Sallust (86-35 B.C.) is generally acknowledged to have been the finest historian of Republican Rome; he may well have been the best classical Rome ever produced. Although he delegated the drudgery of research to assistants (shades of modern academe!), he had a remarkable ability to analyze historical data critically and to create out of it a living, readable story.

A political ally of Julius Caesar, Sallust was a member of the Senate and served Rome in various high military and administrative capacities, capping his political career as governor of Numidia (during which tenure he acquired a fortune, largely through blatant abuse of his office). Following Caesar's assassination in 44 B.C., he retired from public life and devoted his remaining years to good living and historical scholarship (not necessarily compatible pastimes).

In his retirement he composed three short monographic studies of notable recent events. Two are extant today: *The Conspiracy of Catiline* and *The Jugurthine War.* In each work Sallust, himself accused by his enemies of sexual irregularities, profligate living, and extraordinary venality, continually underlined the vicious and immoral nature of the Republic's public arena, from which he had sought refuge.

In the passage below Sallust traces the general course of Roman history in order to set the stage for his history of the Catilinarian conspiracy.

As for me, like most others, I had, in my younger days, a strong desire for a share in the administration; but found many obstructions in my way: for, instead of modesty, justice, and virtue, licentiousness, corruption, and avarice flourished; which, though my soul, as yet untainted with evil habits, utterly abhorred; yet amidst such general depravity, my tender years were caught by ambition; and although I avoided, in the general tenor of my conduct, the corrupt practices of the age, yet, being fired with the same ardour for preferment that others were, I was thence exposed to envy and reproach, as well as they.

As soon, however, as my mind was delivered from the many crosses and dangers attending this pursuit, and I had determined to retire, during the remainder of my life, from the administration, it was not my intention to waste such valuable time in sloth and indolence, nor to pass my days in agriculture, hunting, or the like servile occupations; but resuming my former design, from which the cursed spirit of ambition had diverted me, I resolved to employ myself in writing such parts of the Roman history, as appeared to me to be most deserving of being transmitted to posterity; and this I chose the rather, because my mind was neither influenced by hope or fear, nor attached to any party in the state: accordingly, I shall here, with the utmost veracity, give a short account of Catiline's conspiracy; a memorable attempt, both for the enormous wickedness of it, and the danger it threatened. But before I enter directly upon the story, I shall give a short character of the man.

LUCIUS CATILINE was descended of an illustrious family: he was a man of great vigor both of body and mind; but of a disposition extremely profligate and depraved. From his youth he took pleasure in civil wars, massacres, depredations, and intestine broils: and in these he employed his younger days. His body was formed for enduring cold, hunger, and want of rest, to a degree indeed incredible: his spirit was daring, subtle, and changeable; he was expert in all the arts of simulation and dissimulation; covetous of what belonged to others, lavish of his own; violent in his passions; he had eloquence enough, but a small share of wisdom. His boundless soul was constantly engaged in extravagant and romantic projects, too high to be attempted.

Such was the character of Catiline; who, after Sulla's usurpation, was fired with a violent desire of seizing the government; and, provided he could but carry his point, he was not at all solicitous by what means. His spirit, naturally violent, was daily more and more hurried to the execution of his designs, by his poverty and the consciousness of his crimes; both which evils he had heightened by the practices above mentioned. He was encouraged to it by the wickedness of the state, thoroughly debauched by luxury and avarice; vices equally fatal, though of contrary natures.

Now that I have occasion to mention the Roman manners, I am naturally led to look back a little to past ages, and to give a short account of the institutions of our ancestors, both in war and peace; how they governed the state, and in what grandeur they left it; and how, by a gradual declension, it has fallen from the highest degree of virtue and glory, to the lowest pitch of vice and depravity. . . .

Good morals, therefore, were cultivated both at home and abroad. A spirit of perfect harmony and disinterestedness every where prevailed. Laws had no greater influence in determining them to the practice of justice and equity, than natural disposition. The only quarrels, dissensions, and disputes they exercised, were against the public enemy: all the contests that subsisted among the citizens, were in virtuous deeds. They were magnificent in their offerings to the gods; frugal in their families; and faithful to their friends. Bravery in war, and equity and moderation in peace, were the only means by which they supported themselves and the public affairs: and, as the clearest evidence of these virtues, I find, that, in time of war, such as engaged the enemy contrary to orders, or continued in the field after a retreat was sounded, were more frequently punished, than those who abandoned their standards, or quitted their posts; and in peace, they conducted the administration more by the force of favours than of terror; and, if they received an injury, chose rather to forgive than revenge it.

But when by probity and industry the state was become powerful; when mighty princes were conquered in war; barbarous nations and potent states reduced to obedience; when Carthage, that vied with Rome for the empire of the world, was utterly demolished, and sea and land lay every where open to her power; then fortune began to exert her malice, and throw every thing into confusion. Ease and riches, the grand objects of the pursuit of others, depressed and ruined those, who had, without regret, undergone toils and hardships, distresses and dangers. First a love of money possessed their minds; than a passion for power; and these were the seeds of all the evils that followed. For avarice rooted out faith, probity, and every worthy principle; and, in their stead, substituted insolence, inhumanity, contempt of the gods, and a mercenary spirit. Ambition obliged many to be deceitful, to belie with their tongues the sentiments of their hearts; to value friendship and enmity not according to their real worth, but as they conduced to interest; and to have a specious countenance, rather than an honest heart. These corruptions at first grew by degrees, and were sometimes checked by correction. At last, the infection spreading like a plague, the state was entirely changed, and the government, from being the most righteous and equitable, became cruel and insupportable. . . .

To see the difference between modern and ancient manners, one needs but take a view of the houses of particular citizens, both in town and country, all resembling, in magnificence, so many cities; and then behold the temples of the gods, built by our ancestors, the most religious of all men. But they thought of no other ornament for their temples, than devotion; nor for their houses, but glory: neither did they take any thing from the conquered, but the power of doing hurt. Whereas their descendants, the most effeminate of all men, have plundered from their allies, by the most flagrant injustice, whatever their brave ancestors left to their conquered enemies; as if the only use of power was to do wrong.

It is needless to recount other things, which none but those who saw them will believe; as the levelling of mountains by private citizens, and even covering the sea itself with fine edifices. These men appear to me to have sported with their riches, since they lavished them in the most shameful manner, instead of enjoying them with honour. Nor were they less addicted to lewdness, and all manner of extravagant gratifications: men prostituted themselves like women; women laid aside all regard to chastity. To procure dainties for their tables, sea and land were ransacked. They indulged to sleep, before nature craved it; the returns of hunger and thirst were anticipated with luxury; and cold and fatigue were never so much as felt. The Roman youth, after they had spent their fortunes, were prompted by such depravations to commit all manner of enormities; for their minds, impregnated with evil habits, and unable to resist their craving appetites, were violently bent upon all manner of extravagances, and all the means of supplying them.

In so great and debauched a city, Catiline had always about him, what was no difficult matter to find in Rome, bands of profligate and flagitious wretches, like guards to his person.

8.   LIVY: FROM THE FOUNDATION OF THE CITY

Livy (59 B.C.-17 A.D.), Rome's self-appointed national historian, composed a monumental prose epic, which traced the development of Roman civilization from its legendary origins (hence its title, *From the Foundation of the City*) down to his own day: Some 770 years of myth and history. His work eventually encompassed 142 books (approximately 12,000 modern printed pages), of which only 35 books have survived unabridged into modern times.

Livy's period of mature productivity was roughly coterminous with the long reign of Caesar Augustus. The Augustan Age—the end of the Republic, the beginning of the Empire—was one of the most fruitful periods in Roman history; it was apparent to contemporaries that Augustus was restoring order and providing a new foundation for Roman civilization. He was the new Romulus—the second founder—who promised to end Rome's progressive degeneration and restore its divinely directed mission, to bring Roman peace to the world. Augustus' New Order was successful to the point that Roman civilization continued to flourish for several centuries after his death.

Politically, Livy was a Republican, who had no desire to see Rome governed by an emperor, and he possessed an independent skepticism concerning the efficacy of Augustus' sumptuary laws. But he also enjoyed the friendship and patronage of the emperor for forty years and, in turn, supported Augustus' earnest drive to reform the moral and spiritual life of Roman society.

In his approach to the art of history writing, Livy was far more influenced by the Greek rhetoricians than by Thucydides or Sallust. History for him was a vast storehouse of useful moral examples which must, above all else, be presented artfully. Accuracy and credibility were far less important than style and edification. Livy's work was immediately successful largely because he wrote "apple pie and motherhood" history. The virtues he magnified—Discipline, Orderliness, Courage, Perseverance, Piety, Simplicity, Chastity, Prudence, Sobriety, Dignity—were the essential elements of the Roman self-image. They also constituted the heart of Stoic ethical teaching.

Stoicism was the non-Hebraic, Hellenistic world's attempt to construct a reasonable and just world ordered according to divine principles. This philosophical school, which had arisen in Athens during the late fourth and early third centuries B.C., taught that a transcendental Reason provides the universe with its natural harmony. That harmony can be realized in the microcosm of human society through the agency of virtuous and wise men who seek after the Good in life and order their lives and those of their neighbors accordingly.

Probably because Stoicism's practical ethical values corresponded so closely to Roman society's traditional virtues, a significant percentage of the Roman intelligentsia embraced this philosophy, especially during the two centuries bracketing the Augustan Age. As with everything else they borrowed from the Greeks, the Romans modified the teaching of the Stoic school to suit their needs and visions. Roman Stoicism tended to emphasize a universe guided by this unknown Intelligence toward the predestined end of universal peace and brotherhood. In the light of the Roman imperial experience and the resultant *Pax Romana,* educated popularizers of what had originally been a subtle school of ethical philosophy now identified Rome as the vital agent of an active, creative Reason. Livy, himself no original philosopher, accepted this simplified Neostoicism and centered his history on the theme of Rome's necessary, predetermined development into greatness—predetermined by Reason which he identified as Fortune; necessary because Rome was to become the harmonizing element in the world through its mastery over it.

Excerpted below is a tale out of Book V. The story concerns the siege and capture of large sections of Rome by invading Gauls in 390 B.C. and Rome's almost miraculous recovery under the direction of the dictator Camillus. More than simply illustrating Livy's manner of anecdotal moralizing, this selection serves as an example of Livy's neostoic vision of a linear history under the guidance of Reason—here identified with the traditional Roman deity, Fortune. The reader should note how Livy, like the anonymous Hebrew authors, juxtaposes individual human actions and free will with the overriding historical designs of Fortune.

Fortune herself, in order to test the Roman character, led the Gauls, after they had departed from the City, to Ardea, where Camillus was spending his exile. Even here, while wasting away, he grieved more for Rome's fortune than his own, and in his misery he blamed both the gods and men. Burning with indignation, he wondered where those heroes were who had taken Veii and Falerii with him and who had won other wars more through courage than luck. Suddenly

he heard of the approach of the Gallic army and also that the citizens of Ardea
were deliberating in alarm about what to do. As if divinely inspired, Camillus re-
gally strode into the midst of their assembly, even though up to this time he was
accustomed to absent himself from such meetings, and there he addresses them:

"Men of Ardea, my old friends and, now more recently, my fellow
citizens (since your kindness would have it so, and *my fortune* has made
it so), let none of you imagine that I've come forward forgetful of my
condition. However, our common peril makes it necessary for everyone
to contribute to the public good whatever service he is able to perform in
these alarming times. And when shall I repay you for your important
services to me, if now I'm remiss? How else could I serve you, if not
in war? It was through the art of war that I supported myself in my
homeland, and when I was banished during peacetime by my ungrateful
countrymen, I was still a soldier who had never been conquered. Now,
men of Ardea, Fortune presents you with an opportunity to repay the
Romans for all the favors which they have formerly conferred on you
(You remember the magnitude of these favors; I do not need to mention
them). It is also an opportunity for this city to acquire a great military
reputation among our common enemy. The foe which now marches
toward us in disorder is one to whom nature has given courage and
bodies, both of which are great but undisciplined. For this reason their
main weapon is terror rather than military ability. As proof, consider the
disaster which befell the Romans. The Gauls captured the undefended
City; yet once a stand is made on the Citadel and Capitol by a handful of
men, the Gauls retire, worn out now by the slow process of the siege,
and now roam about the countryside, gorged with food and wine hastily
gulped down. When night comes, they stretch out helter-skelter, like
wild animals near the water. They build no trench, post no sentries, set
up no advanced posts. Now more than ever, they throw caution to the
winds because of their success. If you wish to defend your walls and not
allow this entire area to become Gallic, take up arms at the first watch
and follow me to slaughter, not to battle. If I do not deliver them to you
fettered by sleep, ready to be butchered like cattle, then I accept the
same fate at Ardea that I suffered at Rome."

[Camillus leads the Ardentine army to victory over the sleeping Gauls. Rome,
however, remains under siege and invites Camillus back to assume the extraordinary office of dictator].

. . . Meanwhile, the Citadel and Capitol of Rome were in great danger. The Gauls either saw the track of a human foot where a messenger from Veii had passed, or noted that the rock at the temple of Carmentis afforded an easy ascent. So on a brightly lit night, they first sent out an unarmed person to try the way; then handing their arms to those ahead whenever any difficulty occurred, and alternately supporting and being supported by one another, they pulled each other up whenever the terrain required it. They climbed to the summit in such silence that they not only escaped the notice of the sentries but did not even alarm the dogs—animals which are sensitive to nocturnal noises. However, they did not escape the notice of the geese. Since these animals are sacred to Juno, the besieged Romans had not eaten them, even though food was scarce. *This act proved to be Rome's salvation.* For the animals' cackling and clapping of wings awoke Marcus Manlius, a war hero who had been consul three years previous. He snatched up his armor and sounded the alarm at the same time. Hastening to the spot, he uses the raised ornament on his shield to dislodge a Gaul who had already got a footing on the summit. (Meanwhile the rest of the Roman army is still milling about in confusion). As this Gaul tumbled down, he carried along with him those nearest to him. Several other Gauls threw away their weapons out of fear and clung to the rocks. These Manlius killed. By now the rest of the Romans had organized and began hurling javelins and stones at the enemy. As a result, the entire band of Gauls, having lost their footing, were hurled down the precipice to their death.

After the din of battle subsided the rest of the night was spent in rest—at least as much rest as the Romans' disturbed state of mind would allow, for even though the danger was now past, the thought of it kept them in a high pitch of excitement. At dawn the soldiers were summoned by trumpet to an assembly presided over by the tribunes. Here valor was to be rewarded and bad conduct punished. First of all, Manlius was commended for his courage and presented gifts, not only by the authority of the military tribunes, but also with the consent of the army. Each soldier carried to Manlius' home (which was located in the Citadel) a gift of half a pound of grain and half a pint of wine. In the telling, this appears to be a trifling present, but the prevailing scarcity of food made it a strong token of affection, since each soldier deprived himself of food necessary to maintain his own body in order to contribute to the honor of one man. Then the sentries on duty at the spot where the enemy had climbed up unobserved were summoned. Quintus Sulpicius declared that he would punish them all as military law dictated, but he was deterred by the united cries of the soldiers who threw the blame on a single sentry. So he spared the rest and, with the approval of everyone, flung from the cliff the one who was clearly guilty of the crime.

From this time onward the sentries on both sides were more vigilant—the Gauls because the rumor spread that messengers were passing between Veii and Rome, the Romans because of their memory of the peril they had been in during that night. . . .

[Both the Romans and Gauls continue to suffer during the siege. Finally, famine brings the Romans to the point of despair, especially since Camillus, their dictator and hoped for savior, has not yet arrived.]

. . . No longer could the Romans disguise or endure their hunger. The dictator is personally commanding troops at Ardea, ordering his cavalry commander, Lucius Valerius to lead forces up from Veii, and making the necessary arrangements so that he could attack the enemy on equal terms. But meanwhile the army in the Capitol is worn out from picket and sentry duty. Although they have to this point overcome all human suffering, there was one—hunger—which nature made it impossible to conquer. Daily they searched for any assistance which might come from the dictator. Finally hope runs out along with the food. As they march to their sentry posts, their weapons virtually crush their feeble bodies down. So now the Romans insisted on surrendering or being ransomed at whatever possible price. The Gauls, on their part, intimated plainly that they could be persuaded to abandon the siege for a modest price.

The senate was convened and instructions were given to the military tribunes to surrender. Terms were then reached in a conference between the military tribune, Quintus Sulpicius, and the Gallic chief Brennus. One thousand pounds of gold was fixed as the ransom of a people who presently would rule the world. And insult was added to this humiliating transaction. The Gauls brought false weights, and when a tribune objected, the insolent Gaul added his sword to the pile and an exclamation intolerable to the Romans was heard, ''Woe to the vanquished.''

But both gods and men combined to prevent the Romans from living the lives of ransomed captives. By some chance, before the abominable payment was completed (due to the fact that all the gold was not weighed out owing to the altercation), the dictator arrives and orders the gold carried away and the Gauls to clear out. When they refused, maintaining that they had concluded a bargain, he denied that the agreement was valid, for it had been made after he had been named dictator, through a magistrate of inferior rank, and without the dictator's orders. So he gives notice to the Gauls to prepare for battle and orders his own men to throw their baggage into a heap and to ready their weapons. They are to recover their homeland with iron not gold, having before their eyes the temples of their gods, their wives and children, the soil of their land disfigured by the calamities of war, and all those objects which solemn duty required them to defend, recover, and revenge. He then drew the army up in a line (as well as the terrain allowed), on the site of this half demolished city, which lay on naturally uneven ground, and he saw to it that his soldiers had every advantage in preparation and position such as his knowledge of the art of war suggested. The Gauls, alarmed at the turn of events, take up arms and, more in rage than good judgement, rushed upon the Romans.

Fortune had now changed; now divine favor and human wisdom were on the Roman side. At the first charge the Gauls were routed with no greater difficulty than they had experienced in their victory at Allia. Following this they fought a more systematic battle eight miles out on the Gabine road, where the Gauls had retreated following their initial defeat. There they were beaten again by the inspired generalship of this same Camillus. The slaughter was total; their camp was taken, and there was not one person left to carry home news of the disaster. The dictator having thus recovered his homeland from the enemy, returns to the city in triumph, and in addition to the crude military jests which are bandied about on such occasions, he is hailed with justly deserved praise as Romulus and Father of the Fatherland and, moreover, second founder of the City.

SOURCE NOTES

1. From C. Crispus Sallustius, *The History of the Conspiracy of Catiline and the Jugurthine War,* translated by William Rose (Philadelphia: Thomas Wardle, 1837), pp. 2-5.
2. From T. Livii Patavini, *Historiarum Libri,* ed. by J. T. Kreyssig (Oxford, 1840), I, pp. 334-341. Translation by A. J. Andrea.

4.
EARLY CHRISTIANITY

The message of primitive Christianity transcended time and space, and Faith was demanded of its devotees, not rational analysis. Still, from its earliest days Christianity was a religious movement grounded upon historical consciousness.

Its founder (and God) was a known historical figure, and although the "historical Jesus" was far less important to Christians than the Divine Christ, Jesus' earthly deeds were of interest. The synoptic gospels of Matthew, Mark, and Luke, all composed probably during the first century A.D. when the memory of Jesus was still fresh, were meant, in part, to be history. By placing Christ within a historical framework, these evangelists intended to illustrate how He was the fulfillment of Jewish history and how, through His life and death, had instituted a new Linear History, whose goal was Himself—His Second Coming and the concomitant end to all time. They also attempted to show that He had given his Church on earth a temporal as well as spiritual mission: To preach penance and remission of sins in His name unto all nations (*Luke:* 24, 47). Now all humanity shared fully in the Divine Historical Plan.

Christian history was, therefore, universal history. It cut across all ethnic and national boundaries; it even bridged the sex gap. Hebrew history had had a few heroines, since it was the history of an entire chosen people. For much the same reason, even Livy celebrated the virtuous deeds of several exceptional Roman women. Yet, on the whole, classical Greek and Roman historiography ignored women. The histories of the Greeks and Romans were secular and politically oriented, and in these societies citizenship was exercised by men alone. However, within the Christian Church, women shared, through grace, the same supernatural citizenship as men and could rise to equal heights of spiritual greatness.

They could become saints. And, to the Christian mind, it was these saints, not statesmen and generals, who were most worthy of being remembered and emulated throughout history. Christians, building upon Jewish models, introduced to the Gentile world a new form of historical biography—hagiography—histories of holy men and women performing in finite, human time deeds reflective of the infinite, timeless Virtues of Christ.

Time itself was very important to Christian historians. All human history from the date of creation was now, in a sense, Christian history (although Christian historians did distinguish between the sacred history of Jews and Christians and the profane history of everyone else). Therefore, the history of all peoples had to be synchronized and a world-wide chronological standard of time established. Christian writers from the third century onward prepared Christian world chronologies that, in time, became the basis of our modern system of historical dating.

These would remain essential elements of the Christian historiographical vision for at least two millennia. But within the general outline of this Christ-centered Linear History there was room for different emphases. The first four centuries of the Christian Era saw two major schools of Christian historical thought develop, each formed by different social and political realities. One stressed the temporal dimensions of the Church and believed it natural and inevitable that the Church should work in harmony with earthly governments for the realization of Christ's Kingdom. The other emphasized the mystical nature of Divine History and taught there could be no harmony between the earthly and the spiritual: Although Christians operated *in* the world, they were not *of* the world.

9.   EUSEBIUS: ECCLESIASTICAL HISTORY

Eusebius (*ca.* 260-*ca.* 340), Greek bishop of Caesarea in Palestine, was a prolific writer, whose interests ranged over a broad spectrum of practical and speculative theological topics. His reputation as a historian rests upon two works, the *Chronicle* and the *Ecclesiastical History.*

The former was an attempted synopsis and chronological concordance of all sacred and profane history. A superior work of scholarship, it served as the model for subsequent medieval world histories. The *Ecclesiastical History* established its author as the first great Chruch historian. Its prose was not artful, but the work was thoroughly researched and its conclusions were well argued. Eusebius diligently incorporated large amounts of evidence into the text and exhibited throughout a determination to write critical, accurate history. This did not negate, however, the *Ecclesiastical History*'s apologetical tone and theological message.

Eusebius lived and suffered through the period of the Great Persecution (303-311), and he witnessed the miracle of the Emperor Constantine's conversion to Christianity after the Battle of Milvian Bridge in 312. During the persecution Eusebius was imprisoned and saw many of his friends martyred; during Constantine's reign he enjoyed imperial patronage and friendship.

Sometime before the Great Persecution, Eusebius began a detailed history of the Church down to his own day. The work was completed in seven volumes around 303. It was later enlarged to ten books to include the history of Christian fortunes down to 324. The last of these books, which dealt with the Emperor Constantine, expressed the sentiment that the new Christian Roman Empire was the handiwork of Providence and would provide mankind with a new and lasting basis of solidarity and peace.

The selections below have been culled from Books, V, VIII, and X, respectively.

Other writers of history record the victories of war and trophies won from enemies, the skill of generals, and the manly bravery of soldiers, defiled with blood and with innumerable slaughters for the sake of children and country and other possessions. But our narrative of the government of God will record in ineffaceable letters the most peaceful wars waged in behalf of the peace of the soul, and will tell of men doing brave deeds for truth rather than country, and for piety rather than dearest friends. It will hand down to imperishable remembrance the discipline and the much-tried fortitude of the athletes of religion, the trophies won from demons, the victories over invisible enemies, and the crowns placed upon all their heads. . . .

Up to the sixth year the storm had been incessantly raging against us. Before this time there had been a very large number of confessors of religion in the so-called Porphyry quarry in Thebais, which gets its name from the stone found there. Of these, one hundred men, lacking three, together with women and infants, were sent to the governor of Palestine. When they confessed the God of the universe and Christ, Firmilianus, who had been sent there as governor in the place of Urbanus, directed, in accordance with the imperial command, that they should be maimed by burning the sinews of the ankles of their left feet, and that their right eyes with the eyelids and pupils should first be cut out, and then destroyed by hot irons to the very roots. And he then sent them to the mines in the province to endure hardships with severe toil and suffering.

But it was not sufficient that these only who suffered such miseries should be deprived of their eyes, but those natives of Palestine also, who were mentioned just above as condemned to pugilistic combat, since they would neither receive food from the royal storehouse nor undergo the necessary preparatory exercises. Having been brought on this account not only before the overseers, but also before Maximinus himself, and having manifested the noblest persistence in confession by the endurance of hunger and stripes, they received like punishment with those whom we have mentioned, and with them other confessors in the city of Cæsarea. Immediately afterwards others who were gathered to hear the Scriptures read, were seized in Gaza, and some endured the same sufferings in the feet and eyes; but others were afflicted with yet greater torments and with most terrible tortures in the sides. One of these, in body a woman, but in understanding a man, would not endure the threat of fornication, and spoke directly against the tyrant who entrusted the government to such cruel judges. She was first scourged and then raised aloft on the stake, and her sides lacerated. As those appointed for this purpose applied the tortures incessantly and severely at the command of the judge, another, with mind fixed, like the former, on virginity as her aim,—a woman who was altogether mean in form and contemptible in appearance, but, on the other hand, strong in soul, and endowed with an understanding superior to her body,—being unable to bear the merciless and cruel and inhuman deeds, with a boldness beyond that of the combatants famed among the Greeks, cried out to the judge from the midst of the crowd:

"And how long will you thus cruelly torture my sister?" But he was greatly enraged, and ordered the woman to be immediately seized. Thereupon she was brought forward and having called herself by the august name of the Saviour, she was first urged by words to sacrifice, and as she refused she was dragged by force to the altar. But her sister continued to maintain her former zeal, and with intrepid and resolute foot kicked the altar, and overturned it with the fire that was on it. Thereupon the judge, enraged like a wild beast, inflicted on her such tortures in her sides as he never had on any one before, striving almost to glut himself with her raw flesh. But when his madness was satiated, he bound them both together, this one and her whom she called sister, and condemned them to death by fire. It is said that the first of these was from the country of Gaza; the other, by name Valentina, was of Cæsarea, and was well known to many. . . .

Thanks for all things be given unto God the Omnipotent Ruler and King of the universe, and the greatest thanks to Jesus Christ the Saviour and Redeemer of our souls, through whom we pray that peace may be always preserved for us firm and undisturbed by external troubles and by troubles of the mind. Since in accordance with thy wishes, my most holy Paulinus, we have added the tenth book of the Church History to those which have preceded, we will inscribe it to thee, proclaiming thee as the seal of the whole work; and we will fitly add in a perfect number the perfect panegyric upon the restoration of the churches, obeying the Divine Spirit which exhorts us in the following words: "Sing unto the Lord a new song, for he hath done marvelous things. His right hand and his holy arm hath saved him. The Lord hath made known his salvation, his righteousness hath he revealed in the presence of the nations." And in accordance with the utterance which commands us to sing the new song, let us proceed to show that, after those terrible and gloomy spectacles which we have described, we are now permitted to see and celebrate such things as many truly righteous men and martyrs of God before us desired to see upon earth and did not see, and to hear and did not hear. But they, hastening on, obtained far better things, being carried to heaven and the paradise of divine pleasure. But, acknowledging that even these things are greater than we deserve, we have been astonished at the grace manifested by the author of the great gifts, and rightly do we admire him, worshiping him with the whole power of our souls, and testifying to the truth of those recorded utterances, in which it is said, "Come and see the works of the Lord, the wonders which he hath done upon the earth; he removeth wars to the ends of the world, he shall break the bow and snap the spear in sunder, and shall burn the shields with fire." Rejoicing in these things which have been clearly fulfilled in our day, let us proceed with our account.

The whole race of God's enemies was destroyed in the manner indicated, and was thus suddenly swept from the sight of men. So that again a divine utterance had its fulfillment: "I have seen the impious highly exalted and raising himself like the cedars of Lebanon; and I have passed by, and behold, he was not; and I have sought his place, and it could not be found." And finally a bright and splendid day, overshadowed by no cloud, illuminated with beams of heavenly light the churches of Christ throughout the entire world. And not even those without our communion were prevented from sharing in the same blessings, or at least from coming under their influence and enjoying a part of the benefits bestowed upon us by God.

All men, then, were freed from the oppression of the tyrants, and being released from the former ills, one in one way and another in another acknowledged the defender of the pious to be the only true God. And we especially who placed our hopes in the Christ of God had unspeakable gladness, and a certain inspired joy bloomed for all of us, when we saw every place which shortly before had been desolated by the impieties of the tyrants reviving as if from a long and death-fraught pestilence, and temples again rising from their foundations to an immense height, and receiving a splendor far greater than that of the old ones which had been destroyed. But the supreme rulers also confirmed to us still more extensively the munificence of God by repeated ordinances in behalf of the Christians; and personal letters of the emperor were sent to the bishops, with honors and gifts of money. It may not be unfitting to insert these documents, translated from the Roman into the Greek tongue, at the proper place in this book, as in a sacred tablet, that they may remain as a memorial to all who shall come after us. . . .

To him, therefore, God granted, from heaven above, the deserved fruit of piety, the trophies of victory over the impious, and he cast the guilty one with all his counselors and friends prostrate at the feet of Constantine. For when Licinius carried his madness to the last extreme, the emperor, the friend of God, thinking that he ought no longer to be tolerated, acting upon the basis of sound judgment, and mingling the firm principles of justice with humanity, gladly determined to come to the protection of those who were oppressed by the tyrant, and undertook, by putting a few destroyers out of the way, to save the greater part of the human race. For when he had formerly exercised humanity alone and had shown mercy to him who was not worthy of sympathy, nothing was accomplished; for Licinius did not renounce his wickedness, but rather increased his fury against the peoples that were subject to him, and there was left to the afflicted no hope of salvation, oppressed as they were by a savage beast. Wherefore, the protector of the virtuous, mingling hatred for evil with love for good, went forth with his son Crispus, a most beneficent prince, and extended a saving right hand to all that were perishing. Both of them, father and son, under the protection, as it were, of God, the universal King, with the Son of God, the Saviour of all, as their leader and ally, drew up their forces on all sides against the enemies of the Deity and won an easy victory; God having prospered them in the battle in all respects according to their wish. Thus, suddenly, and sooner than can be told, those who yesterday and the day before breathed death and threatening were no more, and not even their names were remembered, but their inscriptions and their honors suffered the merited disgrace. And the things which Licinius with his own eyes had seen come upon the former impious tyrants he himself likewise suffered, because he did not receive instruction nor learn wisdom from the chastisements of his neighbors, but followed the same path of impiety which they had trod, and was justly hurled over the same precipice. Thus he lay prostrate.

But Constantine, the mightiest victor, adorned with every virtue of piety, together with his son Crispus, a most God-beloved prince, and in all respects like his father, recovered the East which belonged to them; and they formed one united Roman empire as of old, bringing under their peaceful sway the whole world from the rising of the sun to the opposite quarter, both north and south, even to the extremities of the declining day. All fear therefore of those who had formerly afflicted them was taken away from men, and they celebrated splendid and festive days. Everything was filled with light, and those who before were downcast beheld each other with smiling faces and beaming eyes. With dances and hymns, in city and country, they glorified first of all God the universal King, because they had been thus taught, and then the pious emperor with his God-beloved children. There was oblivion of past evils and forgetfulness of every deed of impiety; there was enjoyment of present benefits and expectation of those yet to come. Edicts full of clemency and laws containing tokens of benevolence and true piety were issued in every place by the victorious emperor. Thus after all tyranny had been purged away, the empire which belonged to them was preserved firm and without a rival for Constantine and his sons alone. And having obliterated the godlessness of their predecessors, recognizing the benefits conferred upon them by God, they exhibited their love of virtue and their love of God, and their piety and gratitude to the Deity, by the deeds which they performed in the sight of all men.

10. ST. AUGUSTINE: CITY OF GOD

A century later Eusebius' dream was dying in the chaos occasioned by barbarian incursions into the Empire. Eternal Rome itself was captured and pillaged in 410, and large numbers of pagans asserted that Rome's misfortunes were due to its abandonment of the old gods and ancient virtues.

In 413 St. Augustine (354-430), bishop of Hippo in North Africa and the dominant figure in the early Latin Church, began to compose a defense of Christianity. The project took thirteen years. Somehow, this busy churchman found time to publish serially twenty-two books, known collectively as the *City of God*.

The *City of God* was a theology of world history. In its first ten books Augustine outlined the calamities suffered by pre-Christian Rome and the dark and barbarous side of pagan life. His purpose was to show that the pagan past was not only as equally oppressive as the present but even more so, because the moderating influence of the true religion had been absent. All of this was prologue, however. Augustine refused to base his defense of Christianity upon any promise of earthly peace or temporal benefits.

The central argument of the *City of God* lay in the last twelve books. In a discursive survey of both sacred and profane history, Augustine divided all humanity into two mystical, invisible camps, the City of God and the City of Man. Their differences were spiritual: Those who loved God; those who loved self. One was a tiny minority of pilgrims, traveling as strangers through life toward a supernatural goal. The other was the vast majority of mankind, wedded to things of the flesh and only interested in the peace of this world. The whole course and meaning of history was nothing more or less than the spiritual voyage through time of the citizens of the City of God. Therefore, while God's divine plan controls the destinies of all, mundane problems and the affairs of men really do not matter. The heart of Augustine's message was that Christianity could and would continue to perform its mission till the end of time, no matter what happened to empires, the Christian Roman Empire included.

As history, the *City of God* had many flaws. Augustine had taught Latin rhetoric prior to his conversion to Christianity. Among rhetoricians of his day (as among sociologists in ours) history was considered to be nothing more than a grab bag of colorful illustrations to support one's arguments. The *City of God* used history in this manner. Eusebius' pious but critical history had not been alien to the highest standards of Greek rationalism. Augustine, on the other hand, maintained that faith precedes reason and enlightens it. Rational inquiry without faith results in error. The *City of God* was, above all else, a work grounded upon faith.

Augustine, himself, realized that the historical sections of his work needed fuller development. Having neither the time nor the inclination to do it himself, he commissioned one of his students, a young Spanish priest, Paulus Orosius (*ca.* 380-*ca.* 420?), to research and compose a world history that would support in detail the arguments of the first ten books of the *City of God*.

In 418 the pupil presented his master with *Seven Books of Histories Against the Pagans*. It was essentially a catalog of calamities that had befallen pagan societies, proving that their gods and virtues had failed to provide them any security.

During the Middle Ages both works were widely read and commented upon. Together, Augustine and Orosius dominated the historical world view of the Christian West for the next millennium, but never to the extent that the dream of Eusebius ever ceased to inflame imaginations and excite hopes.

Our selection comes from Book V of the *City of God,* in which Augustine describes the fortunes of the Roman Empire before and after the reign of Constantine. The reader should compare Augustine's description of the fortunes of the Christian emperors with the selection above from Eusebius' Book X.

. . . we do not attribute the power of giving kingdoms and empires to any save to the true God, who gives happiness in the kingdom of heaven to the pious alone, but gives kingly power on earth both to the pious and the impious, as it may please Him, whose good pleasure is always just. For though we have said something about the principles which guide His administration, in so far as it has seemed good to Him to explain it, nevertheless it is too much for us, and far surpasses our strength, to discuss the hidden things of men's hearts, and by a clear examination to determine the merits of various kingdoms. He, therefore, who is the one true God, who never leaves the human race without just judgment and help, gave a kingdom to the Romans when He would, and as great as He would, as He did also to the Assyrians, and even the Persians, by whom, as their own books testify, only two gods are worshipped, the one good and the other evil,—to say nothing concerning the Hebrew people, of whom I have already spoken as much as seemed necessary, who, as long as they were a kingdom, worshipped none save the true God. The same, therefore, who gave to the Persians harvests, though they did not worship the goddess Segetia, who gave the other blessings of the earth, though they did not worship the many gods which the Romans supposed to preside, each one over some particular thing, or even many of them over each several thing,—He, I say, gave the Persians dominion, though they worshipped none of those gods to whom the Romans believed themselves indebted for the empire. And the same is true in respect of men as well as nations. He who gave power to Marius gave it also to Caius Cæsar; He who gave it to Augustus gave it also to Nero; He also who gave it to the most benignant emperors, the Vespasians, father and son, gave it also to the cruel Domitian; and, finally, to avoid the necessity of going over them all, He who gave it to the Christian Constantine gave it also to the apostate Julian, whose gifted mind was deceived by a sacrilegious and detestable curiosity, stimulated by the love of power. . . . Manifestly these things are ruled and governed by the one God according as He pleases; and if His motives are hid, are they therefore unjust? . . .

For neither do we say that certain Christian emperors were therefore happy because they ruled a long time, or, dying a peaceful death, left their sons to succeed them in the empire, or subdued the enemies of the republic, or were able both to guard against and to suppress the attempt of hostile citizens rising against them. These and other gifts or comforts of this sorrowful life even certain worshippers of demons have merited to receive, who do not belong to the kingdom of God to which these belong; and this is to be traced to the mercy of God, who would not have those who believe in Him desire such things as the highest good. But we say that they are happy if they rule justly; if they are not lifted up amid the praises of those who pay them sublime honors, and the obsequiousness of those who salute them with an excessive humility, but remember that they are men; if they make their power the handmaid of His majesty by using it for the greatest possible extension of His worship; if they fear, love, worship God; if more than their own they love that kingdom in which they are not afraid to have partners; if they are slow to punish, ready to pardon; if they apply that punishment as necessary to government and defence of the republic, and not in order to gratify their own enmity; if they grant pardon, not that iniquity may go unpunished, but with the hope that the transgressor may amend his ways; if they compensate with the lenity of mercy and the liberality of benevolence for whatever severity they may be compelled to decree; if their luxury is as much restrained as it might have been unrestrained; if they prefer to govern depraved desires rather than any nation whatever; and if they do all these things, not through ardent desire of empty glory, but through love of eternal felicity, not neglecting to offer to the true God, who is their God, for their sins, the sacrifices of humility, contrition, and prayer. Such Christian emperors, we say, are happy in the present time by hope, and are destined to be so in the enjoyment of the reality itself, when that which we wait for shall have arrived. . . .

For the good God, lest men, who believe that He is to be worshipped with a view to eternal life, should think that no one could attain to all this high estate, and to this terrestrial dominion, unless he should be a worshipper of the demons,—supposing that these spirits have great power with respect to such things,—for this reason He gave to the Emperor Constantine, who was not a worshipper of demons, but of the true God Himself, such fullness of earthly gifts as no one would even dare wish for. To him also He granted the honor of founding a city, a companion to the Roman empire, the daughter, as it were, of Rome itself, but without any temple or image of the demons. He reigned for a long period as sole emperor, and unaided held and defended the whole Roman world. In conducting and carrying on wars he was most victorious; in overthrowing tyrants he was most successful. He died at a great age, of sickness and old age, and left his sons to succeed him in the empire. But again, lest any emperor should become a Christian in order to merit the happiness of Constantine, when every one should be a Christian for the sake of eternal life, God took away Jovian far sooner than Julian, and permitted that Gratian should be slain by the sword of a tyrant. But in his case there was far more mitigation of the calamity than in the case of the great Pompey, for he could not be avenged by Cato, whom he had left, as it were, heir to the civil war. But Gratian, though pious minds require not such consolations, was avenged by Theodosius, whom he had associated with himself in the empire, though he had a little brother of his own, being more desirous of a faithful alliance than of extensive power.

SOURCE NOTES

1. From Eusebius, *Church History,* translated by Arthur C. McGiffert in A Select Library of Nicene and Post-Nicene Fathers, Second Series, Volume I (New York: The Christian Literature Company, 1890), pp. 211, 349-350, 369-370, 386-387.
2. From St. Augustin, *City of God,* translated by Marcus Dods in A Select Library of Nicene and Post-Nicene Fathers, First Series, Vol. II (Buffalo: The Christian Literature Company, 1887), pp. 102-105.

5.
THE EARLY MIDDLE AGES

Western society underwent profound changes in the period from *ca*. 400 to *ca*. 1000 A.D. During these centuries a new civilization—the First Europe—emerged out of the clash and fusion of Christian, Graeco-Roman, and Germanic ideas and institutions. This was the blustery, early springtime of Western European civilization. Marked by a great deal of destruction and the loss of many of the cultural achievements of Graeco-Roman civilization, this age was no stranger to chaos and turbulence. All too often in these days life was brutish, rude, and short. But to dismiss the era as the Dark Ages is to overlook its promise and accomplishments. Largely under the guidance of the Latin Church, these first Europeans struggled successfully to reorder society along new and ultimately very fruitful lines.

History writing during these centuries was generally the province of churchmen, particularly monks. As we might expect, these historians exhibited a preoccupation with the miraculous and the ecclesiastical, and the histories they wrote were often artistically crude and critically naive. Yet, this very artlessness proved to be a colorful and dramatic medium for narrating the violent events of their day, far more effective than the pedantically tortured prose of late classical antiquity.

Early medieval historial writings break down into three major groups: Hagiographies, annals and chronicles, and narratives of specific periods, peoples, or events. Hagiographies tended to be semifictional fabrications in which a list of standardized miracles and pious deeds were ascribed to a saint, who might or might not have existed. Chronicles developed out of ecclesiastical annals. In this largely illiterate age, official Easter tables were widely distributed in order to assure a uniform observance of the shifting holy day. The wide margins of these tables offered scribes sufficient space to jot down one or two memorable events and disasters (often the latter) for each year. Usually these were affairs of only local interest. In time, some of these annals became chronicles. A chronicle remained basically a record of remarkable events with little or no effort at interpretation, but it was more than a series of random notes on disconnected matters. It possessed a continuity in style and subject, often described incidents in detail, and exhibited a wide scope of interest. During the High Middle Ages a significant number of chroniclers would raise their craft from an anecdotal to an analytical level, thus writing fullfledged histories. But histories, strictly defined, were rare during the Early Middle Ages. The few that were composed generally were extended narratives about some Germanic group, such as the sixth century *History of the Franks* by St Gregory of Tours and Paul the Deacon's eighth century work, *History of the Lombards*. The two selections below represent early medieval histories and chronicles at their best.

11. VENERABLE BEDE: ECCLESIASTICAL HISTORY OF THE ENGLISH PEOPLE

St. Bede (672/673-735), monk, priest, theologian, scholar, and teacher, was born in the English kingdom of Northumbria. His parents gave him over to the care and education of the Church at age seven, and several years later he professed monastic vows at the abbey of Jarrow. Here he remained until his death, leaving only infrequently to visit other monastic houses for short periods.

Cloister walls enclosed his person, but never his mind or his fame. In later life he was well-known throughout Christian Europe for his spirituality and erudition. He was an outstanding classical scholar, a student of Greek and Hebrew as well as a master of Latin, who used his monastery's well stocked library to advantage. A prolific author, his publications ranged over a wide area of interests and included such diverse subjects as biblical exegesis, hymnody, moral philosophy, Latin grammar and spelling, and poetry. His contributions to the art of history included two treatises on chronology, a *History of the Saints,* a *Matyrology,* four biographies, and the work for which he is best remembered today, the *Ecclesiastical History of the English People.*

The account traced the fortunes of Christianity in England down to 731. More than any other single work, it popularized in the West the convention of dating all history in relation to the Year of Grace (Jesus' birth). It also preserved for modern scholars a large amount of early English history which would otherwise be lost. Moreover, it is a great work of history.

Bede's precision, accuracy, and painstaking research techniques marked him as a first rate historian in an age that little appreciated or understood historical scholarship. He scrupulously investigated every available source in order to uncover all relevant facts. His work bore the imprint of an orderly, as well as inquisitive, mind; extraneous materials were culled, so that nothing detracted from the central theme, the triumphal progress of the Christian faith in England.

Bede was a great historian, but he also shared the beliefs of his age. The *Ecclesiastical History* abounds with tales of the miraculous, many of which strike the modern reader as totally beyond belief. But Bede accepted the veracity of these stories and expected his reader would also. By combining a highly critical approach to natural historical phenomena and evidence with an ingenuous, almost totally uncritical acceptance of the supernatural, Bede manifested the two sides of the medieval mind.

The following excerpt from Book II recounts some of the trials and triumphs of the fledgling missionary Church in England between the years 605 and 624.

Laurentius succeeded Augustine in the bishopric, having been ordained thereto by the latter, in his lifetime, lest, upon his death, the state of the church, as yet unsettled, might begin to falter, if it should be destitute of a pastor, though but for one hour. Wherein he also followed the example of the first pastor of the church, that is, of the most blessed prince of the apostles, Peter, who, having founded the church of Christ at Rome, is said to have consecrated Clement his assistant in preaching the Gospel, and at the same time his successor. Laurentius, being advanced to the degree of an archbishop, laboured indefatigably, both by frequent exhortations and examples of piety, to raise to perfection the foundations of the church, which had been so nobly laid. In short, he not only took care of the new church formed among the English, but endeavored also to employ his pastoral solicitude among the ancient inhabitants of Britain, as also the Scots, who inhabit the island of Ireland, which is next to Britain. For when he understood that the course of life and profession of the Scots in their aforesaid country, as well as of the Britons in Britain, was not truly ecclesiastical, especially that they did not celebrate the solemnity of Easter at the due time, but thought that the day of the resurrection of our Lord was, as has been said above, to be celebrated between the 14th and 20th of the moon; he wrote, jointly with his fellow bishops, an exhortatory epistle, entreating and conjuring them to observe unity of peace, and conformity with the church of Christ spread throughout the world. The beginning of which epistle is as follows:

"To our most dear brothers, the lords bishops and abbats throughout all Scotland, Laurentius, Mellitus, and Justus, servants of the servants of God. When the apostolic see, according to the universal custom which it has followed elsewhere, sent us to these western parts to preach to pagan nations, we came into this island, which is called Britain, without possessing any previous knowledge of its inhabitants. We held both the Britons and Scots in great esteem for sanctity, believing that they had proceeded according to the custom of the universal church; but coming acquainted with the errors of the Britons, we thought the Scots had been better; but we have been informed by Bishop Dagan, coming into this aforesaid island, and the Abbat Columbanus in

France, that the Scots in no way differ from the Britons in their behaviour; for Bishop Dagan coming to us, not only refused to eat with us,
but even to take his repast in the same house where we were entertained."

The same Laurentius and his fellow bishops wrote a letter to the priests of
the Britons, suitable to his rank, by which he endeavored to confirm them in
Catholic unity; but what he gained by so doing the present times still declare.

About this time, Mellitus, bishop of London, went to Rome to confer with
Pope Boniface about the necessary affairs of the English church. And the same
most reverend pope, assembling a synod of the bishops of Italy, to prescribe
orders for the life and peace of the monks, Mellitus also sat among them, in the
eighth year of the reign of the Emperor Phocas, the thirteenth indiction, on the
27th of February, to the end that he also by his authority might confirm such
things as should be regularly decreed, and at his return into Britain might carry
the same to the churches of the English, to be prescribed and observed; together
with letters which the same pope sent to the beloved of God, Archbishop
Laurentius, and to all the clergy; as likewise to King Ethelbert and the English
nation. This pope was Boniface, who came fourth after Pope Gregory, and who
obtained of the Emperor Phocas that the temple called by the ancients Pantheon,
as representing all the gods, should be given to the Church of Christ; wherein he,
having purified it from contamination, dedicated a church to the holy mother of
God, and to all Christ's martyrs, to the end that, the devils being excluded, the
blessed company of the saints might have therein a perpetual memorial.

Laurentius, being about to follow Mellitus and Justus, and to quit Britain,
ordered his bed to be laid the night before in the church of the blessed apostles,
Peter and Paul, which has been often mentioned before; wherein having laid
himself to take some rest, after he had poured out many prayers and tears to God
for the state of the church, he fell asleep; in the dead of night, the blessed prince
of the apostles appeared to him, and scourging him a long time with apostolical
severity, asked of him, "Why he would forsake the flock which he had committed to him? or to what shepherds he would commit Christ's sheep that were in the
midst of wolves? Have you," said he, "forgotten my example, who, for the sake
of those little ones, whom Christ recommended to me in token of his affection,
underwent at the hands of infidels and enemies of Christ, bonds, stripes, imprisonment, afflictions, and lastly, the death of the cross, that I might at last be
crowned with him?" Laurentius, the servant of Christ, being excited by these
words and stripes, the very next morning repaired to the king, and taking off his
garment, showed the scars of the stripes which he had received. The king, astonished, asked, "Who had presumed to give such stripes to so great a man?"

And was much frightened when he heard that the bishop had suffered so much at the hands of the apostle of Christ for his salvation. Then abjuring the worship of idols, and renouncing his unlawful marriage, he embraced the faith of Christ, and being baptized, promoted the affairs of the church to the utmost of his power.

He also sent over into France, and recalled Mellitus and Justus, and commanded them freely to return to govern their churches, which they accordingly did, one year after their departure. Justus, indeed, returned to the city of Rochester, where he had before presided; but the Londoners would not receive Bishop Mellitus, choosing rather to be under their idolatrous high priests; for King Eadbald had not so much authority in the kingdom as his father, nor was he able to restore the bishop to his church against the will and consent of the pagans. But he and his nation, after his conversion to our Lord, diligently followed the Divine precepts. Lastly, he built the church of the holy Mother of God, in the monastery of the most blessed prince of the apostles, which was afterwards consecrated by Archbishop Mellitus.

In this king's reign, the holy Archibshop Laurentius was taken up to the heavenly kingdom: he was buried in the church and monastery of the holy Apostle Peter, close by his predecessor Augustine, on the 2nd day of the month of February. Mellitus, who was bishop of London, was the third archbishop of Canterbury from Augustine; Justus, who was still living, governed the church of Rochester. These ruled the church of the English with much industry and labour, and received letters of exhortation from Boniface, bishop of the Roman apostolic see, who presided over the church after Deusdedit, in the year of our Lord 619. Mellitus laboured under an infirmity of body, that is, the gout; but his mind was sound, cheerfully passing over all earthly things, and always aspiring to love, seek, and attain to those which are celestial. He was noble by birth, but much nobler in mind.

In short, that I may give one testimony of his virtue, by which the rest may be guessed at, it happened once that the city of Canterbury, being by carelessness set on fire, was in danger of being consumed by the spreading conflagration; water was thrown over the fire in vain; a considerable part of the city was already destroyed, and the fierce flame advancing towards the bishop, when he, confiding in the Divine assistance, where human failed, ordered himself to be carried towards the raging fire, that was spreading on every side. The church of the four crowned Martyrs was in the place where the fire raged most. The bishop being carried thither by his servants, the sick man averted the danger by prayer, which a number of strong men had not been able to perform by much labour.
Immediately, the wind, which blowing from the south had spread the conflagra-

tion throughout the city, turning to the north, prevented the destruction of those places that had lain in its way, and then ceasing entirely, the flames were immediately extinguished. And thus the man of God, whose mind was inflamed with the fire of Divine charity, and who was wont to drive away the powers of the air by his frequent prayers, from doing harm to himself, or his people, was deservedly allowed to prevail over the worldly winds and flames, and to obtain that they should not injure him or his.

This archbishop also, having ruled the church five years, departed to heaven in the reign of King Eadbald, and was buried with his predecessors in the monastery and church, which we have so often mentioned, of the most blessed prince of the apostles, in the year of our Lord's incarnation 624, on the 24th day of April.

12. ANGLO-SAXON CHRONICLE

The *Anglo-Saxon Chronicle,* which cataloged the more remarkable events in English history from the fifth century to the mid-twelfth, is the earliest known historical work written in a Teutonic vernacular tongue. It was originally compiled during the reign of King Alfred the Great of Wessex (871-899) from a nucleus of scattered annals, genealogies, episcopal and regnal lists, and Bede's *Ecclesiastical History,* and thereafter continued down to 1154 in several variant forms at different monasteries throughout England.

The following selections illustrate the type of events whose memory monastic chroniclers thought worthy of preserving. The army to which the chronicler refers was an invading Danish (Viking) force, which had made a permanent, large-scale landing in 865. The Kingdom of Wessex under Alfred led the long, eventually successful Anglo-Saxon defense that resulted in the first united English kingdom under Alfred and his successors.

A. 878. This year, during midwinter, after twelfth night, the army stole away to Chippenham, and overran the land of the West-Saxons, and sat down there; and many of the people they drove beyond sea, and of the remainder the greater part they subdued and forced to obey them, except king Alfred: and he, with a small band, with difficulty retreated to the woods and to the fastnesses of the moors. And the same winter the brother of Hingwar and of Halfdene came with twenty-three ships to Devonshire in Wessex; and he was there slain, and with him eight hundred and forty men of his army; and there was taken the war-flag which they called the RAVEN. After this, at Easter king Alfred with a small band constructed a fortress at Athelney; and from this fortress, with that part of the men of Somerset which was nearest to it, from time to time they fought against the army. Then in the seventh week after Easter he rode to Brixton, on the east side of Selwood; and there came to meet him all the men of Somerset, and the men of Wiltshire, and that portion of the men of Hampshire which was on this side of the sea; and they were joyful at his presence. On the following day he went from that station to Iglea [Iley], and on the day after this to Heddington, and there fought against the whole army, put them to flight, and pursued them as far as their fortress: and there he sat down fourteen days. And then the army delivered to him hostages, with many oaths, that they would leave his kingdom, and also promised him that their king should receive baptism: and this they accordingly fulfilled. And about three weeks after this king Gothrun came to him, with some thirty men who were of the most distinguished in the army, at Aller, which is near Athelney: and the king was his godfather at baptism; and his chrism-loosing was at Wedmore: and he was twelve days with the king; and he greatly honoured him and his companions with gifts....

A. 886. This year the army which before had drawn eastward, went westward again, and thence up the Seine, and there took up their winter quarters near the town of Paris. That same year king Alfred repaired London; and all the English submitted to him, except those who were under the bondage of the Danish-men; and then he committed the town to the keeping of Ethered the ealdorman.

A. 887. This year the army went up through the bridge at Paris, and thence up along the Seine as far as the Marne, and thence up the Marne to Chezy, and then sat down, there, and on the Yonne, two winters in the two places. And that same year Charles king of the French died; and six weeks before he died, Arnulf his brother's son bereaved him of the kingdom. And then was that kingdom divided into five, and five kings were consecrated thereto. This, however, was done by permission of Arnulf: and they said that they would hold it from his hand, because none of them on the father's side was born thereto except him alone. Arnulf then dwelt in the land east of the Rhine: and Rodulf then succeeded to the middle kingdom, and Oda to the western part, and Beorngar and Witha to the land of the Lombards and to the lands on that side of the mountain: and that they held in great discord, and fought two general battles, and oft and many times laid waste the land, and each repeatedly drove out the other. And that same year that the army went up beyond the bridge at Paris, Ethelhelm the ealdorman carried the alms of the West-Saxons and of king Alfred to Rome.

A. 888. This year Beeke the ealdorman carried the alms of the West-Saxons and of king Alfred to Rome; and queen Ethelswith, who was king Alfred's sister, died on the way to Rome, and her body lies at Pavia. And that same year Athelred archbishop of Canterbury, and Ethelwold the ealdorman died in the same month.

A. 889. In this year there was no journey to Rome, except that king Alfred sent two couriers with letters.

A. 890. This year abbat Bernhelm carried the alms of the West-Saxons and of king Alfred to Rome. And Gothrun the Northern king died, whose baptismal name was Athelstan; he was king Alfred's godson, and he abode in East-Anglia, and first settled that country. And that same year the army went from the Seine to St. Lo, which is between Brittany and France; and the Bretons fought against them, and had the victory, and drove them out into a river and drowned many of them. This year Plegmund was chosen of God and of all the people to be archbishop of Canterbury.

A. 891. This year the army went eastward; and king Arnulf, with the East-Franks and Saxons and Bavarians, fought against that part which was mounted before the ships came up, and put them to flight. And three Scots came to king Alfred in a boat without any oars from Ireland, whence they had stolen away, because they desired for the love of God to be in a state of pilgrimage, they recked not where. The boat in which they came was made of two hides and a half; and they took with them provisions sufficient for seven days; and then about the seventh day they came on shore in Cornwall, and soon after went to king Alfred. Thus they were named: Dubslane, and Macbeth, and Maelinmun. And Swinney, the best teacher among the Scots, died.

A. 892. And that same year after Easter, about Rogation week or before, the star appeared which in Latin is called *cometa;* some men say in English that it is a hairy star, because a long radiance streams from it, sometimes on the one side, and sometimes on each side.

SOURCE NOTES

1. From Venerable Bede, *Ecclesiastical History of England,* trans. J. A. Giles (London: George Bell and Sons, 1894), pp. 74-79.
2. From *Anglo-Saxon Chronicle,* trans. J. A. Giles (London: George Bell and Sons, 1894), pp. 356-357 and 359-360.

6.

THE HIGH MIDDLE AGES

Western Europe produced a vigorous economy and relative political stability during the High Middle Ages (*ca*. 1050-*ca*. 1250). One result was a remarkable flowering of European culture and intellectual life. Universities, Romanesque and Gothic cathedrals, radically new forms of Latin and vernacular literature, the revival of legal, philosophical, and theological studies, political theory, historical writing, and the beginnings of European science: These were some of the products of an era which might better be termed the Medieval Christian Renaissance.

If the medieval period was not a monolithic bloc of 1000 unchanging years, neither was the High Middle Ages culturally or intellectually homogeneous. Yet, while richly diverse, it was still basically an Age of Faith, and Christianity continued throughout these centuries to be Europe's single most important unifying element.

During this period Christian expression was changing. New trends were infusing Western Europe's religion. As Europe the besieged became a memory, emphasis on God the Chastiser and Judge gave way to a new spirituality—worship of the Merciful Christ, True Man as well as True God, and devotion to the loving Virgin, Mother of all mankind. By the early thirteenth century Europe was ready for St. Francis, whom it took to its heart and made a saint.

Western Christians of the High Middle Ages did not abandon the idea that history is the God-directed spiritual progress of His Church through time. But as Europeans became more secure and prosperous, they saw more clearly the goodness of God's world; they lowered their gaze from the heavens and the hereafter to the mundane now. Their interests became more secular, but this secularism was not irreligious; they saw themselves as individuals who had been given an earthly as well as a

83

spiritual destiny by a Loving Father. As their religious expressions became more personal, they emphasized more man's role in effecting his own salvation and in influencing history. As their world became more sophisticated, their religion became more genteel. The Augustinian world view was too much a part of medieval man's intellectual baggage to be abandoned, but it was certainly softened during the High Middle Ages.

To illustrate this change in religious-historical perception we have chosen three historians. Each wrote on an aspect of the crusade movement; but each viewed the crusades from a different perspective.

13. FULCHER OF CHARTRES:
HISTORY OF THE EXPEDITION TO JERUSALEM

Fulcher (1058/1059-1127?), a priest of Chartres, participated in the First Crusade as chaplain to Count Baldwin of Flanders, one of the principal leaders of the crusade and later king of Jerusalem. Following the Latin capture of Jerusalem in 1099, Fulcher settled down in Palestine, where he remained for the rest of his life. Around 1101 he began to write a history of the crusade and the subsequent fortunes of the Latin Kingdom of Jerusalem, in order to celebrate the holy deeds, especially the "martyrdoms," of the crusaders and to attract new blood from the West.

Fulcher's account of the First Crusade brings to mind the qualities and attitudes of the contemporary *Song of Roland* (*ca.* 1100) and similar *chansons de geste*. His Christianity was militant and straightforward, and he portrayed the warfare between Muslim and Christian in simple terms: It was a battle between the enemies of the Lord and His friends. Fulcher did not doubt that the crusaders were the new Chosen People—sanctified instruments through which God effected His ends. Toward such Christian heroes, Fulcher exhibited warmth, charity, and deep human empathy. Even when apparent disaster overtook the crusaders, Fulcher was able to discover in it evidence of the almighty wisdom, mercy, and goodness of God. In his words, " . . . He has permitted the Christians to be slain for the augmentation of their salvation, the Turks, however, for the damnation of their souls." (Bk. I, Chap. 16). The infidel enemy neither merited nor received any of Fulcher's sympathies. They were the new Philistines—a people to be dealt with mercilessly.

In the two selections below, Fulcher describes the start of the crusade and its end.

Such then was the immense assemblage which set out from the West. Gradually along the march, and from day to day, the army grew by the addition of other armies, coming from every direction and composed of innumerable people. Thus one saw an infinite multitude, speaking different languages and come from divers countries. All did not, however, come together into a single army until we had reached the city of Nicaea. What shall I add? The isles of the sea and the kingdoms of the whole earth were moved by God, so that one might believe fulfilled the prophecy of David, who said in the Psalm: "All nations whom Thou hast made shall come and worship before Thee, O Lord; and shall glorify Thy name,'' and that all those who reached the holy places afterwards said justly: "We will worship where His feet have stood." Concerning this journey we read very many other predictions in the prophets, which it would be tedious to recall.

Oh, how great was the grief, how deep the sighs, what weeping, what lamentations among the friends, when the husband left the wife so dear to him, his children also, and all his possessions of any kind, father, mother, brethren or kindred! And yet in spite of these floods of tears which those who remained shed for their friends about to depart, and in their very presence, the latter did not suffer their courage to fail, and, out of love for the Lord, in no way hesitated to leave all that they held most precious, believing without doubt that they would gain that hundred-fold in receiving the recompense which God has promised to those who love Him.

Then the husband announced to his wife the time of his return, assuring her that if he lived by God's grace he would return to her. He commended her to the Lord, gave her a kiss, and, weeping, promised to return. But the latter, who feared that she would never see him again, overcome with grief, was unable to stand, fell lifeless to the ground, and wept over her dear one whom she was losing in life, as if he were already dead. He then, as if he had no pity—and nevertheless he was filled with pity—and was not moved by the grief of any friends—and yet he was secretly moved—departed with a firm purpose. The sadness was for those who remained, and the joy for those who departed. What more can we say? "This is the Lord's doings, and it is marvelous in our eyes."

On the seventh of June the Franks besieged Jerusalem. . . .

When the Franks saw how difficult it would be to take the city, the leaders ordered scaling ladders to be made, hoping that by a brave assault it might be possible to surmount the walls by means of ladders and thus take the city, God helping. So the ladders were made, and on the day following the seventh, in the early morning, the leaders ordered the attack, and, with the trumpets sounding, a splendid assault was made on the city from all sides. The attack lasted till the sixth hour, but it was discovered that the city could not be entered by the use of ladders, which were few in number, and sadly we ceased the attack.

Then a council was held, and it was ordered that siege machines should be constructed by the artisans, so that by moving them close to the wall we might accomplish our purpose, with the aid of God. This was done.

In the mean time, while we did not suffer because of any lack of meat or bread, our men and their animals were unable to obtain a sufficient supply of drinking water, for, as I have said, the region is dry and without streams of water. Accordingly, it was necessary to bring water to camp in the skins of animals, from places four or five miles distant.

Moreover, the machines were being prepared for the attack, rams, and hurling machines. Among other siege devices a wooden tower was constructed from small timbers, for we had a very small supply of wood. According to a command that was issued, the parts of this tower were carried by night to a corner of the city. In the morning it was very quickly set up and equipped with petrariæ and other machines, at a safe distance from the wall. When the tower had been put together and had been covered with hides, it was moved nearer to the wall. Then knights, few in number, but brave, at the sound of the trumpet, took their places in the tower and began to shoot stones and arrows. The Saracens defended themselves vigorously, and, with slings, very skilfully hurled back burning firebrands, which had been dipped in oil and fresh fat. Many on both sides, fighting in this manner, often found themselves in the presence of death.

On the other side of the city from Mount Zion, a great attack was also made on the city by Raymond and his men, where machinery was likewise used. However, on the side where duke Godfrey, Robert, count of Normandy, and Robert of Flanders were fighting, the battle was fiercest. Such was the work of that day. On the following day the work again began at the sound of the trumpet, and to such purpose that the rams, by continual pounding, made a hole through one part of the wall. The Saracens suspended two beams before the opening, supporting them by ropes, so that by piling stones behind them they would make an obstacle to the rams. However, what they did for their own protection became, through the providence of God, the cause of their own destruction. For, when the tower was moved nearer to the wall, the ropes that supported the beams were cut; from these same beams the Franks constructed a bridge, which they cleverly extended from the tower to the wall. About this time one of the towers in the stone wall began to burn, for the men who worked our machines had been hurling firebrands upon it until the wooden beams within it caught fire. The flames and smoke soon became so bad that none of the defenders of this part of the wall were able to remain near this place. At the noon hour on Friday, with trumpets sounding, amid great commotion and shouting "God help us," the Franks entered the city. When the pagans saw one standard planted on the wall, they were completely demoralized, and all their former boldness vanished, and they turned to flee through the narrow streets of the city. Those who were already in rapid flight began to flee more rapidly.

Count Raymond and his men, who were attacking the wall on the other side, did not yet know of all this, until they saw the Saracens leap from the wall in front of them. Forthwith, they joyfully rushed into the city to pursue and kill the nefarious enemies, as their comrades were already doing. Some Saracens, Arabs, and Ethiopians took refuge in the tower of David, others fled to the temples of the Lord and of Solomon. A great fight took place in the court and porch of the temples, where they were unable to escape from our gladiators. Many fled to the roof of the temple of Solomon, and were shot with arrows, so that they fell to the ground dead. In this temple almost ten thousand were killed. Indeed, if you had been there you would have seen our feet colored to our ankles with the blood of the slain. But what more shall I relate? None of them were left alive; neither women nor children were spared.

This may seem strange to you. Our squires and poorer footmen discovered a trick of the Saracens, for they learned that they could find byzants in the stomachs and intestines of the dead Saracens, who had swallowed them. Thus, after several days they burned a great heap of dead bodies, that they might more easily get the precious metal from the ashes. Moreover, Tancred broke into the temple of the Lord and most wrongfully stole much gold and silver, also precious stones, but later, repenting of his action, after everything had been accounted for, he restored all to its former place of sanctity. . . .

The carnage over, the crusaders entered the houses and took whatever they found in them. However, this was all done in such a sensible manner that whoever entered a house first received no injury from any one else, whether he was rich or poor. Even though the house was a palace, whatever he found there was his property. Thus many poor men became rich.

Afterward, all, clergy and laymen, went to the Sepulcher of the Lord and His glorious temple, singing the ninth chant. With fitting humility, they repeated prayers and made their offering at the holy places that they had long desired to visit.

14. WILLIAM OF MALMESBURY: DEEDS OF THE KINGS OF THE ENGLISH

Almost a half century ago, Charles Homer Haskins made popular the term Renaissance of the Twelfth Century to describe the quickening of European cultural and intellectual life during the High Middle Ages, and he maintained that one of the clearest expressions of this renaissance was the volume and excellence of its historical writing. Of all the outstanding historians of the twelfth century, William of Malmesbury (*ca.* 1095-1143?) was the ablest.

The son of a Norman French knight and an English mother, William was a monk who, like Bede, had been given over to the Church, in this case Malmesbury Abbey, as a youth. An industrious scholar, he was an expert in the Latin classics, penned three major works of history, wrote numerous devotional works and learned treatises, and supervised his monastery's library, adding substantially to its collection. One pictures William as a person with an insatiable taste for books.

Scholarly he was, bookish he was not. Far from dull, his writings crackled with life and even today entertain as well as enlighten. As a monk William probably manifested the required signs of humility; as a historian he was far from self-effacing. He had little respect for the critical abilities of most other historians and believed that England had produced only two historians of merit, Bede and himself. William never tired of preaching what he practised to a high degree—critical and diligent scouring of every available source and devotion to the principle of truth.

Our selection comes from his *Deeds of the Kings of the English,* a work that traced the history of the English crown from 449 to 1125. In Book IV of this history William described the First Crusade. One of the major sources upon which he based his narrative was Fulcher of Chartres. William's debt to Fulcher is clear, but he did not copy him slavishly. It is interesting to study the manner in which William, a historian of another generation, altered and interpreted Fulcher's material. The tone and message of William's account indicates the direction in which the attitudes and mores of high medieval society were moving. Fulcher would never have believed that the pope could have any ulterior motive for calling the crusade, nor would he have considered it proper to insert a gratuitous witticism into the history of so sacred an event.

I shall now describe the expedition to Jerusalem, relating in my own words what was seen and endured by others. Besides too, as opportunity offers, I shall select from ancient writers, accounts of the situation and riches of Constantinople, Antioch, and Jerusalem; in order that he who is unacquainted with these matters, and meets with this work, may have something to communicate to others. But for such a relation there needs a more fervent spirit, in order to complete effectually, what I begin with such pleasure. Invoking, therefore, the Divinity, as is usual, I begin as follows.

In the year of the incarnation 1095, pope Urban the second, who then filled the papal throne, passing the Alps, came into France. The ostensible cause of his journey, was, that, being driven from home by the violence of Guibert, he might prevail on the churches on this side of the mountains to acknowledge him. His more secret intention was not so well known; this was, by Boamund's advice, to excite almost the whole of Europe to undertake an expedition into Asia; that in such a general commotion of all countries, auxiliaries might easily be engaged, by whose means both Urban might obtain Rome; and Boamund, Illyria and Macedonia. For Guiscard, his father, had conquered those countries from Alexius, and also all the territory extending from Durazzo to Thessalonica; wherefore Boamund claimed them as his due, since he obtained not the inheritance of Apulia, which his father had given to his younger son, Roger. Still nevertheless, whatever might be the cause of Urban's journey, it turned out of great and singular advantage to the Christian world. A council, therefore, was assembled at Clermont, which is the most noted city of Auvergne. The number of bishops and abbats was three hundred and ten. . . .

In this council the pope excommunicated Philip, king of France, and all who called him king or lord, and obeyed or spoke to him, unless for the purpose of correcting him: in like manner too his accursed consort, and all who called her queen or lady, till they so far reformed as to separate from each other: and also Guibert of Ravenna, who calls himself pope: and Henry, emperor of Germany, who supports him.

Afterwards, a clear and forcible discourse, such as should come from a priest, was addressed to the people, on the subject of an expedition of the Christians, against the Turks. This I have thought fit to transmit to posterity, as I have learned it from those who were present, preserving its sense unimpaired. For who can preserve the force of that eloquence? We shall be fortunate, if, treading an adjacent path, we come even by a circuitous route to its meaning. . . .

[There follows William's version of Pope Urban II's speech]

I have adhered to the tenor of this address, retaining some few things unaltered, on account of the truth of the remarks, but omitting many. The bulk of the auditors were extremely excited, and attested their sentiments by a shout; pleased with the speech, and inclined to the pilgrimage. And immediately, in presence of the council, some of the nobility, falling down at the knees of the pope, consecrated themselves and their property to the service of God. Among these was Aimar, the very powerful bishop of Puy, who afterwards ruled the army by his prudence, and augmented it through his eloquence. In the month of November, then, in which this council was held, each departed to his home: and the report of this good resolution soon becoming general, it gently wafted a cheering gale over the minds of the Christians: which being universally diffused, there was no nation so remote, no people so retired, as not to contribute its portion. This ardent love not only inspired the continental provinces, but even all who had heard the name of Christ, whether in the most distant islands, or savage countries. The Welshman left his hunting; the Scot his fellowship with lice; the Dane his drinking party; the Norwegian his raw fish. Lands were deserted of their husbandmen; houses of their inhabitants; even whole cities migrated. There was no regard to relationship; affection to their country was held in little esteem; God alone was placed before their eyes. Whatever was stored in granaries, or hoarded in chambers, to answer the hopes of the avaricious husbandman, or the covetousness of the miser, all, all was deserted; they hungered and thirsted after Jerusalem alone. Joy attended such as proceeded; while grief oppressed those who remained. But why do I say remained? You might see the husband departing with his wife, indeed, with all his family; you would smile to see the whole household laden on a carriage, about to proceed on their journey. The road was too narrow for the passengers, the path too confined for the travellers, so thickly were they thronged with endless multitudes. The number surpassed all human imagination, though the itinerants were estimated at six millions. Doubtless, never did so many nations unite in one opinion; never did so immense a population subject their unruly passions to one, and almost to no, direction. For the strangest wonder to behold was, that such a countless multitude marched gradually through various Christian countries without plundering, though there was none to restrain them. Mutual regard blazed forth in all; so that if any one found in his possession what he knew did not belong to him, he exposed it everywhere for several days to be owned; and the desire of the finder was suspended, till perchance the wants of the loser might be repaired.

In the fourth year, then, of the expedition to Jerusalem, the third after the capture of Nice, and the second after that of Antioch, the Franks laid siege to

Jerusalem,—a city well able to repay the toils of war, to soothe its labours, and to requite the fondest expectation. . . . As they saw, therefore, that the city was difficult to carry on account of the steep precipices, the strength of the walls, and the fierceness of the enemy, they ordered engines to be constructed. But before this, indeed, on the seventh day of the siege, they had tried their fortune by erecting ladders, and hurling swift arrows against their opponents: but, as the ladders were few, and perilous to those who mounted them, since they were exposed on all sides and nowhere protected from wounds, they changed their design. There was one engine which we call the Sow, the ancients, Vinea; because the machine, which is constructed of slight timbers, the roof covered with boards and wickerwork, and the sides defended with undressed hides, protects those who are within it, who, after the manner of a sow, proceed to undermine the foundations of the walls. There was another, which, for want of timber, was but a moderate sized tower, constructed after the manner of houses: they call it Berefreid: this was intended to equal the walls in height. The making of this machine delayed the siege, on account of the unskilfulness of the workmen and the scarcity of the wood. And now the fourteenth day of July arrived, when some began to undermine the wall with the sows, others to move forward the tower. To do this more conveniently, they took it towards the works in separate pieces, and, putting it together again at such a distance as to be out of bowshot, advanced it on wheels nearly close to the wall. In the meantime, the slingers with stones, the archers with arrows, and the cross-bow-men with bolts, each intent on his own department, began to press forward and dislodge their opponents from the ramparts; soldiers, too, unmatched in courage, ascend the tower, waging nearly equal war against the enemy with missile weapons and with stones. Nor, indeed, were our foes at all remiss; but trusting their whole security to their valour, they poured down grease and burning oil upon the tower, and slung stones on the soldiers, rejoicing in the completion of their desires by the destruction of multitudes. During the whole of that day the battle was such that neither party seemed to think they had been worsted; on the following, which was the fifteenth of July, the business was decided. For the Franks, becoming more experienced from the event of the attack of the preceding day, threw faggots flaming with oil on a tower adjoining the wall, and on the party who defended it, which, blazing by the action of the wind, first seized the timber and then the stones, and drove off the garrison. Moreover the beams which the Turks had left hanging down from the walls in order that, being forcibly drawn back, they might, by their recoil, batter the tower in pieces in case it should advance too near, were by the Franks dragged to them, by cutting away the ropes; and being placed from the engine to the wall, and covered with hurdles, they formed a bridge of communication from the ramparts to the tower. Thus what the infidels had contrived for their defence became the means of their destruction; for then the enemy, dismayed by the smoking masses of flame and by the courage of our soldiers, began to give way. These advancing on the wall, and thence into the city, manifested the excess of their joy by the strenuousness of their exertions. This success took place on the side of Godfrey and of the two Roberts; Raymond knew nothing of the circumstance, till the cry of the fugitives and the alarm of the people, throwing themselves from the walls, who thus met death while flying from it, acquainted him that the city was taken. On seeing this, he rushed with drawn sword on the runaways, and hastened to avenge the injuries of God, until he had satiated his own animosity. Moreover, adverting to the advantages of quiet for the moment, he sent unhurt to Ascalon five hundred Ethiopians, who, retreating to the citadel of David, had given up the keys of the gates under promise of personal safety. There was no place of refuge for the Turks, so indiscriminately did the insatiable rage of the victors sweep away both the suppliant and the resisting. Ten thousand were slain in the temple of Solomon; more were thrown from the tops of the churches, and of the citadel. After this, the dead bodies were heaped and dissolved into the aery fluid by means of fire; lest putrifying in the open air, they should pour contagion on the heavy atmosphere. The city being thus expiated by the slaughter of the infidels, they proceeded with hearts contrite and bodies prostrate to the sepulchre of the Lord, which they had so long earnestly sought after, and for which they had undergone so many labours. By what ample incense of prayer, they propitiated heaven, or by what repentant tears they once again brought back the favour of God, none, I am confident, can describe; no, not if the splendid eloquence of the ancients could revive or Orpheus himself return; who, as it is said, bent e'en the listening rocks to his harmonious strain. Be it imagined then, rather than expressed.

15. JOINVILLE: HISTORY OF ST LOUIS

Comparatively few laymen wrote history during the Middle Ages, but the handful that did managed to produce some outstanding works, especially in the area of crusade memoirs. The Seventh Crusade (1248-1254), led by St Louis IX of France, provided the framework around which Jean, Sire de Joinville (*ca.* 1224-1317) constructed the *History of St Louis*. During this expedition the young Joinville, a member of the nobility of Champagne, became a close friend of King Louis, a position he enjoyed for the rest of the king's life. Early in the fourteenth century, the then aged peer dictated in French a biography of his friend, who recently had been canonized a saint by the Roman Church.

Joinville centered his work around the theme of Louis' sanctity, but his history did not follow the hagiographical traditions of an earlier age. The saint whom Joinville described was no stock character; he was flesh and blood, and his biographer attempted to delineate accurately his personal, human qualities. In this history Louis performed no miracles; he was not even portrayed as having lived an exceptionally ascetic life. His claim to sainthood followed from his having lived the life of a Christian gentleman to the fullest and having performed his royal duties conscientiously. As Joinville described him, this holy man was always a moderate and sensible practitioner of the highest ideals of Christian chivalric society.

We have chosen two selections to illustrate Joinville's treatment of the king and the changing attitudes of polite society. The first relates some of the king's virtues; the second concerns an incident during the Seventh Crusade. Louis' army had suffered a disastrous defeat in Egypt, and the king, along with most of his army, was taken prisoner. Louis and many of his nobles won their release by negotiating a huge ransom, but most of the common soldiers remained captive. It was in this context that Louis contemplated returning to France in 1250.

This holy man, King St. Louis, loved and feared God during his life above all things, and, as is very apparent, was in consequence favoured in all his works. As I have before said that our God died for his people, so in like manner did St. Louis several times risk his life and incur the greatest dangers for the people of his realm, as shall be touched on hereafter.

The good king, being once dangerously ill at Fontainebleau, said to my Lord Louis, his eldest son, "Fair son, I beseech thee to make thyself beloved by the people of thy kingdom; for, in truth, I should like better that a Scotsman, fresh from Scotland, or from any other distant and unknown country, should govern the subjects of my realm well and loyally, than that thou shouldst rule them wickedly and reproachfully."

The holy king loved truth so much, that even to the Saracens and infidels, although they were his enemies, he would never lie, nor break his word in any thing he had promised them, as shall be noticed hereafter. With regard to his food, he was extremely temperate; for I never in my whole life heard him express a wish for any delicacies in eating or drinking, like too many rich men; but he sat and took patiently whatever was set before him.

In his conversation he was remarkably chaste; for I never heard him, at any time, utter an indecent word, nor make use of the devil's name, which, however, is now very commonly uttered by every one, by which I firmly believe is so far from being agreeable to God, that it is highly displeasing to him.

He mixed his wine with water by measure, according to the strength of it, and what it would bear. He once asked me, when at Cyprus, why I did not mix water with my wine. I answered what the physicians and surgeons had told me, that I had a large head and a cold stomach, which would not bear it. But the good king replied, that they had deceived me, and advised me to add water; for that if I did not learn to do so when young, and was to attempt it in the decline of life, the gout and other disorders, which I might have in my stomach, would greatly increase; or, perhaps, by drinking pure wine in my old age, I should frequently intoxicate myself; and that it was a beastly thing for an honourable man to make himself drunk.

My good lord the king asked me at another time, if I should wish to be honoured in this world, and afterward to gain paradise; to which I answered, that I should wish it were so. "Then," replied he, "be careful never knowingly to do or say any thing disgraceful, that should it become public, you may not have to blush, and be ashamed to say I have done this, or I have said that." In like manner he told me never to give the lie, or contradict rudely whatever might be said in my presence, unless it should be sinful or disgraceful to suffer it, for oftentimes contradiction causes coarse replies and harsh words, that bring on quarrels, which create bloodshed, and are the means of the deaths of thousands.

He also said, that every one should dress and equip himself according to his rank in life, and his fortune, in order that the prudent and elders of this world may not reproach him, by saying such a one has done too much, and that the youth may not remark, that such a one has done too little, and dishonours his station in society.

Not long after the king's arrival at Acre he summoned his brothers, and all the other nobles, on a certain Sunday, and, when assembled, he addressed them: "My lords, I have called you together, to give you some news from France. In truth, my lady-mother, the queen, has sent for me, and it is necessary that I return with the utmost haste, for my kingdom is in great danger, inasmuch as there exists neither peace nor truce with the king of England. The people here wish to detain me, assuring me that if I depart their country will be destroyed, and insist on following me. I beg you will maturely consider what I have said, and give me your opinions within eight days."

On the Sunday following, we all presented ourselves before the king to give him our opinions, as he had charged us, whether he should depart or stay. Sir Guion de Malvoisin was our spokesman, and said, "Sire, my lords your brothers, and the other nobles now present, have fully considered your situation, and they are of opinion, that you cannot remain longer in this country with honour to yourself or profit to your kingdom. For, in the first place, of all the knights whom you led to Cyprus, amounting to 2,800, not one hundred remain. Secondly, you have not any habitation in this country, nor have your army any money; for these reasons, which we have maturely weighed, we unanimously advise that you return to France to reinforce yourself with men-at-arms, and supply yourself with money, so that you may hastily repair again hither, and take vengeance on the enemies of God and of his holy religion."

The king was not pleased with this advice of Sir Guy, but demanded from each person his private opinion on the business, beginning with the counts d'Anjou, de Poitiers, and the other nobles near him. All of them replied, they agreed in the advice of Sir Guy de Malvoisin. The count de Japhe was hard pressed to give his opinion, for he had castles and possessions in those countries; but when the king insisted on having it, he said, that if the king could keep the field, it would redound more to his honour to remain, than thus discomfited to return. I, who was the fourteenth in rank, answered in my turn that I was of the same opinion with the count de Japhe; moreover, giving these additional reasons, that it was reported the king had not as yet expended any of the money from the royal treasury, but had employed that which was in the hands of the clerks of finance; and that the king should send to the Morea, and the adjoining countries, to seek powerful reinforcements of men-at-arms, who, when they should learn the high pay the king was willing to give, would hasten to join him from all parts, and by this means the king might deliver the multitude of poor prisoners who had been captured in the service of God, which would never be the case unless it were done as now proposed.

You must know, that at this moment none reproved me for my opinion, but many began to weep, for there was scarcely one among us who had not some of his relations in the prisons of the Saracens.

Sir William de Belmont spoke next, and said that my advice was very good, and that he agreed in it. When all had delivered their opinions, the king was much confounded at their diversity, and took eight days more to declare which he should follow. When we had left the presence of the king, the great nobles made a violent attack on me, and, through jealousy and envy, said, "Ha! certainly the king must be mad, if he do not follow your opinion, lord de Joinville, in preference to that of the whole French council." But to this I made not any reply.

The tables were soon after laid for dinner, and the king, who had usually made me sit down near him when his brothers were absent, and during the repasts had conversed with me, did not now open his lips, nor even turn his face toward me. I then thought he was displeased with me for having said that he had not employed his own money, when he had expended such very large sums. After he had said grace, and returned thanks to God for his dinner, I retired to a window near the head of the king's bed, and, passing my hand through the grating, remained there musing. I said to myself, that if the king should now return to France, I would go to the prince of Antioch, who was a relation of mine.

While I was thus meditating, the king leant on my shoulders, and held my head between his hands. I thought it was Sir Philip de Nemours, who had been fretting me all the day for the advice which I had given the king, and said to him, "Sir Philip, do leave me quiet in my misfortune." As I turned round, the king covered my face with his hands, and I then knew it was the king from an emerald on his finger. I wished to make some reparation, as one that had improperly spoken; but the king made me be silent, and continued, "Now, lord de Joinville, tell me how you, who are so young a man, could have the courage to advise me to remain in these countries contrary to the opinion of all my greatest nobles?" I replied, that if I had advised him well, he should follow it; if the contrary, he ought not to think more on what I had said. "And will you remain with me, if I should stay?" "Yes, certainly," answered I, "were it at my own or at another's expense." The king said, that he was pleased with the advice I had given, but ordered me to tell this to no one.

I was so rejoiced that whole week with what he had told me, that I was insensible to my illness, and defended myself boldly against the other lords when they attacked me.

You must know, in these countries the peasant is called Poulain,* and I was told by my cousin Sir Peter d'Avallon, that I was called Poulain, because I had advised the king to remain with the Poulains. This information he gave me, that I might defend myself against those who should call me so, and tell them that I would rather be a Poulain* than such recreant knights as themselves.

On the Sunday we all again assembled in the presence of the king, who began by signing himself with the cross, saying that it was from the instructions of his mother he did so, who had thus ordered him, and likewise to invoke the name of God and the aid of his Holy Spirit, whenever he was about to make a speech. He then continued: "My lords, I feel equally thankful to those who have advised our return to France as to those who have recommended our stay here. But, since I last saw you, I have fully considered this matter, and believe, that should we remain here, my kingdom will not the sooner be in great danger from it; for my lady-mother the queen has a sufficiency of men-at-arms to defend it. I have thought much on what the knights of this country say, that if I depart, the kingdom of Jerusalem will be lost, since no one will remain here after me. Now, my lords, having told my resolution, let such speak out boldly who wish to remain with me; and I promise to give them emoluments, that the fault shall not be mine but their own, if they do not remain. Those that may not choose to stay, God be with them."

When the king had done speaking, several were as if thunderstruck, and began to weep bitterly. After the king had declared his resolution, he gave permission to his brothers to return to France; but I know not if he did this at their requests, or whether it was the will of the king. This passed about St. John Baptist's day.

SOURCE NOTES

1. From "Urban and the Crusaders," trans. by Dana C. Munro in *Translations and Reprints from the Original Sources of European History* (Philadelphia: University of Pennsylvania, 1902), Vol. I, No. 2, pp. 22-23.

   From "The Capture of Jerusalem in 1099," trans. by August C. Krey in *Parallel Source Problems in Medieval History,* ed. by Frederic

---

*The offspring of a Syrian father and a European mother.

Duncalf and A. C. Krey (New York: Harper and Brothers, 1912), pp. 109-115, *passim*.

2. From William of Malmesbury, *Chronicle of the Kings of England,* trans. J. A. Giles (London: Henry G. Bohn, 1847), pp. 355-358, 363-365, and 387-389.

3. From John Lord de Joinville, *Memoirs of Louis IX, King of France (Commonly Called Saint Louis),* trans. by Colonel Johnes in *Chronicles of the Crusades* (London: Bell and Daldy, 1871), pp. 351-353 and 463-467.

7.
THE FOURTEENTH AND FIFTEENTH CENTURIES

The period *ca.* 1300-*ca.* 1517 has been variously characterized as an age of rebirth, an age of death; one of breakthroughs, one of breakdown; a period of promise, a period of crisis; the Renaissance, the Waning of the Middle Ages. Each characterization is very much an oversimplification and fails, by itself, to encompass adequately the variety of moods and movements within European society during these centuries.

Whatever else it was, this was a period of dramatic, transitional change, and much of the change was turbulent: International conflict on an unprecedented scale; destructive civil wars; schism within the Church; violent rebellions among the lowest classes and savage repression; a crisis of religious and secular leadership at all levels of society; famine and economic depression; new schools of thought and spirituality that called old values into question; and the Black Death. But not all was decay. A general economic upswing followed the depression, and Western monarchs were able to reassert their authority in new and ultimately more effective ways. Brilliant new modes of art, literature, and music were created, and a new world was discovered.

Some of the paradoxes of this epoch become less confusing when we consider Europe as two separate, but related, geographic entities: The Late Medieval North and Renaissance Italy. Europe north of the Alps suffered more grievously than Italy from the troubles of this age. The result was that Northern European art and literature largely abandoned the joyous motifs and lighthearted exuberance of the High Middle Ages and became positively morbid. Because the North was still anchored in the medieval feudal world, with its French-centered culture, the forms it used to express this new pessimism remained essentially Gothic. Its intellectual and artistic products, such as the brawling, brutally realistic poetry of François Villon, were sophisticated, technically advanced, and often works of genius, but they also carried the odor of a dying medieval order. To the south, urban, commercial, nonfeudal Italy was producing self-consciously classical modes of life and expression, which collectively we term the Renaissance. By the latter half of the fifteenth century these new trends would cross the Alps and begin infusing the culture of the North.

The three historians chosen to represent these two centuries illustrate in turn the world views of the late medieval North, early Renaissance France, and Renaissance Italy in full bloom.

16. FROISSART: CHRONICLES OF ENGLAND, FRANCE, AND SPAIN

Jean Froissart (1337?-1410?), priest, courtier, and traveller, sprang from the merchant class of Flanders but attached himself to the nobility of England and France and shared their chivalric values. The Hundred Years' War, which he chronicled in his native Walloon French, was for him essentially a long series of knightly deeds, and he was lavish in his praise of gallantry wherever he found it. The chivalry that he valued so highly was originally a creation of the Church and feudal nobility of the High Middle Ages. Perhaps during the twelfth and thirteenth centuries it served a useful function and somehow corresponded to societal realities. By Froissart's day it was in an advanced state of decay, but he was incapable of perceiving the emptiness of its highly formalized trappings. To the deeper implications of this conflict Froissart was either blind or indifferent. He certainly lacked all understanding and sympathy for the violent lower class rebels engendered by the crises of this age—crises which were often caused or exacerbated by the "honorable and valorous" deeds of late medieval nobles.

We have seen where medieval monastic historians treated the natural and supernatural as two different categories of phenomena. The following selections illustrate how Froissart employed different standards in judging the actions of nobles and commoners. The first excerpt concerns the Battle of Poitiers (1356); the second the Peasants' Rebellion of 1381.

The next day was Sunday, and early in the morning, after he had heard mass and received the communion, the King of France, who was very impatient for battle, ordered his whole army to prepare. Upon this the trumpet sounded, and everyone mounted his horse, and made for that part of the plain where the King's banner was planted. There were to be seen all the nobility of France richly dressed in brilliant armor, with banners and pennons gayly displayed; for no knight or squire, for fear of dishonor, dared to remain behind. The army was divided into three battalions, each consisting of 16,000 men; the first was commanded by the Duke of Orleans, the second by the Duke of Normandy and his two brothers, the Lord Lewis and Lord John, and the third by the King himself. The King was armed in royal armor, and to prevent discovery nineteen others were armed like him. . . .

It chanced on that day that Sir John Chandos had ridden out near one of the wings of the French army, and Lord John de Clermont, one of the French King's marshals, had done the same to view the English; as each knight was returning to his quarters, they met; both had the same device upon the surcoats which they wore over their clothes. On seeing this Lord Clermont said, "Chandos, how long is it since you have taken upon you to wear my arms?" "It is you who have mine," replied Chandos, "for the arms are as much mine as yours." "I deny that," said the Lord Clermont, "and were it not for the truce between us, I would soon show that you have no right to wear them." "Ha!" answered Chandos, "you will find me to-morrow in the field, ready prepared to defend, and to prove by force of arms what I have said." The Lord Clermont replied, "These are the boastings of you English, who can invent nothing new, but take for your own whatever you see handsome belonging to others;" with that they parted, and each returned to his army. As soon as the cardinal's negotiations were ended, the Prince of Wales thus addressed his army: "Now, my gallant fellows, what though we be a small number compared with our enemies, do not be cast down; victory does not always follow numbers; it is the Almighty who bestows it. I entreat you to exert yourselves, and to combat manfully, for if it please God and St. George you shall see me this day act like a true knight." The whole army of the prince, including everyone, did not amount to 8,000; while the French, counting all sorts of persons, were upward of 60,000 combatants, among whom were more than 3,000 knights; however, the English were in high spirits; Sir John Chandos placed himself near the prince, to guard him, and never during that day would he on any account quit his post. The Lord James Audley also remained near him a considerable time, but when he saw that they must certainly engage, he said to the prince, "Sir, I have ever most loyally served my lord your father, and yourself, and shall continue to do so as long as I have life. Dear sir, I must now acquaint you that formerly I made a vow that if ever I should be engaged in any battle where the King your father, or any of his sons were, I would be the foremost in the attack, and the best combatant on his side, or die in the attempt; I beg, therefore, most earnestly, as a reward for any services I may have done, that you will grant me permission honorably to quit you, that I may post myself in such wise to accomplish my vow." The prince granted this request, and holding out his hand to him, said, "Sir James, God grant that this day you may shine in valor above all other knights." . . .

. . . . The Lord James Audley, attended by his four squires, was always engaged in the heat of the battle; he was severely wounded, but as long as his strength and breath permitted him, he maintained the fight, and continued to advance. At length, when quite exhausted, his four squires, who were his body guard, led him out of the engagement toward a hedge, that he might cool himself, and take breath; they disarmed him as gently as they could, in order to examine his wounds, dress them, and sew up the most dangerous.

King John, on his part, proved himself a good knight; indeed, if the fourth of his people had behaved as well, the day would have been his own. Those also who were more immediately about him acquitted themselves to the best of their power, and were either slain or taken prisoners. Scarcely any attempted to escape. . . .

It happened in the midst of the general pursuit, that a squire from Picardy, named John de Helennes, had quitted the King's division, and meeting his page with a fresh horse, had mounted, and made off as fast as he could; there was near to him at the time the Lord of Berkeley, a young knight who had that day for the first time displayed his banner, and he immediately set off in pursuit of him. When the Lord of Berkeley had followed for some time John de Helennes turned about, put his sword under his arm in the manner of a lance, and thus advanced upon his adversary, who, taking his sword by the handle, flourished it, and lifted up his arm in order to strike the squire as he passed. John de Helennes, seeing the intended stroke, avoided it, but did not miss his own; for, as they passed each other, by a blow on the arm he made Lord Berkeley's sword fall to the ground. When the knight found that he had lost his sword, and that the squire retained his own, he dismounted, and made for the place where his sword lay; but before he could get there the squire gave him a violent thrust, which passed through both his thighs, so that he fell to the ground. John, upon this, dismounted, and seizing the sword of the knight, advanced to him and asked if he were willing to surrender. The knight required his name. "I am John de Helennes," said he; "what is your name?" "In truth, companion," replied the knight, "my name is Thomas and I am Lord of Berkeley, a very handsome castle situated on the river Severn, on the borders of Wales." "Lord of Berkeley," said the squire, "you shall be my prisoner; I will place you in safety, and take care that you are well treated, for you appear to me to be badly wounded." The knight answered, "I surrender myself willingly, for you have loyally conquered me." Accordingly he gave him his word in token that he would be his prisoner, rescued or not. John then drew his sword out of the knight's thighs, bound the wounds up tightly, and placing him on his horse, led him at a footpace to Châtellerault, where he continued with him, out of friendship, fifteen days, and had medicines administered to him. As soon as the knight was a little recovered the squire caused him to be placed on a litter, and conducted safely to his house in Picardy; here he remained more than a year before he was quite well; and when he departed he paid for his ransom 6,000 nobles, so that this squire became a knight by the large sum which he got from the Lord of Berkeley.

The English continued the pursuit of the enemy even to the city of Poitiers, where there was great slaughter, both of men and horses, for the inhabitants had shut the gates, and would suffer none to enter. The Lord of Pons, a powerful baron of Poitou, was there slain. During the whole engagement the Lord de Chargny, who was near the King, and carried the royal banner, fought most bravely; the English and Gascons, however, poured so fast upon the King's division, that they broke through the ranks by force, and in the confusion the Lord de Chargny was slain, with the banner of France in his hand. There was now much eagerness manifested to take the King; and those who were nearest to him, and knew him, cried out, "Surrender yourself, surrender yourself, or you are a dead man." In this part of the field was a young knight from St. Omer, engaged in the service of the King of England, whose name was Denys de Morbeque; for three years he had attached himself to the English on account of having been banished from France in his younger days for a murder committed during an affray at St. Omer. Now it fortunately happened for this knight, that he was at the time near to the King of France, to whom he said in good French, "Sire, sire, surrender yourself." The King, who found himself very disagreeably situated, turning to him asked, "To whom shall I surrender myself? Where is my cousin, the Prince of Wales? If I could see him I would speak to him." "Sire," replied Sir Denys, "he is not here; but surrender yourself to me, and I will lead you to him." "Who are you?" said the King. "Sire, I am Denys de Morbeque, a knight from Artois; but I serve the King of England because I cannot belong to France, having forfeited all I possessed there." The King then gave him his right-hand glove, and said, "I surrender myself to you."

The Prince of Wales, who was as courageous as a lion, took great delight that day in combating his enemies. Sir John Chandos, who was near his person, and indeed had never quitted it during the whole of the engagement, nor stopped to make any prisoners, said to him toward the end of the battle, "Sir, it will be proper for you to halt here, and plant your banner on the top of this bush, which will serve to rally your forces, as they seem very much scattered; for I do not see any banners or pennons of the French, or any considerable bodies ably to rally against us, and you must refresh yourself a little, for I perceive you are very much heated." Upon this the banner of the prince was placed on a high bush, the minstrels began to play, and the trumpets and clarions to do their duty. The prince took off his helmet, and the knights attendant on his person were soon ready, and pitched a small pavilion of crimson color, which he entered. As soon as the prince's marshals were come back, he asked them if they knew anything of the King of France. They replied, "No, sir, nothing for a certainty, but we believe he must be either killed or made prisoner, since he has never quitted his battalion." The prince, then addressing the Earl of Warwick and Lord Cobham, said, "I beg of you to mount your horses and ride over the field, so that on your return you may bring me some certain intelligence respecting him." The two barons immediately mounting their horses left the prince, and made for a small hillock, that they might look about them; from this position they perceived a crowd of men-at-arms on foot, advancing very slowly. The King of France was in the midst of them, and in great danger, for the English and Gascons had taken him from Sir Denys de Morbeque, and were disputing who should have him; some bawling out, "It is I that have got him;" "No, no," replied others, "we have him." The King, to escape from this perilous situation, said, "Gentlemen, gentlemen, I pray you to conduct me and my son, in a courteous manner, to my cousin the prince, and do not make so great a riot about my capture, for I am a great lord, and I can make all sufficiently rich." These words, and others which fell from the King, appeased them a little; but the disputes were always beginning again, and the men did not move a step without rioting. When the two barons saw this troop of people they descended from the hillock, and sticking spurs into their horses, made up to them. On their arrival they asked what was the matter, and were informed that the King of France had been made prisoner, and that upward of ten knights and squires challenged him at the same time as belonging to each of them. The two barons then pushed through the crowd by main force, and ordered all to draw aside. They commanded in the name of the prince, and under pain of instant death, that everyone should keep his distance, and none approach unless ordered to do so. All then retreated behind the King, and the two barons, dismounting, advanced to the royal prisoner with profound reverence, and conducted him in a peaceable manner to the Prince of Wales. . . .

Lord James Audley had not long left the prince's presence, when the Earl of Warwick and Lord Reginald Cobham entered the pavilion and presented the King of France to him. The prince made a very low obeisance to the King and gave him all the comfort as he was able. He ordered wine and spices to be brought, which, as a mark of his great affection, he presented to the King himself.

. . .There happened great commotions among the lower orders in England, by which that country was nearly ruined. In order that this disastrous rebellion may serve as an example to mankind, I will speak of all that was done from the information I had at the time. It is customary in England, as well as in several other countries, for the nobility to have great privileges over the commonalty; that is to say, the lower orders are bound by law to plough the lands of the gentry, to harvest their grain, to carry it home to the barn, to thrash and winnow it; they are also bound to harvest and carry home the hay. All these services the prelates the gentlemen exact of their inferiors; and in the counties of Kent, Essex, Sussex, and Bedford, these services are more oppressive than in other parts of the kingdom. In consequence of this the evil disposed in these districts began to murmur, saying, that in the beginning of the world there were no slaves, and that no one ought to be treated as such, unless he had committed treason against his lord, as Lucifer did against God; but they had done no such thing, for they were neither angels nor spirits, but men formed after the same likeness as these lords who treated them as beasts. This they would bear no longer; they were determined to be free, and if they labored or did any work, they would be paid for it. A crazy priest in the county of Kent, called John Ball, who for his absurd preaching had thrice been confined in prison by the Archbishop of Canterbury, was greatly instrumental in exciting these rebellious ideas. Every Sunday after mass, as the people were coming out of church, this John Ball was accustomed to assemble a crowd around him in the market-place and preach to them. On such occasions he would say, "My good friends, matters cannot go on well in England until all things shall be in common; when there shall be neither vassals nor lords; when the lords shall be no more masters than ourselves. How ill they behave to us! For what reason do they thus hold us in bondage? Are we not all descended from the same parents, Adam and Eve? And what can they show, or what reason can they give, why they should be more masters than ourselves? They are clothed in velvet and rich stuffs, ornamented with ermine and other furs, while we are forced to wear poor clothing. They have wines, spices, and fine bread, while we have only rye and the refuse of the straw; and when we drink it must be water. They have handsome seats and manors, while we must brave the wind and rain in our labors in the field; and it is by our labor they have wherewith to support their pomp. We are called slaves, and if we do not perform our service we are beaten, and we have no sovereign to whom we can complain or who would be willing to hear us. Let us go to the King and remonstrate with him; he is young, and from him we may obtain a favorable answer, and if not we must ourselves seek to amend our condition."

With such language as this did John Ball harangue the people of his village every Sunday after mass. The archbishop, on being informed of it, had him arrested and imprisoned for two or three months by way of punishment; but the moment he was out of prison, he returned to his former course. Many in the city of London, envious of the rick and noble, having heard of John Ball's preaching, said among themselves that the country was badly governed, and that the nobility had seized upon all the gold and silver. These wicked Londoners, therefore, began to assemble in parties, and to show signs of rebellion; they also invited all those who held like opinions in the adjoining counties to come to London, telling them that they would find the town open to them and the commonalty of the same way of thinking as themselves, and that they would so press the King that there should no longer be a slave in England.

By this means the men of Kent, Essex, Sussex, Bedford, and the adjoining counties, in number about 60,000, were brought to London, under command of Wat Tyler, Jack Straw, and John Ball. This Wat Tyler, who was chief of the three, had been a tiler of houses—a bad man and a great enemy to the nobility. When these wicked people first began their disturbances, all London, with the exception of those who favored them, was much alarmed. The mayor and rich citizens assembled in council and debated whether they should shut the gate and refuse to admit them; however, upon mature reflection they determined not to do so, as they might run the risk of having the suburbs burned. The gates of the city were therefore thrown open, and the rabble entered and lodged as they pleased. True it is that full two-thirds of these people knew neither what they wanted, nor for what purpose they had come together; they followed one another like sheep. . . .

In order that gentlemen and others may take example and learn to correct such wicked rebels, I will most amply detail how the whole business was conducted. On the Monday preceding the feast of the Holy Sacrament in the year 1381, these people sallied forth from their homes to come to London, intending, as they said, to remonstrate with the King, and to demand their freedom. At Canterbury, they met John Ball, Wat Tyler, and Jack Straw. On entering this city they were well feasted by the inhabitants, who were all of the same way of thinking as themselves; and having held a council there, resolved to proceed on their march to London. They also sent emissaries across the Thames into Essex, Suffolk, and Bedford, to press the people of those parts to do the same, in order that the city might be quite surrounded. It was the intention of the leaders of this rabble that all the different parties should be collected on the feast of the Holy Sacrament on the day following. At Canterbury the rebels entered the Church of St. Thomas, where they did much damage; they also pillaged the apartments of the archbishop, saying as they were carrying off the different articles, ''The

Chancellor of England has had this piece of furniture very cheap; he must now give us an account of his revenues, and of the large sums which he has levied since the coronation of the King.'' After this they plundered the abbey of St. Vincent, and then, leaving Canterbury, took the road toward Rochester. As they passed they collected people from the villages right and left, and on they went like a tempest, destroying all the houses belonging to attorneys, King's proctors, and the archbishop, which came in their way. . . .

In other counties of England the rebels acted in a similar manner, and several great lords and knights, such as the Lord Manley, Sir Stephen Hales, and Sir Thomas Cossington, were compelled to march with them. Now observe how fortunately matters turned out, for had these scoundrels succeeded in their intentions, all the nobility of England would have been destroyed; and after such success as this the people of other nations would have rebelled also, taking example from those of Ghent and Flanders, who at the time were in actual rebellion against their lord; the Parisians, indeed, the same year acted in a somewhat similar manner; upward of 20,000 of them armed themselves with leaden maces and caused a rebellion, which I shall speak of as we go on; but I must first finish my account of these disturbances in England. . . .

On Friday morning the rebels, who lodged in the square of St. Catherine's, before the Tower, began to make themselves ready. They shouted much and said, that if the King would not come out to them, they would attack the Tower, storm it, and slay all who were within. The King, alarmed at these menaces, resolved to speak with the rabble; he therefore sent orders for them to retire to a handsome meadow at Mile-end, where, in the summer time, people go to amuse themselves, at the same time signifying that he would meet them there and grant their demands. Proclamation to this effect was made in the King's name, and thither, accordingly, the commonalty of the different villages began to march; many, however, did not care to go, but stayed behind in London, being more desirous of the riches of the nobles and the plunder of the city. Indeed, covetousness and the desire of plunder was the principal cause of these disturbances, as the rebels showed very plainly. When the gates of the Tower were thrown open, and the King, attended by his two brothers and other nobles, had passed through, Wat Tyler, Jack Straw, and John Ball, with upward of 400 others, rushed in by force, and running from chamber to chamber, found the Archbishop of Canterbury, by name Simon, a valiant and wise man, whom the rascals seized and beheaded. The prior of St. John's suffered the same fate, and likewise a Franciscan friar, a doctor of physic, who was attached to the Duke of Lancaster, also a sergeant-at-arms whose name was John Laige.

The heads of these four persons the rebels fixed on long spikes and had them carried before them through the streets of London; and when they had made sufficient mockery of them, they caused them to be placed on London Bridge, as if they had been traitors to their King and country. . . .

[Wat Tyler is Killed in the presence of King Richard II]

When the rebels found that their leader was dead, they drew up in a sort of battle array, each man having his bow bent before him. The King at this time certainly hazarded much, though it turned out most fortunately for him; for as soon as Tyler was on the ground, he left his attendants, giving orders that no one should follow him, and riding up to the rebels, who were advancing to revenge their leader's death, said, "Gentlemen, what are you about? you shall have me for your captain: I am your King, remain peaceable." The greater part, on hearing these words, were quite ashamed, and those among them who were inclined for peace began to slip away; the riotous ones, however, kept their ground. The King returned to his lords, and consulted with them what next should be done. Their advice was to make for the fields; but the mayor said, that to retreat would be of no avail. "It is quite proper to act as we have done; and I reckon we shall very soon receive assistance from our good friends in London." . . .

When the rabble had dispersed, the King and his lords, to their great joy, returned in good array to London, whence the King immediately took the road to the Wardrobe, to visit the princess, his mother, who had remained there two days and two nights under the greatest apprehension. On seeing her son, the good lady was much rejoiced, and said, "Ah, ah, fair son, what pain and anguish have I not suffered for you this day!" "Madam," replied the King, "I am well assured of that; but now rejoice, and thank God, for it behooves us to praise him, as I have this day regained my inheritance—the kingdom of England, which I had lost." . . .

John Ball and Jack Straw were found hidden in an old ruin, where they had secreted themselves, thinking to steal away when things were quiet; but this they were prevented doing, for their own men betrayed them. With this capture the King and his barons were much pleased, and had their heads cut off, as was that of Tyler, and fixed on London Bridge, in the room of those whom these wretches themselves had placed there.

News of this total defeat of the rebels in London was sent throughout the neighboring counties, in order that all those who were on their way to London might hear of it; and as soon as they did so, they instantly returned to their homes, without daring to advance farther.

17. COMMINES: MEMOIRS

The Alps have never been an effective barrier between Italy and the North. Throughout the fifteenth century the warm breeze of an Italianate Renaissance wafted northward. Finally in 1494 French troops under Charles VIII invaded Italy, beginning a centuries-long involvement of the European monarchies in Italy. Italy became the battleground for European dynastic conflicts; it also became the new school of Europe. Ironically, France, the artistic and intellectual center of the Gothic North, was the first transalpine country to experience the imprint of the new Italian culture. As we look at France around 1500 we can, in the immortal words of a freshman essayist, see a society "that stood with one foot planted in the Middle Ages and with the other saluted the rising sun of the Renaissance."

France's ablest historian of this period, Philippe de Commines (*ca.* 1447-1511), reflected the dichotomous nature of North European Renaissance civilization. He was France's last great medieval historian and its first modern political observer.

Commines, born into the Flemish nobility, spent a long, checkered career as councillor and foreign minister for three kings and several peers of France. Much of his diplomatic life was spent directing French interests in Italy, where he served as ambassador of Charles VIII to both Venice and Milan. At least as early as 1485 Commines began recording his experiences and probably completed the task during a period of forced retirement under Louis XII. One of the outstanding diplomats of his age, Commines realized fully his own worth and the importance of his observations, and he intended his *Memoirs* to serve as a practical guide for princes and other statesmen.

One of the major facets of Renaissance society was its intensification of a secular spirit, which found expression in a renewed emphasis on statecraft and a return to a pre-Augustinian disposition to view politics as the most important element in history. In the Renaissance North this new political awareness magnified the position of the traditional (medieval), hereditary prince, whose public actions now were judged not in the light of Christian or chivalric codes of conduct but in terms of their political ramifications. The good prince was not necessarily a moral man. He was one who governed effectively. For this reason, Louis XI, an amoral, in many respects repulsive, person, who happened to be a skilled and brutally efficient monarch, assumed a heroic role in Commines' *Memoirs*. Yet, Renaissance secularism did not preclude medieval values or attitudes. Commines' treatment of Louis' last days, of which selections appear below, illustrates the manner in which this Renaissance man retained, without apparent contradiction, the religious convictions of an earlier age and considered the state of an individual's soul proper historical material.

    . . . all endeavours to prolong his [Louis XI] life proved ineffectual; his time was come, and he must follow his predecessors. Yet in one thing God Almighty favoured him in a peculiar manner, for, as he had made him more prudent, liberal, virtuous, and greater in every thing than the contemporary princes, who were his neighbours and enemies; so he suffered him to survive them, though it was not very long. For Charles Duke of Burgundy, the duchess his daughter, King Edward of England, Duke Galeas of Milan, and John King of Arragon, were all dead: but King Edward and the Duchess of Austria a very little before him. In all of them there was a mixture of bad as well as good, for they were but mortals. But, without flattery, I may say of our king, that he was possessed of more qualifications suitable to the majesty and office of a prince, than any of the rest, for I knew the greatest part of them, and was acquainted with most of their transactions, so that I do not speak altogether by guess or hearsay.

    . . . In all his sickness he never was the man that complained, which most other people do when they are ill, at least I am of that nature, and I have known several of the same temper, and the common opinion is, that complaining does alleviate our pain.

    He was continually discoursing on some subject or another, and always with a great deal of sense and judgment. His last fit (as I said before) continued from Monday to Saturday night. Upon which account I will now make comparison between the evils and sorrows which he brought upon others, and what he suffered in his own person: for I hope his sufferings and torments here on earth, have translated him into Paradise, and will be a great part of his purgatory: and if, in respect of their greatness and duration, his sufferings were inferior to what he had brought upon other people, yet, if you consider the grandeur and dignity of his office, and that he had never before suffered any thing in his own person, but been obeyed by all people, as if all Europe had been created for no other end, but to serve and be commanded by him; you will find that little which he endured was so contrary to his nature and custom, that he was as great a sufferer as any. . . .

Never man was more fearful of death, nor used more things to prevent it than he. He had, all his life long, commanded and requested his servants, and me among the rest, that whenever we saw him in any danger of death, we should not use any long stories, but admonish him at a distance to confess himself, without ever mentioning that cruel and shocking word Death, which he did believe he should not be able to bear with any tolerable patience. However, he endured that and several more things as terrible, when he was ill, and indeed more than any man I ever saw die. He spoke several things, which were to be delivered to his son, whom he called king; confessed himself very devoutly, said several prayers according to the sacraments he received, and called for them himself. He spoke as judiciously as if he had never been sick, discoursed of all things which might be necessary for his son's instruction, and among the rest gave orders that the Lord des Cordes should not stir from his son in six months; and that he should be desired to attempt nothing against Calais, or elsewhere, declaring, that though he had designed himself to undertake such enterprises as those, and with good intention both to the king and the kingdom, yet they were very dangerous, especially that of Calais, lest the English should resent it; and he left it in charge, that for six or seven years after his death, they should, above all things, preserve the kingdom in peace, which during his life he would never suffer. And indeed it was no more than was necessary; for, though the kingdom was large and fertile, yet it was grown very poor, upon the marching and counter-marching of the soldiers up and down in their motions from one country to another, as they have done since, and in a worse manner. He also ordered that nothing should be attempted against Bretagne, but that Duke Francis should be suffered to live quietly and in peace; that both he and his neighbours might be secure, and the king and kingdom remain free from wars, till the king should be of age, to take upon him the administration of affairs himself.

In a preceding paragraph I began to compare the evils, which he made several others suffer, who lived under his dominion, with those he endured himself before his death; that it might appear, though they were not perhaps of so long a duration, that they were as great and terrible, considering his station and dignity, which required more obedience than any private person's and had found more; so that the least opposition was a great torment to him. Some five or six months before his death, he began to grow jealous of every body, especially of those who were most capable and deserving of the administration of affairs. . . .*

The king had ordered several cruel prisons to be made, some of iron, and some of wood, but covered with iron plates both within and without, with terrible

---

*Commines probably is referring to himself.

cages about eight foot wide and seven high; the first contriver of them was the Bishop of Verdun, who was the first that hanseled them, being immediately put in one of them, where he continued fourteen years. Many bitter curses he has had since, for his invention, and some from me, having lain in one of them eight months together, in the minority of our present king. . . .

Is it possible then to keep a prince, (with any regard to his quality,) more strictly confined than he kept himself? The cages which were made for other people, were about eight feet square; and he, (though so great a monarch,) had but a small court of the castle to walk in, and seldom made use of that; but generally kept himself in the gallery, out of which he went into the chambers, and from thence to mass, but not through the court. Who can deny but he was a sufferer as well as his neighbours? considering his being locked up, guarded, afraid of his own children and relations, and changing every day those very servants whom he had brought up and advanced; and though they owed all their preferment to him, yet he durst not trust any of them, but shut himself up in those strange chains and enclosures. If the place where he confined himself was larger than a common prison, his quality was as much greater than a common prisoner's. It may be urged that other princes have been more given to jealousy than he, but it was not in our time; and, perhaps, their wisdom was not so eminent, nor their subjects so good. They too might, probably, be tyrants, and bloody-minded, but our king never did any person a mischief who had not offended him first. I have not recorded these things purely to represent our master as a suspicious and mistrustful prince; but to shew, that by the patience which he expressed in his sufferings, (like those which he inflicted on other people) they may be looked upon, in my judgment, as a punishment which God inflicted upon him in this world, in order to deal more mercifully with him in the next, as well in those things before-mentioned, as in the distempers of his body, which were great and painful, and much dreaded by him before they came upon him; and, likewise, that those princes, who are his successors, may learn by this example, to be more tender and indulgent to their subjects, and less severe in their punishments than our master had been. I will not accuse him, or say I ever saw a better prince; for though he oppressed his subjects himself, he would never see them injured by any body else.

After so many fears, sorrows, and suspicions, God, by a kind of miracle, restored him both in body and mind, as is His divine method in such kind of wonders. He took him out of the world in perfect ease, understanding, and memory; having called for all the sacraments himself, discoursing without the least twinge, or expression of pain, to the very last moment of his life. He gave directions for his own burial, appointed who should attend his corps to the grave, and declared that he desired to die on a Saturday of all days in the week; and that, he hoped Our Lady would procure him that favour, in whom he had always placed great part of his trust, and served her devoutly. And so it happened; for he died on Saturday, the 30th of August, 1483, about eight at night, in the castle of Plessis, where his fit took him on the Monday before. His soul, I hope, is with God, and enjoys an everlasting rest in the kingdom of Paradise.

18. MACHIAVELLI: HISTORY OF FLORENCE

Niccolo Machiavelli (1469-1527), Florentine patriot, republican politician, warrior, diplomat, political and military theorist, comic playwright, poet, and historian, has often been compared with Commines (whom he possibly met). The similarities between their political histories are striking, the differences revealing.

In Machiavelli's *History of Florence* we encounter a more pronounced secular spirit. He was conventionally religious, taking care to avail himself of the comforts of religion before he died, but totally avoided all elements of the spiritual when he wrote history. Commines centered his *Memoirs* around the exploits of two kings whom he had served; Machiavelli's history had one hero—his beloved Florence. Commines, who knew no Latin, wrote in French, and his allusions to ancient history were minimal. In Florence the dominant intellectual force was Latin humanism—study of classical Roman authors—and Machiavelli had received a proper education. He wrote his history in Italian, but its spirit and dress were Roman. Livy's Republican Rome was the touchstone by which Machiavelli judged Florence and its citizens, and like Livy he used history to teach civic virtues, in this case by contrasting ancient Roman Republican virtues with modern Florentine failings.

Since the late fourteenth century "civic humanism" had been one of the many intellectual-educational currents within Florentine classicism. Civic humanists maintained that the proper end of education was the creation of good citizens who conformed to ancient models. These scholars generally abandoned such traditionally medieval subjects as logic, metaphysics, and theology and concentrated on classical rhetoric, moral philosophy, and history—subjects necessary for one who wished to play an active political role.

Machiavelli's *History of Florence*, composed between 1520 and 1525, was within this tradition. His implied message was that because it lacked the virtues that had made Rome great, Florence had been subjected to internal disorders and its republican forms of government had failed.

The following excerpts are taken from the author's introduction and the first chapter of Book III.

When I first determined to write the History and Deeds of the Florentines at home and abroad, I designed to begin with the year 1434, when the family of the

Medici, by the merits of Cosimo, and of his father Giovanni, had acquired greater power than any other in Florence. Leonardo d' Arezzo and Marco Poggio, two excellent historians, seemed to have given a sufficiently minute account of the events which happened before that period.

But after carefully perusing their writings to see the method and order they had adopted, that I might recommend my own by imitating theirs, I found, although they had been very accurate in their relation of the wars of the Florentines with foreign States and Princes, they were either totally silent about their civil dissensions, and domestic animosities, and their consequences, or had touched them in so cursory and superficial a manner, the reader was neither profited nor entertained.

They adopted this course, I suppose, either because they thought those occurrences too insignificant to be transmitted to future times; or from fear of offending the descendants of those they would have been obliged to mention with dishonor. Both reasons, if I may be allowed to say it, seem to be altogether unworthy of great men. For, if anything be either instructive or entertaining in history, it is a minute narration of facts. If any lesson be useful to citizens who govern republics, it is a knowledge of the causes of animosities and divisions in commonwealths; by which they may be made wise by the fate of others, and learn to preserve their union. If every lesson drawn from the history of republics impresses mankind, the admonitions which come from their own are certain to impress them still deeper, and prove more useful.

If the factions of any republic are worthy of notice, they must be those that have distracted Florence. For while most other commonwealths of which we have any knowledge have only been divided between two rival parties, which either added strength to the State, or caused its destruction, this city has been subject to a thousand factions. In Rome, as every one knows, after the expulsion of their kings, a contest arose between the Patricians and Plebeians, which continued till the utter dissolution of that republic. This, too, was the fate of Athens, and all the commonwealths that flourished in those early ages. But in Florence, the first dissension was among the nobles; the second between the nobility and the citizens; and the last between the citizens and plebeians; and not unfrequently the party in the ascendant divided again. These divisions were followed by assassinations, executions, banishments and dispersions of families, without a parallel in the history of any people whose annals have descended to our times.

But nothing, it seems to me, demonstrates the strength of our city so clearly as the effects of those divisions, which were sufficient to have subverted the most powerful state in the world. Ours, on the contrary, seems to have emerged from these divisions stronger than ever. For such was the virtue, the patriotism, and the ambition of the citizens to aggrandize their country, that some who escaped those evils contributed more effectually to its exaltation than the malignity of faction had done to crush it. And, without doubt, had a form of government been fortunately established in Florence which would have kept the citizens firmly united, after shaking off the yoke of the empire, I know of no commonwealth, ancient or modern, that could have been deemed its superior, so glorious would she have become in arms and in commerce. For it is well known, that after the Ghibellines had been banished in such numbers, that Tuscany and Lombardy swarmed with the exiles, the Guelphs and those that remained, raised an army of twelve thousand foot, and twelve hundred heavy-armed horse, among their own citizens, for the expedition against Arezzo, only one year before the battle of Compaldino. And afterwards, in the war with Philip Visconti, Duke of Milan, when their own forces had been destroyed, and they were obliged to trust to mercenary soldiers, the Florentines expended three millions, five hundred thousand florins, during the five years it lasted; and it was no sooner ended than they became dissatisfied with the peace, and desirous of making a further display of their strength, marched an army to the siege of Lucca.

I can see no reason, therefore, why civil dissensions should not be thought worthy of a particular relation. And if those noble authors were deterred from it only by the fear of injuring the memory of some of whom they would have been obliged to speak, they not only deceived themselves, but showed they knew little of the ambition of mankind, and their desire to have their names and those of their ancestors perpetuated. They forgot, that many who never had any opportunity of signalizing themselves by laudable achievements, have perpetuated their memory by the most flagitious crimes. Nor did they consider that powerful movements, like those of states and governments, reflect more honor than infamy upon their actors, whatever may have been their motives, or in whatever light they may be represented.

These considerations induced me to alter my first plan, and begin my history from the foundation of our city. And since it is not my intention to tread in the footsteps of others, I shall relate such things only as happened within the city to the year 1434, taking no further notice of foreign transactions than will be necessary to understand what occurred at home: after this period, I shall give a distinct narration of foreign as well as domestic affairs. And that we may be more perfectly understood throughout, before I treat of the affairs of Florence, I shall show by what means Italy became subject to those princes who governed it at that time. All this will be included in the first four books.

The first will contain a brief recital of the principal events that happened in Italy from the decline of the Roman Empire to the year 1434. The second, a general account of affairs from the foundation of the city of Florence to the war against the Pontiff, after the expulsion of the Duke of Athens. The third will conclude with the death of Ladislaus, King of Naples; and the fourth will bring us down to the year 1434; after which we shall give a particular narrative of events which transpired in Florence and throughout the Peninsula down to our own times.

The bitter animosities which prevail between the people and nobility, from ambition in the one to command, and a reluctance in the other to obey, are the natural sources of all those calamities which spring up in free states; for all other evils that disturb their peace are inflamed by this universal hostility. This kept Rome divided. This, too, if we may compare great things with small, was the bane of Florence, although its fruits were very different in the two cities.

The animosities that first arose between the nobles and the people of Rome were determined by debate; those of Florence, by the sword. A feud in Rome was settled by a law; a dispute in Florence by the death and banishment of many of her citizens. The quarrels of Rome augmented her military virtue; those of Florence utterly extinguished it. The struggles of Rome annihilated the original equality of her citizens, and brought the masses under the sway of the few; while the war in Florence brought the old nobility to the feet of the people, and put every man upon the same level. This diversity of effects was necessarily owing to the widely different views entertained by the two cities. The people of Rome were willing to share with the nobility the honors of the state, but the people of Florence fought for the supreme control of the government, to the utter exclusion of the nobles. And as the desire of the Roman people was more reasonable, the nobility the more readily complied with them; and after some little bickerings, which were conducted without any open rupture, a law was made which satisfied the people, and left the nobles in possession of their dignities. But the demands of the Florentine people were so extravagant and humiliating, that the nobility resorted to arms in self-defence, and their quarrels ended in the blood and exile of multitudes of her citizens. The laws afterwards made, were for the victors and not for the good of the public.

The triumph of the people of Rome, too, augmented the grandeur of the state, for they were admitted equally with the nobles to the administration of the magistracies, command of armies and the sway of the empire. They thus became inspired with the same magnanimity; and as their virtue increased, the power of that great city extended. But when the people of Florence had conquered, they divested the nobles of every remnant of authority, and left them no alternative for its recovery, but to conform in appearance and in fact entirely to their government, their spirit and their manner of life. To this cause may be attributed the change of the arms and the titles of noble families, to win favor with the people. Thus that bravery in arms and generosity of soul, which had distinguished the nobility, were utterly annihilated; nor were they to be aroused in the breast of the mass of the people, where they had never been kindled. Florence inevitably became every day more abject and pusillanimous. Rome, by an unprecedented career of victory, at last became too haughty to be governed except by a Prince; Florence, on the contrary, was reduced so low, that a wise legislator might easily have re-organized its government, as we have clearly shown in the Second Book of this History.

SOURCE NOTES

1. From Sir John Froissart, *Chronicles of England, France, and Spain and the adjoining countries*, trans. Thomas Johnes (New York: The Co-operative Publication Society, 1901, revised edition), I, pp. 52-64, 58-63, and II, 211-215, 220-221, and 226-228.
2. From *The Memoirs of Philip de Comines* (London: William Clowes, 1823), II, pp. 84, 87-94, *passim*, and 96-98.
3. From Niccolo Machiavelli, *The Florentine Histories*, trans. C. Edwards Lester (New York: Paine and Burgess, 1845), pp. 15-17 and 129-130.

8.
THE
CONFESSIONAL
AGE

The Age of Reformation (*ca.* 1517-*ca.* 1648) was a period of intensive historical-mindedness. Protestants and Catholics of every hue based their respective ideologies on differing interpretations of the history of the Christian Church, each justifying present actions in the light of an understanding of the past.

Italian Renaissance humanists were the first Europeans to publicize what they believed to have been a meaningful difference between classical antiquity and the period that immediately followed. In their admiration for the ancient world, these scholars characterized the 1000 years that succeeded the demise of Roman civilization as an age of barbarism and illiteracy, from which Europe was only beginning to emerge in their own day. North European humanists generally were more sympathetic toward medieval civilization, but they also admitted a distinction between antiquity and post-Roman European society. Protestantism, essentially a northern movement, was worlds removed from the values of the Italian Renaissance, even though it owed much to the iconoclasm of the humanists. In one respect, however, Protestants agreed with Italian humanists. These new religious enthusiasts accepted and broadened the concept of post-classical debasement. Protestants understood the medieval Church, and especially the Roman papacy, to have perverted classical Christian beliefs and practices. They saw themselves as the new elect of God who would uproot the corruption of the last millennium and return Christendom to its primitive purity. Catholics, of course, defended medieval (therefore, present) practices as divinely established and saw in Protestantism a satanic attempt to defeat the linear progress and purpose of God's history.

Once again Western Europe adopted an Augustinian philosophy of history in order to give meaning to the course of present, past, and future human events. Once again history was viewed as a cosmic struggle. Now the enemy was the Scarlet Woman of Rome or the Protestant Antichrist, depending upon one's confessional allegiance.

Excerpted below are selections from the writings of three men, each a cleric and theologian as well as a historian of outstanding ability. In their different perceptions of the history of Christendom they represent, in turn, the world views of militant Reformed Protestantism, the strict, antirevolutionary Catholic Counter Reformation, and the more secular (liberal?) Catholic Reformation ideals of urban Italy. To illustrate these differences, we will concentrate upon their respective treatments of the English Reformation under Henry VIII and Edward VI.

19. KNOX: HISTORY OF THE REFORMATION OF RELIGION WITHIN THE REALM OF SCOTLAND

John Knox (*ca.* 1514-1572), a former Catholic priest, was the prophet and champion of Reformed Protestantism in his native Scotland and, more than any other individual, was responsible for its victory there. In 1559 he returned to Scotland after an exile of twelve years to undertake again his work of conversion; in this same year he began to write a history of the Scottish Reformation, which he composed and revised over the next thirteen years. At his death he had completed an unpublished manuscript divided into four books, concentrating on the period 1556-1564. An unknown continuator added a fifth book to bring the story down to the deposition of Mary Queen of Scots in 1567.

The *History* was initially printed in 1586, but the first accurate, complete edition did not appear until 1732. Although there have been numerous editions of the work since then, it remains largely unknown and unread—a pity since it is a masterpiece of Elizabethan English prose, a thrilling story told by a first-rate story-teller, and a particularly revealing historical document. It is also good history.

The theme of the *History of the Reformation* is God's solicitude for His Church, against which the devil's Roman Church could never triumph. Knox was not objective in his judgments, but he was honest, neither falsifying evidence nor suppressing relevant material. Although partisan, he strove to record the truth as he knew it. The following selections show Knox's approach to the historical truth. Note not only the different criteria he used to judge Catholic and Protestant deeds, but also the manner in which he treated different Protestants: Henry VIII, who rid England of "popery" but remained basically Catholic in theology and ritual; the boy king Edward VI, whose government was sympathetic to Calvinism; and the self-serving "rascal multitude" at Saint Johnston.

The two passages concerning the English Reformation come from Book I; from Book II we have taken Knox's description of the destruction of the friaries at Saint Johnston.

In this middle time, so did the wisdom of God provide, that Henry VIII. king of England, abolished from his realm the name and authority of the pope of Rome, commanded the Bible to be read in English, suppressed the abbeys, and other places of idolatry, with their idols, which gave great hope to divers realms, that some godly reformation should have thereof enused: And therefore, from this our country, divers learned men, and others that lived in fear of persecution, repaired to that realm; where, albeit they found not such purity as they wished (and therefore divers of them sought other countries*) yet they escaped the tyranny of merciless men, and were reserved to better times, that they might fructify within his church in divers places and parts, and in divers vocations. Alexander Seton remained in England, and publickly (with great praise and comfort of many) taught the gospel in all sincerity certain years. And albeit the craftiness of Gardiner, bishop of Winchester, and of others, circumvented the said Alexander, so that they caused him at Paul's cross to affirm certain things that were repugnant to his former doctrine; yet it is no doubt, but that God potently had assisted him in all his life, and that also in his death (which shortly after followed) he found the mercy of his God, whereupon he ever exhorted all men to depend.

Thus did light and darkness strive within the realm of Scotland: the darkness ever before suppressing the light, from the death of that notable servant of God, Mr. Patrick Hamilton, until the death of Edward VI, the most godly and most virtuous king that had been known to have reigned in England, or elsewhere, these many years bypast, who departed the miseries of this life the sixth of July, anno 1553. The death of this prince was lamented of all the godly within Europe; for the graces given unto him of God, as well of nature, as of erudition and godliness, passed the measure that accustomably is used to be given to other princes in their greatest perfection and yet exceeded he not sixteen years of age. What gravity, above age? what wisdom, wherein he passed all understanding or expectation of man? and what dexterity in answering, in all things proposed, were in that excellent prince, the ambassadors of all countries (yea, some that were mortal enemies to him, and to his realm, amongst whom the queen Dowager of Scotland was not the least) could, and did testify: for the said Queen Dowager, returning from France through England, communed with him at length, and gave record when she came to this realm, that she found more wisdom and solid judgment in young King Edward, than she would have looked for in any three princes that were then in Europe. His liberality towards the godly and learned that were in other realms persecuted, was such, as Germans, Frenchmen, Italians, Scots,

---

*In an autobiographical note, Knox tells us that in 1547 "...wearied of removing from place to place, by reason of the persecution that came upon him . . . [he] was determined to have left Scotland, and to have visited the schools of Germany (of England then he had no pleasure, by reason that the Pope's name being suppressed, his laws and corruptions remained in full vigour)." After being liberated from captivity in a French galley by the more Protestant government of Edward VI, Knox did take up residence in England and remained there until the accession of Mary I.

Spaniards, Polonians, Grecians, and Hebrews born, can yet give sufficient document. For how honourably was Martin Luther, Peter Martyr . . . and many others, upon his public stipends entertained their parents* can witness, and they themselves, during their lives, would never have denied.

After the death of this most virtuous prince, of whom the godless people of England (for the most part) were not worthy, Satan intended nothing less, than the light of Jesus Christ utterly to have been extinguished within the whole isle of Britain. For after him, was raised up, in God's hot displeasure, that idolatrous and mischievous Mary of the Spaniards blood,† a cruel persecutrix of God's people, as the acts of her unhappy reign can sufficiently witness.

And in Scotland, that same time (as we have heard) reigned the crafty practiser, Mary of Lorrain,‡ then named regent of Scotland, who, bound to the devotion of her two brethren, the Duke of Guise, and cardinal of Lorrain, did only abide the opportunity to cut the throat of all those, in whom she suspected any knowledge of God to be, within the realm of Scotland: and so thought Satan, that his kingdom of darkness was in quietness and rest, as well as in the one realm as in the other. But that provident eye of our eternal God, who continually watches for preservation of his church, did so order all things, that Satan shortly after found himself far disappointed of his conclusion taken: for in that cruel persecution used by queen Mary of England, were godly men dispersed into divers nations, of whom it pleased the goodness of God to send some unto us for our comfort and instruction.

The preachers had declared before, how odious idolatry was in God's presence; what commandment he had given for the destruction of the monuments thereof; what idolatry, and what abomination was in the mass. It chanced that the next day, which was the 11th of May [1559], after that the preachers were exiled, after the sermon, which was very vehement against idolatry, a certain priest in contempt would go to the mass; and to declare his malapert presumption, he would open up a glorious tabernacle, which stood upon the high altar: there stood beside certain godly men, and, amongst others, a young boy, who cried with a bold voice, "This is intolerable, that when God by his word hath plainly condemned idolatry, we shall stand and see it used in despite." The priest hereat offended, gave the child a great blow; who, in anger, took up a stone, and casting

---

*An editorial error. The word which Knox wrote was *patents*.

†Mary I daughter of Henry VIII and Catherine of Aragon.

‡Mary Stuart, Queen of Scots.

at the priest, hit the tabernacle, and brake down an image: and immediately the whole multitude threw stones, and put on hands on the said tabernacle, and on all other monuments of idolatry; which they dispatched before the tenth man of the town were advertised, for the most part were gone to dinner. Which noised abroad, the whole multitude assembled, not of the gentlemen, neither of them that were earnest professors, but of the rascal multitude; who finding nothing to do in that church [went] without deliberation to the gray and black friars, and, notwithstanding that they had within them very strong guards kept for their defence, yet were their gates incontinent burst up. The first invasion was upon idolatry, and thereafter the common people began to seek some spoil. And in very deed the Gray-friars was a place so well provided, that unless honest men had seen the same, we would have feared to have reported what provision they had: their sheets, blankets, beds and coverlets were such, that no earl in Scotland had better; their napery was fine; they were but eight persons in the convent, and yet had they eight puncheons of salt beef, (consider the time of the year, the 11th of May) wine, beer and ale, beside store victuals belonging thereto: the like abundance was not in the Black-friars, and yet there was more than became men professing poverty.

The spoil was permitted to the poor: for so had the preachers before threatened all men, that for covetousness sake none should put their hand to such a reformation; that no honest man was enriched thereby the value of a groat: their conscience so moved them, that they suffered those hypocrites* to take away what they could, of that which was in their places; the prior of the Charter-house was permitted to take with him even us† much gold and silver as he was able to carry. So were mens consciences beaten with the word, that they had no respect to their own particular profit, but only to abolish idolatry, the places and monuments thereof; in which they were so busy, and so laborious, that within two days these three great places, monuments of idolatry, viz. the Black and Gray thieves, and Charter house Monks (a building of wondrous cost and greatness) was so destroyed, that the walls only remained of all those great edifices. . . . we [the preachers] . . . returned to our own houses, leaving in St. Johnston John Knox, to instruct the people, because they were young and rude in Christ. . . .

---

*The friars and monks.

†Editorial error. *As.*

20. SANDERS: RISE AND GROWTH OF THE ANGLICAN SCHISM

Nicholas Sanders (*ca*. 1530-1581) labored and suffered as much for his Catholic faith as did Knox for Reformed Protestantism. Indeed, the two men had more in common than either would ever have admitted. The similarity of their world views indicates that, despite its rancor and brutality, the Reformation was a family squabble.

An Oxford graduate and lecturer in canon law, Sanders fled England shortly after Elizabeth I's accession. Ordained a priest at Rome, where he acquired the degree of Doctor of Divinity, Sanders served as an official theologian at the Council of Trent and taught theology at the University of Louvain. During his later years he was active in promoting the military invasion of England in order to crush Elizabeth's Protestant regime. In 1579 he secretly landed in Ireland, as a papal agent instructed with the mission of promoting rebellion among the Catholic Irish. There he died, presumably of hunger and cold in the Irish hills.

During his days of continental exile Sanders penned a number of theological and apologetical tracts. These included a history of the English Reformation that he composed mainly for the edification of English exiles, among whom it circulated in various Latin manuscripts. The first pirnted edition of the work appeared posthumously in 1585, with revisions and additions by the editor.

Tolerance and sobriety were virtues little admired or exercised by Protestants and Catholics during the sixteenth century, and Sanders' scandal-mongering history was no exception. He was all too willing to accept and repeat the most malicious gossip concerning the enemies of Catholicism, including the now discredited story that Anne Boleyn was Henry VIII's daughter. Despite the partisan nature of his history, Sanders wrote a work that showed industrious research, and because it was and remains so controversial, it is a book that continues to stimulate and entertain. The greatest strength of the work is its vivid portraiture, of which there are several examples below. In addition, we have included a short discourse by Sanders on the workings of Divine Providence.

There was some difference in age between Henry and Catherine, and a still greater difference in their lives. She was older than her husband in years, at the utmost five years, but more than a thousand years in character. Catherine used to rise at midnight in order to be present at matins sung by religious. At five o'clock she dressed herself, but as quickly as she could, saying that the only time wasted was the time spent in dressing. She was a member of the third Order of St. Francis, and wore the habit thereof under her royal robes. She fasted every Friday and Saturday, and on bread and water on the eves of our Lady's feasts. She went to confession every Wednesday and Friday, and on Sunday received communion. She said the office of our Lady daily, and was present every morning in church for six hours together during the sacred offices. After dinner, and in the midst of her maids of honour, she read the lives of saints for two hours. That done, she went to church, and generally remained there till it was time for supper, which was with her a very scanty meal. She always prayed on her knees, without a cushion or anything else between them and the pavement. Can any one be astonished that so saintly a woman was to be tried in a greater fire of tribulation, so that the fragrance of her goodness might be the more scattered over the Christian world?

Meanwhile Henry was giving the reins to his evil desires, and living in sin, sometimes with two, sometimes with three of the queen's maids of honour, one of whom, Elizabeth Blount, gave birth to a son, whom Henry made duke of Richmond. The king, indeed, admired the sanctity of his wife, but followed evil counsels himself.

Anne Boleyn was the daughter of Sir Thomas Boleyn's wife; I say of his wife, because she could not have been the daughter of Sir Thomas, for she was born during his absence of two years in France on the king's affairs. Henry VIII. sent him apparently on an honourable mission in order to conceal his own criminal conduct; but when Thomas Boleyn, on his return at the end of two years, saw that a child had been born in his house, he resolved, eager to punish the sin, to prosecute his wife before the delegates of the archbishop of Canterbury, and obtain a separation from her. His wife informs the king, who sends the marquis of Dorset with an order to Thomas Boleyn to refrain from prosecuting his wife, to forgive her, and be reconciled to her.

Sir Thomas Boleyn saw that he must not provoke the king's wrath, nevertheless he did not yield obedience to his orders before he learned from his wife that it was the king who had tempted her to sin, and that the child Anne was the daughter of no other than Henry VIII. His wife then entreated him on her knees to forgive her, promising better behaviour in the future. The marquis of Dorset and other personages, in their own and in the king's name, made the same request, and then Sir Thomas Boleyn became reconciled to his wife, and had Anne brought up as his own child.

But his wife had borne Sir Thomas another daughter before this one, named Mary. Upon her the king had cast his eyes when he used to visit her mother, and now, after the return of Sir Thomas, he had her brought to the court, and ruined her. The royal household consisted of men utterly abandoned—gamblers, adulterers, panders, swindlers, false swearers, blasphemers, extortioners, and even heretics; among these was one distinguished profligate, Sir Francis Bryan, of the blood and race of the Boleyn. This man was once asked by the king to tell him what sort of a sin it was to ruin the mother and then the child. Bryan replied that it was a sin like that of eating a hen first and its chicken afterwards. The king burst forth into loud laughter, and said to Bryan, "Well, you certainly are my vicar of hell." The man had been long ago called the vicar of hell on account of his notorious impiety, henceforth he was called also the king's vicar of hell. The king, who had sinned before with the mother and the elder daughter, turned his thoughts now to the other daughter, Anne.

Anne Boleyn was rather tall of stature, with black hair, and an oval face of a sallow complexion, as if troubled with jaundice. She had a projecting tooth under the upper lip, and on her right hand six fingers. There was a large wen under her chin, and therefore to hide its ugliness she wore a high dress covering her throat. In this she was followed by the ladies of the court, who also wore high dresses, having before been in the habit of leaving their necks and the upper portion of their persons uncovered. She was handsome to look at, with a pretty mouth, amusing in her ways, playing well on the lute, and was a good dancer. She was the model and the mirror of those who were at court, for she was always well dressed, and every day made some change in the fashion of her garments. But as to the disposition of her mind, she was full of pride, ambition, envy, and impurity.

At fifteen she sinned first with her father's butler, and then with his chaplain, and forthwith was sent to France, and placed, at the expense of the king, under the care of a certain nobleman not far from Brie. Soon afterwards she appeared at the French court, where she was called the English mare, because of her shameless behaviour; and then the royal mule, when she became acquainted with the king of France. She embraced the heresy of Luther to make her life and opinions consistent, but nevertheless did not cease to hear mass with the Catholics, for that was wrung from her by the custom of the king and the necessities of her own ambition.

On her return to England she was taken into the royal household, and there easily saw that the king was tired of his wife. She also detected the aims of Wolsey, how much the king was in love with herself, and how quickly he changed in his lawless affections. Not to speak of strangers to her family, she saw how her mother first, and then her sister, had been discarded by the king. What was she, then, to hope for in the end if she did not take care of herself at first? She made up her mind what to do. The more the king sought her, the more she avoided him, sanctimoniously saying that nobody but her husband should find her alone; nevertheless she did not think there was any want of modesty in talking, playing, and even in dancing with the king. In this way she so fed the fires of the king's passion that he became more and more determined to put away Catherine his wife, and to put a woman of such admirable modesty in her place. The news was carried over into France, and there it became a common report that the king of England was going to marry the mule of the king of France.

When God saw the people of England bent on giving up into the hands of its civil rulers the visible government of the Church, wrested from the successor of Peter, to whom our Lord had given it, He brought it most mercifully to pass in the course of His providence that the new supremacy of the Anglican Church should, in the first instance, be given to no other than Henry, the persecutor not only of Catholics, but of Lutherans and Calvinists also, and that it should not be given even upon him but in ways the most dishonourable and utterly hateful. For God did not suffer the king to become the head of the Anglican Church by any other means than by first divorcing Catherine, his most saintly wife, and putting in her place, still living, Anne Boleyn, who was related to him in the first, and more than in the first degree, yea, perhaps his own child. Moreover, after the evil deeds of Henry—and they were so many—when the English maintained that the supremacy belonged of right to the king, God, of His goodness, once more, to check their wickedness by the force of circumstances, did most compassionately provide that the supremacy recently brought in should fall the second time upon a king who was a child, too young to govern himself, to say nothing of the many priests and bishops over whom he was made to rule as supreme even in the things of God.

Then, again, when the English Protestants, thus admonished, would not amend their misdoings, God, unwearied in His goodness, brought it to pass for the third time that the successor of this boy, the supreme head of the Church of England, should be none other than a woman,* who, as they had learned from

*Queen Elizabeth I. Sanders shared with Knox a deep misogynistic streak.

St. Paul, could not speak with authority in the Church, and certainly ought not therefore to be styled the supreme governor thereof. Even that, brought about by the mercy of God, wrought no amendment; and the people, according to their hardness and impenitent heart, heap up for themselves wrath in the day of wrath, and of the revelation of the just judgment of God.

Oh, how marvellous the wisdom and goodness of God! how deplorable the folly and wickedness of men! For as God made His wisdom and goodness more and more manifest by leaving to the English Protestants no way of falling into sin but one that was most foul, then another more foul than that, and in the end another unutterably loathsome, so the Protestants, going further and further in their sin, fill up by degrees the measure of their iniquities. They first go from the successor of Peter to the successor of Nero, from the Pontiff to the king, from the priest to the layman, and what a layman! Then among laymen from a man to a boy, of whose deeds I am going now to speak; but from the boy they go to a woman, of whom also I shall speak further on.

21. SARPI: HISTORY OF THE COUNCIL OF TRENT

One of the currents binding the Renaissance to the Age of Reformation was the movement known as Christian Humanism. For the most part the Christian Humanists advocated reform of the Church without revolution, cleansing without schism. When the break finally came, most Christian Humanists opted to remain within the Catholic Church, working to reform it internally. But whether they remained Catholics or became Protestants, the Christian Humanists were advocates of moderation in an immoderate age. Although distrusted by both Catholic and Protestant extremists, these humanists were not only apostles of reconciliation, they also influenced the course of the Catholic Reformation, a movement distinguished from the militant Counter-Reformation by its goals—the eradication of those abuses within the Church that had helped occasion the Protestant revolt. Fra Paolo Sarpi (1552-1623) was such a reformer and much more.

Born into a minor Venetian mercantile family, Sarpi became a Servite friar at age fifteen and was ordained a priest in 1574. He rose quickly to a position of prominence within his religious order, finally serving as its Vicar General from 1599 to 1604. If ever there was a Renaissance "universal man," that person was Sarpi. His genius ranged over such diverse fields as theology, philosophy, law, classical languages, politics, history, and the natural sciences. He has been credited with original discoveries in both physics and anatomy. Scholars believe he anticipated Harvey's discovery of the circulation of the blood, and Galileo bestowed upon him the title of Europe's best mathematician. Unfortunately none of Sarpi's many scientific works are known to be extant.

As a theologian he was heavily influenced by the anti-papal Nominalism of William of Ockham. When Venice named him its official state theologian he entered the lists against the ultra Counter-Reformation papalism of Paul V. Resistance to papal power had been a leitmotif of Italian urban politics since the twelfth century, and Sarpi, loyal son of Venice, believed his antipapalism to be consistent with his Catholic faith. He and his fellow Venetians, also loyal Catholics, saw no reason why the pope should govern the affairs of Venice. (The papacy did not quite agree and plotted Sarpi's assassination.) For his troubles, Sarpi was excommunicated in 1607 but continued to function as a priest. He appears to have died unreconciled with the papacy but, although he had Protestant associations, to have considered himself a good Catholic to his dying day.

Sarpi's *History of the Council of Trent,* the first full account of the synod, presented the theme that the council, called to heal the wounds of the Reformation, became the final wedge that split Christendom, because of the intransigence of the papacy and the machinations of the Jesuits. A work of monumental scholarship, his conclusions were based upon materials within the Venetian archives and his association with men who had played major roles in the council. Although a partisan study, it was the fruit of honesty and industry, and none of its detractors (largely Jesuits) have ever been able to destroy its credibility.

The papacy banned the work while it was still in manuscript form, but Protestant England published it in 1619 (perhaps without Sarpi's consent), and within ten years it had gone through several editions and five translations.

Excerpted below is Sarpi's treatment of the schism of Henry VIII, and some observations on the commonly accepted practice of executing heretics. Combined they serve to illustrate the temper of his mind.

This year* the pope, instead of regaining Germany, lost the obedience of England by proceeding with passion rather than with the wisdom necessary in such great negotiations. The event was of great importance and greater consequence, and to set it down clearly, it is necessary to begin with the first causes from which it had its origin.

Catherine infanta of Spain, sister to the mother of Charles the Emperor, was married to Henry VIII, King of England, and was before, the wife of Arthur, Prince of Wales, Henry's eldest brother. After Arthur's death, her father gave her in marriage to Henry, who remained successor, by the dispensation of Pope Julius II. This Queen was with child often and always either miscarried or brought forth a creature of short life, except one only daughter; King Henry, either out of displeasure against the Emperor, or because of a desire for a male heir, or for some other cause, conceived a scruple in his mind that the marriage was not good. Taking counsel with his bishops, he separated himself from her company. The bishops advised the Queen to be contented with a divorce, saying that the Pope's dispensation was neither good nor true. The Queen would

*1534.

not give ear to them, but had recourse to the Pope, to whom the King also had applied for a divorce. The Pope, who was still retired in Orvieto, hoped for good conditions in his affairs, if the favors of France and England (which still they performed) were continued, by molesting the Emperor in the Kingdom of Naples. He sent into England the Cardinal Campeggio, delegating the affair unto him and the Cardinal of York. From these and from Rome, the King had hope given him that in the end the sentence should be on his side. Indeed, to facilitate the matter (so that the solemnities of the judgment might not draw it out too long), a brief was framed, in which he was declared free from that marriage by reason of the most ample causes that ever were put into any Pope's Bull, and a cardinal was sent into England with order to present it after a few proofs were given, which he* was sure would easily be made. And this happened in the year 1524. But Clement†, judging it fitter for realizing his designs upon Florence, as has been declared in its proper place, to join himself with the Emperor rather than to continue in the friendship of France and England, in the year 1529 sent Francis Campana to Campeggio with order to burn the brief and to proceed slowly in the case. Campeggio began first to prolong the case and afterwards to renege on the promises made to the King. Whereby being assured that the judge and his adversaries were in collusion, Henry sent to the universities of Italy, France, and Germany for consultation in his case. Among these Doctors of Theology, some were contrary and some were favorable to his cause. The greater part of the Parisians were on his side, and some believed that the King's gifts more persuaded them than reason.

But the Pope, either to gratify the Emperor, or out of fear that the Cardinal of York might create in England something contrary to Papal plans, and also to give Campeggio an excuse to depart from England, reserved the case to himself. The King impatient of delay, either because he knew their cunning, or for some other cause, published the divorce with his wife and married Anne Boleyn in the year 1533. Yet still the case was pending before the Pope, in which he was resolved to proceed slowly in order to satisfy the Emperor and not offend the King. Therefore some by-points were handled rather than the merits of the case. And the argument developed around the Article of Attentas, in which the Pope gave sentence against the King, declaring that it was not lawful for him, by his own

*Pope Julius II.

†Pope Clement VII.

authority, without ecclesiastical judgment, to separate himself from his wife. As a result, the King in the beginning of this year 1534, denied the Pope obedience, commanding all his subjects not to carry any money to Rome nor to pay the ordinary Peter's pence.

. . . For the Pope should be Bishop of Rome and himself (Henry) the sole Lord of his Kingdom, and he would follow the ancient fashion of the Eastern Church, not abandoning the life of a good Christian, nor allowing the Lutheran heresy or any other to be brought into his Kingdom. And so he did. He published an edict, wherein he declared himself head of the Church of England and punished capitally all who said that the Pope of Rome had any authority there. He chased out the collector of the Peterpence and caused the Parliament to approve all these things. Here it was determined that all the bishoprics of England should be conferred by the Archbishop of Canterbury, without sending to Rome, and that the clergy should pay to the King one hundred and fifty thousand pounds sterling yearly, for the defense of the Kingdom against all enemies.

The action of the King was variously evaluated. Some thought him wise for freeing himself from the subjection of Rome without any innovation in Religion, without putting his subjects in danger of sedition, and without referring himself to a Council, a thing which they saw hard to be effected and dangerous also for him, it being impossible that a Council, composed of ecclesiastical persons, should not maintain the Pope's power, which is the main pillar of their Order. Through the Papacy, the clergy is above all Kings and the Emperor, but without it is subject to them, there being no ecclesiastical person who has superiority but the Pope. But the Court of Rome maintained that it could not be said that there was no change in Religion since the first and principal Article was changed, which is the supremacy of the Pope, and seditions would arise because of this alone, as well as for all the other reasons. Events showed this to be true. For the King was inclined to proceed severely against some of his subjects, whom he loved and esteemed. It cannot be expressed what grief was felt in Rome and by all the clergy for the alienation of such a great Kingdom from the Pope's subjection. It illustrated the imbecillity of human affairs, wherein, for the most part, great damages proceed from those things from which the greatest benefits were formerly received. For by matrimonial dispensations and by sentences of divorce (those granted and those denied), the Papacy gained much in former times, sheltering the Princes with the name of the Vicar of Christ. . . . But the misfortune which then arose might be ascribed to the hastiness of Clement, who, in this case, knew not how to manage his authority. . . .

But because mention is made of the Edict of the King of England in matter of Religion, it will not be amiss to recount here how Henry VIII in the time of the Diet of Frankfort, either because he thought to do God Service by not permitting innovation of Religion within his Kingdom, or to show constancy in what he had written against Luther, or to give the Pope the lie, who had accused him in his Bull that he had published heretical doctrine in his Kingdom, made a public edict. In it he commanded that the real presence of the true and natural Body and Blood of our Lord Jesus Christ, under the appearances of Bread and Wine, there remaining no substance of those Elements, was to be believed throughout all England, and also that Christ was wholly contained under either one or the other; that the communion of the cup was not necessary; that it was not lawful for priests to marry; that religious men, after their profession and vows of chastity, were bound always to keep them and to live in monasteries; that secret and auricular confession was not only profitable but also necessary; that the celebration of Mass even private, was a holy thing, which he commanded should be observed in his Kingdom. He prohibited all to do or teach any thing contrary to these articles upon pain of being punished as Heretics. It is to be marvelled at how the Pope,* who a little before thundered against the King, was constrained to praise his actions and to propose him to the Emperor as an example to be imitated. So a man's proper interest makes him commend and blame the same person.

The Parliament continued until the midst of January 1555:* all the ancient edicts of the Kings to punish Heretics and concerning the jurisdiction of Bishops were renewed; the primacy and all prerogatives of the Pope restored; all contrary decrees made within the past twenty years, by Henry as well as by Edward, abolished; the penal Laws against Heretics revived: and many were burned, especially bishops who would persevere in the now abolished Reformation. It is certain that one hundred and seventy-six persons of quality were burned that year for Religion, in additon to many commoners. This little pleased those people who also were displeased that Martin Bucer and Paulus Fagius already dead four years, were cited and condemned, as if they had been living, and their bodies dug up and burned; this action, commended by some as revenge for what Henry VIII had done against St. Thomas, was by others compared to that which Popes Stephan VI and Sergius III did against the corpse of Pope Formosus.†

*Paul III.

*The Parliament of the Catholic Queen, Mary I.

†In the ninth century.

Many also were at the same time burned in France for religion, not without the indignation of honest men, who knew that the diligence used against those poor people was not for piety or religion but to satiate the covetousness of Diana Valentina, the King's mistress, to whom he had given all goods confiscated for reason of heresy in the Kingdom. It was wondered at also that those of the new Reformation should meddle with blood for the sake of Religion. For Michael Servetus of Tarragona, a physician turned theologian, renewing the old opinion of Paulus Samosatenus and Marcellus Ancirarus that the Word of God was not consubstantial with the Father (and therefore that Christ was a pure man) was put to death for it in Geneva, by counsel of the ministers of Zurich, Berne, and Schiaffusa. And John Calvin, who was blamed for it by many, wrote a book, arguing that the magistrate may punish heretics with loss of life. This doctrine being variously understood (as it is understood both strictly and loosely and also the name of Heretic is understood differently), may sometime do hurt to him, whom another time it has helped.

SOURCE NOTES

1. John Knox, *The History of the Reformation of the Church of Scotland* (Paisley, Scotland: John Neilson, 1791), I, pp. 127-128, 262-264, and 327-329.
2. Nicholas Sander *(sic), Rise and Growth of the Anglican Schism,* trans. David Lewis (London: Burns and Oates, 1877), pp. 7-8, 23-26, 167-168.
3. Pietro Soave Polano (Paulo Sarpi), *The History of the Council of Trent,* trans. Nathanael Brent (London: J. Macock, 1676), pp. 64, 63, 68, *(sic),* 84, 362-363. [Spelling and syntax modernized.]

9.
THE
SEVENTEENTH
CENTURY

For few periods is it as difficult to discover a common denominator, an intellectual tendency or world view expressive of the "Spirit of the Age," as it is for the seventeenth century. Contradiction and tension are of the very essence of the period.

The century can be viewed as the Age of the Scientific Revolution and the beginning of the Age of Reason: But John Kepler, who completed the revolution of men's view of the cosmos by reconciling the Copernican Hypothesis with observed data, was also an adept of astrology and alchemy, and sought to discover the principle of the music of the spheres through his astronomical and mathematical researches. Isaac Newton, that epitome of scientific genius, the great synthesizer of the new view of the physical universe, spent much of his life in pursuing the hidden meanings of biblical prophecy. He studied alchemy, numerology, and other aspects of the occult. Never were such interests and concerns more widespread and vital than in that age of anxiety, haunted by witches and omens.

The century has also been labeled as the Age of Absolutism; indeed it saw the development of centralized, secular, bureaucratic state power based on principles of rationality and functional efficiency. But contrary tendencies abounded: In Britain, individual and corporate rights and privileges were vindicated against the power of the Throne, and egalitarian, democratic doctrines and groups played an important role; in Poland, a feudal aristocracy prevailed over monarchy; the Holy Roman Empire became a shadow; and over most of the European continent social developments were characterized by the strengthening of special privilege and the heightening of barriers between the classes of society.

And so it is in all spheres: The secular, skeptical challenge to the world view of traditional faith, exemplified in these pages by Bayle, on the one side, on the other the intense religiosity of the Counter-Reformation, of French Jansenism, Lutheran orthodoxy, and British non-conformity; radical rationalism side by side with mysticism; *raison d'etat* à la Richelieu coexisting with uncompromising doctrines of sacred Divine Right Monarchy; religious toleration, emerging as the solution to the existence under one political authority of groups of different religious persuasions, challenged by spectacular acts of persecution: In every field of human life and endeavor we find this age characterized by paradox, unresolved conflict, and stresses. On the international level, these find expression in incessant warfare, in which the concept of a European balance of power painfully emerged from clashing hegemonial ambitions, warfare that had catastrophic effects on the material and cultural standard of civilization of much of the European continent.

It is for these reasons that contemporary historians speak of the Crisis of the Seventeenth Century. Divergent and opposed forces and ideas were in delicate balance, and their stresses threatened to tear apart the fabric of Western Civilization. "Modernity," that is, the scientific, materialist, secular world outlook, man's increasing ability to understand and thus to use the forces of nature, and to organize his social and political life for rational, purposive ends, emerged out of this crisis.

With this many-faceted, ambiguous character of the age, there is not a single historian, or school of history, that can be said to exemplify its historical world view. Nor is it possible, in the scope of this volume, to illustrate all the elements of this complexity. The following selections illustrate merely a few of the major themes: the increasing power of the monarchical state, the tension between the Christian world view, based on revelation, and the new knowledge, based on human reason and experience, and the secularist skepticism that developed out of this tension.

22. BACON: THE HISTORIE OF
THE REIGNE OF KING HENRY VII

Sir Francis Bacon (1561-1626) is primarily remembered as a prophet of the new scientific method. In his *Novum Organum* he attacked the scholastic method of deducing truth from first principles, and called for a new approach to scientific investigation based on inductive reasoning from observed phenomena. However, while Bacon's broad range of interests extended to science, and his prescription for empirical investigation was to be vastly influential, he was not in any sense a scientist: Trained as a lawyer, he rose to political power and great wealth and influence at the courts of Elizabeth I and James I, not only through his ability, but also by inveterate obsequiousness and opportunism, finally becoming Lord Chancellor in 1618. Corrupt in his judicial dealings, he was impeached and removed from office in 1621.

His *Historie of the Reigne of Henry VII*, first published in 1622, is political history in more than one sense: Not only does it deal primarily with the political events of that reign, but one of Bacon's purposes in writing it was to regain the monarch's favor, by flattering his ancestor and extolling the greatness of his family. The work illustrates the spirit and nature of the New State, in this case, Tudor Monarchy. The King *is* the state, his actions are the affairs of state, and the stuff of history, he is the link that ties men together into a common body. Bacon is traditional enough to offer a supernatural explanation for the events he describes: It was divine vengeance that brought Henry VII to the throne, and that provided ultimate legitimacy to his claim to rule.

After that Richard the third of that name, king in fact only, but tyrant both in title and regiment, and so commonly termed and reputed in all times since, was by divine revenge, favoring the design of an exiled man, overthrown and slain at Bosworth Field: There succeeded in the Kingdom the Earl of Richmond, thenceforth styled Henry the Seventh. The King immediately after the victory, as one that had been bred under a devout mother, and was in his nature, a great observer of religious forms, caused the *Te Deum Laudamus* to be solemnly sung in the presence of the whole army upon the place, and was himself with general applause, and great cries of joy, in a kind of military election, or recognition,

saluted King. Meanwhile the body of Richard after many indignities and re-
proaches (the obsequies of the common people towards tyrants) was obscurely
buried. . . . No man thinking any ignominy or contumely unworthy of him, that
had been the executioner of King Henry the Sixth (that innocent prince) with his
own hands; the contriver of the death of the Duke of Clarence, his brother; the
murderer of his two nephews (one of them his lawful king in the present, and the
other in the future, failing of him) and vehemently suspected to have been the
poisoner of his wife, thereby to make vacant his bed, for a marriage within the
degrees forbidden. And although he were a prince in military virtue approved,
jealous of the honor of the English nation, and likewise a good lawmaker, for the
ease and solace of the common people: yet his cruelties and parricides in the
opinion of all men, weighed down his virtues and merits; and in the opinion of
wise men, even those virtues themselves were conceived to be rather feigned,
and affected things to serve his ambition, than true qualities ingenerate in his
judgment or nature. . . .

But King Henry in the very entrance of his reign . . . met with a point of
great difficulty, and knotty to solve, able to trouble and confound the wisest king
in the newness of his estate; and so much the more, because it could not endure a
deliberation, but must be at once . . . determined. There were fallen to his lot,
and concurrent in his person, three several titles to the imperial crown. The first,
the title of the Lady Elizabeth, with whom, by precedent pact with the party that
brought him in, he was to marry. The second, the ancient and long disputed title
(both by plea, and arms) of the House of Lancaster, to which he was inheritor in
his own person. The third, the title of the sword or conquest, for that he came in
by victory of battle, and that the king in possesion was slain in the field. The first
of these was fairest, and most like to give contentment to the people, who by two
and twenty years reign of King Edward the Fourth, had been fully made capable
of the clearness of the title of the White Rose or House of York; and by the mild
and plausible reign of the same king toward his latter time, were become
affectionate to that line. But then it lay plain before his eyes, that if he relied
upon that title, he could be but a king at courtesy, and have rather a matrimonial
than a regal power: the right remaining in his queen, upon whose decease . . . he
was to give place, and be removed. And though he should obtain by Parliament
to be continued, yet he knew there was a very great difference between a king
that holds his crown by a civil act of Estates, and one that holds it originally by
the Law of Nature, and descent of blood. Neither wanted there even at that time
secret rumors and whisperings (which afterwards gathered strength and turned to

great troubles) that the two young sons of King Edward the Fourth, or one of them (which were said to be destroyed in the Tower) were not indeed murdered, but conveyed secretly away, and were yet living: which if it had been true, had prevented the title of the Lady Elizabeth. On the other side, if he stood upon his own title of the House of Lancaster, inherent in his person; he knew it was a title condemned by Parliament, and generally prejudged in the common opinion of the Realm, and that it tended directly to the disinherison of the line of York, held then the indubiate heirs of the crown. So that if he should have no issue by the Lady Elizabeth, which should be descendants of the double line, . . . the ancient flames of discord and intestine wars upon the competition of both houses, would again return and revive.

As for the conquest notwithstanding, Sir William Stanley, after some acclamations of the soldiers in the field, had put a crown of ornament (which Richard wore in the battle, and was found amongst the spoils) upon King Henry's head, as if there were his chief title; yet he remembered well upon what conditions and agreements he was brought in, and that to claim as conqueror, was to put as well his own party, as the rest, into terror and fear; as that which gave him power of annulling of laws, and disposing of men's fortunes and estates, and the like points of absolute power, being in themselves too harsh and odious, as that William himself, commonly called the Conqueror, howsoever he used and exercised the power of a conqueror, to reward his Normans, yet he forebore to use that claim in the beginning, but mixed it with a titulary pretense grounded upon the will and designation of Edward the Confessor. But the King out of the greatness of his own mind, presently cast the die, and the inconveniences appearing unto him on all parts; and knowing there could not be any interregnum or suspension of title; and preferring his affection to his own line and blood, and liking that title best which made him independent; and being in his nature and constitution of mind not very apprehensive or forecasting of future events afar off, but an entertainer of fortune by the day; resolved to rest upon the title of Lancaster as the main, and to use the other two, that of marriage, and that of battle, but as supporters, the one to appease secret discontents, and the other to bear down upon open murmur and dispute: not forgetting that the same title of Lancaster had formerly maintained a possession of three descents in the crown, and might have proved a perpetuity, had it not ended in the weakness and inability of the last prince. Whereupon the King presently that very day . . . assumed the style of King in his own name, without mention of the Lady Elizabeth at all, or any relation thereunto. . . . The King full of these thoughts, before his departure from Leicester, dispatched Sir Robert Willoughby to the castle of Sheriffe-Hutton in Yorkshire, where were kept in safe custody by King Richard's commandment, both the Lady Elizabeth daughter of King Edward, and Edward Plantagenet, son and heir to George Duke of Clarence. This Edward was by the King's warrant delivered from the Constable of the Castle to the hand of Sir Robert Willoughby; and by him with all safety and diligence conveyed to the Tower of London, where he was shut up close prisoner. Which act of the King's (being an act merely of policy and power) proceeded . . . upon a settled disposition to depress all eminent persons of the line of York. . . .

For the Lady Elizabeth she received also a direction to repair with all convenient speed to London, and there to remain with the Queen Dowager her mother; which accordingly she soon after did. . . . In the mean season the King set forward by easy journeys to the City of London, receiving the acclamations and applause of the people as he went, which indeed were true and unfeigned. . . . For they thought generally that he was a prince as ordained and sent down from Heaven, to unite and put to an end the long dissensions of the two Houses. . . .

He on the other side with great wisdom (not ignorant of the affections and fears of the people) to disperse the conceit and terror of a conquest, had given order that there should be nothing in his journey like unto a warlike march, or manner: but rather like unto the progress of a king in full peace and assurance.

He entered the City upon a Saturday, as he had also obtained the victory upon a Saturday, which day of the week first upon an observation, and after upon memory and fancy, he accounted and chose as a day prosperous unto him.

The Mayor and Companies of the City received him at Shoreditch: whence, with great and honorable attendance and troops of noblemen, and persons of quality he entered the City. . . .

He went first into Saint Paul's Church, where not meaning that the people should forget too soon that he came in by battle, he made offertory of his standards, and had orisons and *Te Deum* again sung, and went to his lodging prepared in the Bishop of London's palace, where he stayed for a time.

23. NEWTON: A SHORT CHRONICLE FROM THE FIRST MEMORY OF THINGS IN EUROPE TO THE CONQUEST OF PERSIA BY ALEXANDER THE GREAT

Isaac Newton (1642-1727), like Bacon, is likely to be far more familiar to students as a towering figure in the history of science than as a historian. History, however, was one of the many concerns of this universal genius. For much of his life he worked on a project designed to systematize and reconcile the chronology of "sacred" and "secular" history of antiquity. This concern points to the tensions and ambiguities of the world view of men in that age. Newton, the father of modern, materialist science, was still seeking to reintegrate the world of faith and the world of reason, and thus to restore the unity of the medieval world picture. God was still the ultimate moving power of human history to Newton, and man's reason and knowledge must be reconciled with divine revelation.

Newton's age possessed only fragmentary knowledge of ancient history. The development of archeological research, which vastly expanded our knowledge of the civilizations of the ancient Near East and Mediterranean, still lay in the future. Thus, Newton's *Chronology of Ancient Kingdoms Amended,* of which the *Short Chronicle* is an abstract, is a curious mixture of fact and fancy, with such figures from Greek mythology as the Argonauts, Hercules, and even the centaur Chiron presented as historical personages. Newton's purpose was to demonstrate that events of early Greek and Near Eastern history, whose antiquity seemed to throw doubt on the biblical account of the origin and development of the human race, and on the primacy and centrality of the history of the people of Israel, occurred much more recently than was generally thought, and thus could be reconciled with the Bible. In the process, Newton shaved some 400 years off the accepted chronology of Greek history. To prove his assertions, Newton used an extraordinary combination of scientific method and lack of critical judgment. By painstaking and exact astronomical calculations, he sought to establish certain dates for events in ancient history from the equinoctial position of the sun in the various zodiacal constellations, as these positions had changed over the ages. This would indeed be a feasible method of fixing historical dates, *if* we had precise data from ancient observers. Newton used a mythical account of Chiron's "invention" of the stellar constellations, and highly ambiguous astronomical statements by some ancient writers, which he interpreted to fit his arguments, as the basis of his calculations. Still, his was the first attempt to enlist the tools of physical science in aid of historical research. He may thus be considered a forerunner of contemporary historians who have used carbon isotope dating, astronomical calculations of the incidence of eclipses, and a host of other methods derived from the physical sciences, for similar purposes, particularly for ascertaining dates of events in the history of non-literate cultures.

The selection exemplifies an important trend in the historiography of the age. The intellectual endeavor of Renaissance humanism had been based on the striving to penetrate to the original sources of classical grace and wisdom, so as to recapture the spirit of what was viewed as a golden age of mankind. Some seventeenth-century historians were motivated by a similar desire to purify history from the accretions of myth and error and to rewrite it on the basis of pure, original sources, critically examined. Given the preoccupations of the age, it is not surprising that the primary examples of this effort are found in the areas of church and religious history (e.g. the monumental *Acta Sanctorum* of the Bollandist community and the works of Jean Mabillon and Richard Simon). The full development of this approach in secular history did not occur until the early nineteenth century.

Although Newton's attempt to disentangle historical truth from "poetical fictions" and the mistakes of past historians was fatally flawed by his preconceptions, and his theories were based on wholly insufficient sources, it foreshadows this development.

The Greek antiquities are full of poetical fictions, because the Greeks wrote nothing in prose before the conquest of Asia by Cyrus the Persian. Then Pherecydes Scyrius and Cadmus Milesius introduced the writing in prose. Pherecydes Atheniensis, about the end of the reign of Darius Hystaspis, wrote of antiquities, and digested his work by genealogies, and was reckoned one of the best genealogers. Epimenides, the historian, proceeded also by genealogies; and Hellanicus, who was twelve years older than Herodotus, digested his history by the ages or successions of the priestesses of Juno Argiva. Others digested theirs by the kings of the Lacedemonians, or archons of Athens. Hippias the Elean, about thirty years before the fall of the Persian empire, published a breviary, or list, of the olympic victors: and about ten years before the fall thereof Ephorus, the disciple of Socrates, formed a chronological history of Greece, beginning with the return of the Heraclidae into Peloponnesus, and ending with siege of

Perinthus, in the twelfth year of Philip the father of Alexander the Great. But he digested things by generations, and the reckoning by olympiads was not yet in use; nor doth it appear that the reigns of kings were yet set down by numbers of years. The Arundelian marbles were composed sixty years after the death of Alexander the Great (an. 4. olymp. 128.) and yet mention not the olympiads. But in the next olympiad Timaeus Siculus published an history in several books down to his own times, according to the olympiads, comparing the ephori, the kings of Sparta, the archons of Athens, and the priestesses of Argos with the olympic victors; so as to make the olympiads, and the genealogies and successions of kings, archons, and priestesses, and poetical histories, suit with one another, according to the best of his judgment. And where he left off, Polybius began and carried on the history.

So then, a little after the death of Alexander the Great, they began to set down the generations, reigns, and successions, in numbers of years; and by putting reigns and successions equipollent to generations, and three generations to an hundred or an hundred and twenty years (as appears by their chronology) they have made the antiquities of Greece three or four hundred years older than the truth: and this was the original of the technical chronology of the Greeks. Eratosthenes wrote about an hundred years after the death of Alexander the Great. He was followed by Apollodorus; and these two have been followed ever since by chronologers.

But how uncertain their chronology is, and how doubtful it was reputed by the Greeks of those times, may be understood by these passages of Plutarch. "Some reckon," saith he, "Lycurgus contemporary to Iphitus, and to have been his companion in ordering the olympic festivals: amongst whom was Aristotle the philosopher, arguing from the olympic disc which had the name of Lycurgus upon it. Others supputing the times by the succession of the kings of the Lacedemonians, as Eratosthenes and Apollodorus, affirm that he was not a few years older than the first olympiad. First, Aristotle and some others made him as old as the first olympiad; then Eratosthenes, Apollodorus, and some others, made him above an hundred years older." And in another place Plutarch tells us: "The congress of Solon, with Croesus, some think they can confute by chronology. But an history so illustrious, and verified by so many witnesses, and (which is more) so agreeable to the manners of Solon, and so worthy of the greatness of his mind and of his wisdom, I cannot persuade myself to reject because of some chronological canons, as they call them; which hundreds of authors correcting, have not yet been able to constitute any certainty among themselves about repugnances." It seems the chronologers had made the legislature of Solon too ancient to consist with that congress.

scarce be remembered above eighty or an hundred years after their deaths: and

For reconciling such repugnances, chronologers have sometimes doubled the persons of men. So when the poets had changed Io, the daugher of Inachus, into the Egyptian Isis, chronologers made her husband Osiris, or Bacchus, and his mistress Ariadne as old as Io; and so feigned there were two Ariadne's, one the mistress of Bacchus, the other the mistress of Theseus, and two Minos's their fathers, and a younger Io the daughter of Jasus; writing Jasus corruptly for Inachus: and so they have made two Pandion's and two Erechtheus's, giving the name of Erechthonius to the first. Homer calls the first Erechtheus. And by such corruptions they have exceedingly perplexed ancient history.

And as for the chronology of the Latins, that is still more uncertain. Plutarch represents great uncertainties in the originals of Rome: and so doth Servius. The old records of the Latines were burnt by the Gauls sixty-four years before the death of Alexander the Great; and Quintus Fabius Pictor, the oldest historian of the Latines, lived an hundred years later then that king.

In sacred history, the Assyrian empire began with Pul and Tiglathpilesar, and lasted about 170 years. And accordingly Herodotus hath made Semiramis only five generations, or about 166 years, older than Nitocris, the mother of the last king of Babylon. But Ctesias has made Semiramis 1500 years older than Nitocris; and feigned a long series of kings of Assyria, whose names are not Assyrian, nor have any affinity with Assyrian names in Scripture.

The priests of Egypt told Herodotus, that Menes built Memphis, and the sumptuous temple of Vulcan in that city: and that Rhampsinitus, Moeris, Asychis, Psammiticus, added magnificent porticos to that temple. And it is not likely that Memphis could be famous before Homer's days, who doth not mention it, or that a temple could be above two or three hundred years in building: and yet the priests of Egypt had so magnified their antiquities before the days of Herodotus, as to tell him, that from Menes to Moeris there were 330 kings, whose reigns took up as many ages, that is, eleven thousand years; and had filled up the interval with feigned kings who had done nothing. And before the days of Diodorus Siculus they had raised their antiquities so much higher, as to place six, eight, or ten, new reigns of kings between those kings whom they had represented to Herodotus to succeed one another immediately.

In the kingdom of Sicyon, chronologers have split Apis, Epaphus, or Epópeus, into two kings, whom they call Apis and Epopeus; and between them have inserted eleven or twelve feigned names of kings who did nothing; and thereby they have made its founder Aegialeus three hundred years older than his brother Phoroneus: and some have made the kings of Germany as old as the Flood. And yet before the use of letters, the names and actions of men could therefore I admit no chronology of things done in Europe above eighty years before Cadmus brought letters into Greece: none of things done in Germany before the rise of the Roman empire.

Now since Eratosthenes and Apollodorus computed the times by the reigns of the kings of Sparta, and (as appears by their chronology still followed) have made the seventeen reigns of those kings between the return of the Heraclidae into Peloponnesus and the battle of Thermopylae take up 622 years, which is after the rate of 36½ years to a reign; and yet a race of seventeen kings of that length is no where to be met with in all true history; and kings, at a moderate reckoning, reign but 18 or 20 years apiece one with another: I have stated the time of the return of the Heraclidae by the last way of reckoning; placing it 345 years before the battle of Thermopylae. And making the Trojan war eighty years older, according to Thucydides; and the Argonautic expedition a generation older; and the wars of Sesostris in Thrace, and death of Ino the daughter of Cadmus, a generation older: I have drawn up the following chronological table, so as to make chronology suit with the course of nature, with astronomy, with sacred history, and with itself, without the many repugnances complained of by Plutarch. I do not pretend to be exact to a year. There may be errors of five or ten years, and sometimes twenty, and not much above.

24. BAYLE: HISTORICAL AND CRITICAL DICTIONARY

Pierre Bayle (1647-1706) was born in southern France, the son of a Protestant pastor. Educated by Jesuits at Toulouse, he became a Catholic in order to qualify for public appointments; his essential attitude to religion, however, became one of indifference. After studying in Geneva, he taught philosophy in Sedan and, from 1681, in Rotterdam in the Dutch Republic. In 1684, Bayle began publishing *Nouvelles de la Republique des Lettres,* one of the earliest journals of literary criticism appealing to the general educated public.

His *Dictionnaire Historique et Critique,* first published in Rotterdam in 1696, represents another important aspect of 17th century intellectual ferment: Essentially, it is one sustained onslaught against the world view of the Christian Middle Ages and its implicit belief in the immediate intervention of supernatural forces in human events. His debunking style is well illustrated in his article on the siege of Constance, an event close to his time. History is reduced to purely material and human factors. The "state of the military art", the "situation of the country," the strength of the contending forces, etc., determine the outcome of military conflict, not divine intervention, or the justice or injustice of a cause. Bayle's scepticism left open the question of any purpose in history (and in historical study). It was left to the philosophy of the Enlightenment and the historiography of the 18th century to furnish a new element of purpose and meaning: Progress and the unfolding of Reason.

Constance, a City of Germany, situated between two Lakes formed by the Rhine, has very long preserved the Form of a Republic; and the better to maintain its Liberty, which the Princes of the House of Austria would fain have taken from it, it entered into a Confederacy with the Cities of Zurich, Lindau, and Uberlingen. It abolished Popery in the Year 1523; but, being put under the Ban of the Empire in 1548, it was so pressed by the Emperor Charles V, that it was forced to submit to him; and then the greatest Part of the Protestants, and particularly Ambrose Blaurer, their chief Minister, retired to other Places. From that time

"Constance," in *Selections from Bayle's Dictionary,* edited by E. A. Beller and M. du P. Lee, Jr. (copyright © 1952 by Princeton University Press), pp. 93-96. Omission of notes. Reprinted by permission of Princeton University Press.

Constance has belonged to the House of Austria; and Moréri is very much
mistaken, who says, in two Places, that it was an Imperial Town. It joined with
the League of Smalcald in 1531; and no doubt this was one Motive to Charles V
to subdue it after he had vanquished the League. The Swedes, under the Command of Marshal Horn, besieged Constance in 1633, but could not take it. The
Besieged wrote a Journal, in which they have inserted abundance of Miracles, or
extraordinary Observations of the Divine Protection, which appeared in their
Favour during the Siege.

[The principal ones were, "I. The Advantages obtained in the weakest parts
of the City, above their Hopes. II. The Courage and incredible Resolution of
their Citizens and Soldiers, besides the good Understanding kept up between
them. III. The frequent and seasonable Convoys thrown at different times into
the Town, and the wonderful Concurrence of favourable Winds to forward them,
although the Air of the Climate is commonly otherwise, and their Lake subject to
frequent Storms in those Months. IV. The little damage done by the Grenados,
and red hot Bullets, notwithstanding the prodigious Number thrown into the
Town, which were sufficient to reduce the City to Ashes, and its Inhabitants to
Beggary. V. The extraordinary Height of the Rhine, which was wont to fall as
soon as the Heat of the Summer was over, but now continued to swell, and
furnished one of the City Mills so abundantly with Water, that they had enough
to supply the Necessities of the besieged, throughout the whole Siege: which was
confirmed by the Report of the Millers, that this Flood of Water ran off as soon as
the Enemy were dislodged, and the Foreign Troops dismissed. VI. The most
Contemplative added, that the fourth Day of the Siege they saw the Blessed Virgin, in open Day, soaring aloft over the Church of the Augustines, with infinite
Splendor. The Swedish Sentinels are also produced in the same Journal, as having seen the like Apparitions, and the Appearance of a Face more than Angelical,
sliding along the Walls, near the Loop Holes, from the Tower of Rewenegg to
the Gate of Creutzlingen."]

A Protestant has criticised a little upon this.

[Frederic Spanheim, who was Minister at Geneva when he wrote the *Swiss
Mercury,* and furnished me with the preceding Remark, adds: "The Swedes
found nothing like this, neither in their Inventory, nor by the Report of their
Men; and they observe, that the Author of the Journal was often forgetful, not
remembering, in the Conclusion of his Narrative, what he had confessed at the
beginning of it, neither the Terror of their Men, nor the Ruins of the City, nor the
Numbers in the Hospitals, nor the Registers of the Dead, which are sufficient to
shew the Effects of the Grenados. They reckon also, as the most dangerous Ap-

paritions, which they saw during the Siege, the Entrance of so many Troops into the Town, by favour of the Lake, the want of Boats, and the Breadth of the Lake, preventing their People from disputing the Passage at such a Distance. Indeed the besieged themselves charge their Registers with Five thousand five hundred Men that entered the Town, during the Siege, besides Count de Wolffegg's Regiment, which was in Garrison there, before the Arrival of the Swedes. The City of Uberlingen furnished them with Two hundred Men; Lindau Four hundred; Bregenz Two hundred; Colonel de Mersy One thousand Two hundred; the Regiment of Embs Five hundred; the Regiment of Altringen Five hundred; Colonel Comargo One thousand; Sergeant Major de Reinach One thousand, and his Lieutenant Five hundred. The Swedes imagine that such powerful succours, so often repeated, together with all necessary Provisions, were not only sufficient to keep their Ground behind good Curtains, against Five or Six thousand Men, who had the Face to besiege them, in the midst of so many Difficulties, and in a Foreign Country; but also to have drove them out of the Field, if these Auxiliary Troops had been as tender of their Honour, as they were of their Persons.''

[You see then that this Minister rejects as false one part of the Miracles, which the Inhabitants of this besieged City gloried in. The other part is of such a Nature, that there is no Country, where such like things may not be observed, where Winds, Rains, the Rise of Rivers, etc. have not favoured or destroyed Military Enterprizes. Now as there is no probability, that God should supersede the general Laws of Nature, but in Cases where the Preservation of his Children requires it, we ought not to take for a Miracle, what happens equally among Believers and Unbelievers. Yet in all Religions People are strangely inclined to think themselves favoured by miraculous Benefits, and perhaps if Frederic Spanheim had writ a History of a Siege, happily sustained by a Protestant Town, he would have made Observations not unlike those which he now confutes. There are some Ministers, who see a Miracle in all Events, which concern their Party. Mr. Jurieu, for example, finds one every where, and lately in what happened to the Inhabitants of the Cevennes. But People, who are acquainted with the Military Art, and know the Situation of the Country, the Disposition of the neighbouring Cities, and all the Particulars of the Insurrection of the Cevennois, discover nothing supernatural in the Continuance and Circumstances of it. I will not enter into the Question, whether a Man, who is persuaded, that a certain Concurrence of second Causes has ruined the Designs of the Enemy, ought to make others believe there was a Miracle in it, and whether he can justify himself, by pretending, that thereby he excites more confidence in the Mind, and greater thankfulness for the Divine Protection; but I dare affirm, that if he hopes by this

means to engage Princes to enter into War, he will find himself greatly
deceived. . . . The Princes will not stir in it, if other political Reasons, which they
know better than he, and do not want his Advice in, do not engage them to assist
those People. They will see clearly into an Affair. Now Miracles to come are an
Object of Faith, and consequently an obscure Object.]

SOURCE NOTES

1. From Francis Bacon, *The Historie of the Reigne of King Henry the
   Seventh* (London: 1629), pp. 1-8. [Spelling modernized.]
2. From Isaac Newton, "A Short Chronicle from the First Memory of
   Things in Europe to the Conquest of Persia by Alexander the Great,"
   Isaaci Newtoni Opera Quae Extant Omnia (London: 1629), vol. V,
   pp. 267-271.
3. From *Selections from Bayle's Dictionary,* ed. by E. A. Beller and M.
   du P. Lee, Jr. (New York: Greenwood Press, 1969). Copyright ©
   1952 by Princeton University Press. Pp. 93-96 reprinted by
   permission of Princeton University Press.

10.

THE
ENLIGHTENMENT

The ideology of the eighteenth century, the Age of the Enlightenment, developed from several of the tendencies referred to in the previous chapter. Questioning of the traditional world view based on authority and revelation led to its rejection. The emphasis on knowledge derived from sense experience, capable of being used for the betterment of the human condition, became absolute. Human nature was seen as static and permanent, as were all the Laws of Nature. Mankind's distinguishing characteristic was its possession of Reason. Reason, operating on evidence derived from empirical observation of natural phenomena, made men increasingly cognizant of the universal laws governing the universe. Once these were fully understood, they could be used, as sailors use their knowledge of the wind, over which they have no control but whose behavior they can predict, to achieve their destination. Nothing must be allowed to stand in the way of human reason: Traditions and customs, institutions and beliefs which inhibited and restrained its development and exercise must give way before it. This was the basic condition for Progress, through which the human condition, if not human nature, would become increasingly perfected.

Following the argument of Carl Becker's *Heavenly City of the Eighteenth-Century Philosophers,* modern historians have pointed out that this world view bore basic similarities to that of Christianity: Reason takes the place of Grace, its unfettering from the shackles of tradition and superstition represents the redemption of mankind, and a secular paradise of peace and plenty, ruled by philosopher kings, is substituted for the spiritual kingdom of God as the end of history.

By and large, this ideology, like that of medieval Christianity, did not provide fertile ground for great historiography: History is not needed

153

in it to explain the condition of man and his world. That is governed by immutable laws, discernible by Reason. The works of most eighteenth-century historians were written to *demonstrate* the existence and workings of these laws: The evil effects of departures from the path of reason, which led to decline and misery, and the rational behavior of great men, which produced progress, happiness, and prosperity.

Seeing themselves at the apex of the still rising crest of Progress, these eighteenth-century writers considered that little could be learned from the detailed investigation of the remote past, which to them reeked of barbarism and superstition. At most, the past might furnish warning examples of the result of departures from the course of Reason: Gibbon's work takes this idea as its sustained theme. For the most part, however, the historical interest of the Enlightenment focused on the recent past. Voltaire argued that our knowledge of recent events was more complete and verifiable, and thus superior (Echoes of Thucydides!); moreover, recent history was considered to be more significant and "moral", less marred by superstition and unreason, and thus more likely to teach positive lessons. Voltaire's treatment of Peter the Great is illustrative of this trend and method. Finally, the record of past accomplishments along the road to enlightenment and emancipation of the human spirit pointed the way into a glorious future. Condorcet's tableau of the progress of the human mind is not so much history as statement of the faith of the Enlightenment. The record of the past is made to demonstrate how human reason has progressively triumphed over the forces of darkness. From its past accomplishments the march towards the future is extrapolated. Essentially Condorcet (and Gibbon and Voltaire as well) did not care about the past. Their concern was with the instruction of the present and the shaping of the future.

25. GIBBON: THE HISTORY OF THE DECLINE AND FALL OF THE ROMAN EMPIRE

Edward Gibbon (1737-1794) was one of the great representatives of British upper-class culture of the eighteenth century. Steeped in classical civilization (he learned Latin at seven, and was writing studies on ancient history at twelve), he moved in a cosmopolitan social circle that brought him into contact with many of his great contemporaries. Sent to Geneva in his teens to cure him of a youthful flirtation with Roman Catholicism (still socially and politically unacceptable to Britain's ruling class), he met Voltaire. During later travels in France he met Diderot, d' Alembert, and other luminaries. In London his active social and club life made him an intimate of such stars of British intellectual and cultural life as Samuel Johnson, James Boswell, Sir Joshua Reynolds, and David Garrick. A member of the landed ruling class, Gibbon sat in Parliament during the 1770's as a supporter of Lord North's ministry, which rewarded him with the sinecure office of Commissioner of Trade and Plantations.

His great history, whose six original volumes relate the events of over 1300 years, from the age of the Antonines to the fall of Constantinople to the Turks in 1453, was conceived during a visit to Italy in 1764, and begun in 1770. The first volume, concluding with Chapter XVI (from which the following excerpt is taken), was published in 1776. It was an immediate success, praised for the grandeur of its style and sweep, condemned for its undisguised attack on Christianity, sustained throughout the remaining volumes, the last of which appeared in 1787.

The History of the Decline and Fall of the Roman Empire, for all its literary merit, and for all of Gibbon's prodigious learning, says at least as much about the author and his age as it does about the fall of Rome. Heavily didactic, it seeks throughout to convey the moral that the latter Romans' departure from values dear to the Enlightenment—secularism, rationalism, and humanism—brought about their doom. "I have described the triumph of barbarism and religion," Gibbon said of his work. In the following passage, the persecuting Roman emperors appear, as it were, as English Whig grandees, reluctantly forced to counteract a menace to society posed by plebeian ignorance and fanaticism.

History, which undertakes to record the transactions of the past, for the instruction of future, ages, would ill deserve that honourable office, if she condescended to plead the cause of tyrants, or to justify the maxims of persecution. It must, however, be acknowledged that the conduct of the emperors who appeared the least favourable to the primitive church is by no means so criminal as that of modern sovereigns who have employed the arm of violence and terror against the religious opinions of any part of their subjects. From their reflections, or even from their own feelings, a Charles V. or a Louis XIV. might have acquired a just knowledge of the rights of conscience, of the obligation of faith, and of the innocence of error. But the princes and magistrates of ancient Rome were strangers to those principles which inspired and authorized the inflexible obstinacy of the Christians in the cause of truth, nor could they themselves discover in their own breasts any motive which would have prompted them to refuse a legal, and as it were a natural, submission to the sacred institutions of their country. The same reason which contributes to alleviate the guilt, must have tended to abate the rigour, of their persecutions. As they were actuated, not by the furious zeal of bigots, but by the temperate policy of legislators, contempt must often have relaxed, and humanity must frequently have suspended, the execution of those laws which they enacted against the humble and obscure followers of Christ. From the general view of their character and motives we might naturally conclude: I. That a considerable time elapsed before they considered the new sectaries as an object deserving of the attention of government. II. That, in the conviction of any of their subjects who were accused of so very singular a crime, they proceeded with caution and reluctance. III. That they were moderate in the use of punishments; and IV. That the afflicted church enjoyed many intervals of peace and tranquillity. . . .

I. By the wise dispensation of Providence, a mysterious veil was cast over the infancy of the church, which, till the faith of the Christians was matured and their numbers were multiplied, served to protect them not only from the malice, but even from the knowledge, of the Pagan world. The slow and gradual abolition of the Mosaic ceremonies afforded a safe and innocent disguise to the more early proselytes of the Gospel. As they were far the greater part of the race of Abraham, they were distinguished by the peculiar mark of circumcision, offered up their devotions in the Temple of Jerusalem till its final destruction, and received both the Law and the Prophets as the genuine inspirations of the Deity. The Gentile converts, who by a spiritual adoption had been associated to the hope of Israel, were likewise confounded under the garb and appearance of Jews, and, as the polytheists paid less regard to articles of faith than to the external worship, the new sect, which carefully concealed, or faintly announced, its future greatness and ambition, was permitted to shelter itself under the general toleration which was granted to an ancient and celebrated people in the Roman empire. It was not long, perhaps, before the Jews themselves, animated with a fiercer zeal and a more jealous faith, perceived the gradual separation of their Nazarene brethren from the doctrine of the synagogue; and they would gladly have extinguished the dangerous heresy in the blood of its adherents. But the decrees of heaven had already disarmed their malice; and, though they might sometimes exert the licentious privilege of sedition, they no longer possessed the administration of criminal justice; nor did they find it easy to infuse into the calm breast of a Roman magistrate the rancour of their own zeal and prejudice. The provincial governors declared themselves ready to listen to any accusation that might affect the public safety; but, as soon as they were informed that it was a question not of facts but of words, a dispute relating only to the interpretation of the Jewish laws and prophecies, they deemed it unworthy of the majesty of Rome seriously to discuss the obscure differences which might arise among a barbarous and superstitious people. The innocence of the first Christians was protected by ignorance and contempt; and the tribunal of the Pagan magistrate often proved their most assured refuge against the fury of the synagogue. If, indeed, we were disposed to adopt the traditions of a too credulous antiquity, we might relate the distant peregrinations, the wonderful achievements, and the various deaths, of the twelve apostles; but a more accurate inquiry will induce us to doubt whether any of those persons who had been witnesses to the miracles of Christ were permitted, beyond the limits of Palestine, to seal with their blood the truth of their testimony. From the ordinary term of human life, it may very naturally be presumed that most of them were deceased before the discontent of the Jews broke out into that furious war which was terminated only by the ruin of Jerusalem. During a long period, from the death of Christ to that memorable rebellion, we cannot discover any traces of Roman intolerance, unless they are to be found in the sudden, the transient, but the cruel persecution, which was exercised by Nero against the Christians of the capital, thirty-five years after the former, and only two years before the latter of those great events. . . .

II. [In 111 A.D.] the younger Pliny was intrusted by his friend and master [The Emperor Trajan] with the government of Bithynia and Pontus. He soon found himself at a loss to determine by what rule of justice or of law he should direct his conduct in the execution of an office the most repugnant to his humanity. Pliny had never assisted at any judicial proceedings against the Christians, with whose name alone he seems to be acquainted; and he was totally uninformed with regard to the nature of their guilt, the method of their conviction, and the degree of their punishment. In this perplexity he had recourse to his usual expedient, of submitting to the wisdom of Trajan an impartial and, in some respects, a favourable account of the new superstition, requesting the emperor that he would condescend to resolve his doubts and to instruct his ignorance. The life of Pliny had been employed in the acquisition of learning, and in the business of the world. Since the age of nineteen he had pleaded with distinction in the tribunals of Rome, filled a place in the senate, had been invested with the honours of the consulship, and had formed very numerous connexions with every order of men, both in Italy and in the provinces. From *his* ignorance, therefore, we may derive some useful information. We may assure ourselves that when he accepted the government of Bithynia there were no general laws or decrees of the senate in force against the Christians; that neither Trajan nor any of his virtuous predecessors, whose edicts were received into the civil and criminal jurisprudence, had publicly declared their intentions concerning the new sect; and that, whatever proceedings had been carried on against the Christians, there were none of sufficient weight and authority to establish a precedent for the conduct of a Roman magistrate.

The answer of Trajan, to which the Christians of the succeeding age have frequently appealed, discovers as much regard for justice and humanity as could be reconciled with his mistaken notions of religious policy. Instead of displaying the implacable zeal of an inquisitor, anxious to discover the most minute particles of heresy and exulting in the number of his victims, the emperor expresses much more solicitude to protect the security of the innocent than to prevent the escape of the guilty. He acknowledges the difficulty of fixing any general plan; but he lays down two salutary rules, which often afforded relief and support to the distressed Christians. Though he directs the magistrates to punish such persons as are legally convicted, he prohibits them, with a very humane inconsistency, from making any inquiries concerning the supposed criminals. Nor was the magistrate allowed to proceed on every kind of information. Anonymous charges the emperor rejects, as too repugnant to the equity of his government; and he strictly requires, for the conviction of those to whom the guilt of Christianity is imputed, the positive evidence of a fair and open accuser. It is likewise probable that the persons who assumed so invidious an office were obliged to declare the grounds of their suspicions, to specify (both in respect to time and place) the secret assemblies which their Christian adversary had frequented, and to disclose a great number of circumstances which were concealed with the most vigilant jealousy from the eye of the profane. If they succeeded in their prosecution, they were exposed to the resentment of a considerable and active party, to the censure of the more liberal portion of mankind, and to the ignominy which, in every age and country, has attended the character of an informer. If, on the contrary, they failed in their proofs, they incurred the severe, and perhaps capital, penalty which, according to a law published by the emperor Hadrian, was inflicted on those who falsely attributed to their fellow-citizens the crime of Christianity. The violence of personal or superstitious animosity might sometimes prevail over the most natural apprehensions of disgrace and danger; but it cannot surely be imagined that accusations of so unpromising an appearance were either lightly or frequently undertaken by the Pagan subjects of the Roman empire. . . .

III. Punishment was not the inevitable consequence of conviction, and the Christians, whose guilt was the most clearly proved by the testimony of witnesses, or even by their voluntary confession, still retained in their own power the alternative of life or death. It was not so much the past offence, as the actual resistance, which excited the indignation of the magistrate. He was persuaded that he offered them an easy pardon, since, if they consented to cast a few grains of incense upon the altar, they were dismissed from the tribunal in safety and with applause. It was esteemed the duty of a humane judge to endeavor to reclaim, rather than to punish, those deluded enthusiasts. Varying his tone according to the age, the sex, or the situation of the prisoners, he frequently condescended to set before their eyes every circumstance which could render life more pleasing, or death more terrible; and to solicit, nay, to intreat them, that they would show some compassion to themselves, to their families, and to their friends. If threats and persuasions proved ineffectual, he had often recourse to violence; the scourge and the rack were called in to supply the deficiency of argument, and every art of cruelty was employed to subdue such inflexible and, as it appeared to the Pagans, such criminal obstinacy. The ancient apologists of Christianity have censured, with equal truth and severity, the irregular conduct of their persecutors, who, contrary to every principle of judicial proceeding, admitted the use of torture, in order to obtain not a confession but a denial of the crime which was the object of their inquiry. The monks of succeeding ages, who, in their peaceful solitudes, entertained themselves with diversifying the death and sufferings of the primitive martyrs, have frequently invented torments of a much more refined and ingenious nature. In particular, it has pleased them to suppose that the zeal of the Roman magistrates, disdaining every consideration of moral virtue or public decency, endeavoured to seduce those whom they were unable to vanquish, and that, by their orders, the most brutal violence was offered to those whom they found it impossible to seduce. It is related that pious females, who were prepared to despise death, were sometimes condemned to a more severe trial, and called upon to determine whether they set a higher value on their religion or on their chastity. The youths to whose licentious embraces they were abandoned received a solemn exhortation from the judge to exert their most strenuous efforts to maintain the honour of Venus against the impious virgin who refused to burn incense on her altars. Their violence, however, was commonly disappointed; and the seasonable interposition of some miraculous power preserved the chaste spouses of Christ from the dishonour even of an involuntary defeat. We should not, indeed, neglect to remark that the more ancient, as well as authentic, memorials of the church are seldom polluted with these extravagant and indecent fictions.

The total disregard of truth and probability in the representation of these primitive martyrdoms was occasioned by a very natural mistake. The ecclesiastical writers of the fourth or fifth centuries ascribed to the magistrates of Rome the same degree of implacable and unrelenting zeal which filled their own breasts against the heretics or the idolaters of their own times. It is not improbable that some of those persons who were raised to the dignities of the empire might have imbibed the prejudices of the populace, and that the cruel disposition of others might occasionally be stimulated by motives of avarice or of personal resentment. But it is certain, and we may appeal to the grateful confessions of the first Christians, that the greatest part of those magistrates who exercised in the provinces the authority of the emperor, or of the senate, and to whose hands alone the jurisdiction of life and death was intrusted, behaved like men of polished manners and liberal educations, who respected the rules of justice, and who were conversant with the precepts of philosophy. They frequently declined the odious task of persecution, dismissed the charge with contempt, or suggested to the accused Christian some legal evasion by which he might elude the severity of the laws. Whenever they were invested with a discretionary power, they used it much less for the oppression than for the relief and benefit of the afflicted church. They were far from condemning all the Christians who were accused before their tribunal, and very far from punishing with death all those who were convicted of an obstinate adherence to the new superstition. Contenting themselves, for the most part, with the milder chastisements of imprisonment, exile, or slavery in the mines, they left the unhappy victims of their justice some reason to hope that a prosperous event, the accession, the marriage, or the triumph of an emperor might speedily restore them, by a general pardon, to their former state. The martyrs, devoted to immediate execution by the Roman magistrates, appear to have been selected from the most opposite extremes. They were either bishops and presbyters, the persons the most distinguished among the Christians by their rank and influence, and whose example might strike terror into the whole sect; or else they were the meanest and most abject among them, particularly those of the servile condition, whose lives were esteemed of little value, and whose sufferings were viewed by the ancients with too careless an indifference. The learned Origen, who, from his experience as well as reading, was intimately acquainted with the history of the Christians, declares, in the most express terms, that the number of martyrs was very inconsiderable. His authority would alone be sufficient to annihilate that formidable army of martyrs whose relics, drawn for the most part from the catacombs of Rome, have replenished so many churches, and whose marvellous achievements have been the subject of so many volumes of holy romance.

26. VOLTAIRE: THE HISTORY OF CHARLES XII, KING OF SWEDEN

Francois-Marie Arouet (1694-1778), who became famous under the pen name Voltaire, was unquestionably the most influential intellect of his age, and the most widely known man in Europe. Read by everyone with a pretense to enlightenment and intellectual respectability, he was sought after and courted by rulers all over Europe, and visited and inundated with correspondence by the famous and the aspiring alike. Playwright, poet, novelist, popularizer of Newton's scientific method and view of the universe, tireless propagandist against all forms of intolerance and persecution, Voltaire also produced voluminous historical writings, of which the *History of Charles XII,* published in 1731, was the earliest. Like his better-known *Age of Louis XIV,* this account is largely based on oral and written evidence of contemporaries. Voltaire felt that such sources, critically examined, provided the surest basis for accurate history. Voltaire's basic ideas are clearly discernable in the following passage dealing with the reign of Peter the Great of Russia (to which he later devoted a separate work): Progress is equated with the widening of tolerance, and the increase of wealth, scientific knowledge, and respect for human rights. Charles XII's heroics bring him glory, but end in failure and desolation. Peter, though not faultless, is the greater figure, for he lays the basis of civilization in a barbarous country.

Peter Alexiowitz had received an education that tended still more to increase the barbarism of this part of the world. His natural disposition led him to caress strangers, before he knew what advantages he might derive from their acquaintance. A young Genevese, named Le Fort, of an ancient family in Geneva, the son of a druggist, was the first instrument he employed, in the course of time, to change the face of affairs in Muscovy. This young man, sent by his father to be a merchant at Copenhagen, quitted his business and followed an ambassador of Denmark to Muscovy, from that restlessness of mind which is always experienced by such as feel themselves superior to their situation. He took it into his head to learn the Russian language. The rapid progress which he made in it excited the curiosity of the Czar, who was yet in his youth. Le Fort became acquainted with him; he insinuated himself into his familiarity; he often talked to him of the advantages of commerce and navigation; he told him how Holland, which had never possessed the hundredth part of the States of Muscovy, made as great a figure by means of her commerce alone, as the Spains, a small province of which she had formerly been, both useless and despised. He entertained him with the refined policy of the Princes of Europe, with the discipline of their troops, the police of their cities, and the infinite number of manufactures, arts and sciences, which render the Europeans powerful and happy. These discourses awakened the young emperor as from a profound lethargy; his mighty genius, which a barbarous education had repressed, but had not been able to destroy, unfolded itself almost at once. . . .

He left Muscovy in 1698, having reigned but two years, and went to Holland, disguised under a common name, as if he had been a domestic servant of the same Mr. Le Fort, whom he sent in quality of Ambassador Extraordinary to the States General. As soon as he arrived at Amsterdam, he enrolled himself among the shipwrights of the India Company's wharf, under the name of Peter Michaeloff, but he was commonly called Peter Bas, or Master Peter. He worked in the yard like the other mechanics. At his leisure hours he learned such parts of the mathematics as are useful to a Prince, fortification, navigation, and the art of drawing plans. He went into the workmen's shops, and examined all their manufactures, in which nothing could escape his observation. From thence he went over to England, where, having perfected himself in the art of ship-building, he returned to Holland, carefully observing every thing that might turn to the advantage of his own country. At length, after two years of travel and labour, to which no man but himself would have willingly submitted, he again made his appearance in Muscovy, with all the arts of Europe in his train. Artists of every kind followed him in crowds. Then were seen for the first time large Russian ships in the Baltick, and on the Black Sea, and the ocean. Stately buildings, of a regular architecture, were raised among the Russian huts. He founded colleges, academies, printing-houses, and libraries. The cities were brought under a regular police. The cloaths and customs of the people were gradually changed, though not without some difficulty; and the Muscovites learned by degrees the true nature of a social state. Even their superstitious rites were abolished; the dignity of the Patriarch was suppressed; and the Czar declared himself the Head of the Church. This last enterprize, which would have cost a Prince less absolute than Peter both his throne and his life, succeeded almost without opposition, and insured to him the success of his other innovations.

After having humbled an ignorant and a barbarous clergy, he ventured to make a trial of instructing them, though by that means he ran the risque of rendering them formidable; but he was too sensible of his own power to entertain any fear of it. He caused philosophy and theology to be taught in the few monasteries that still remained. True it is, this theology still savours of that barbarous period in which Peter civilized his people. . . .

The Monks were not pleased with this reformation. The Czar had hardly erected printing-houses, when they made use of them to decry him. They declared in print that Peter was Anti-christ, for that he deprived the living of their beards, and allowed the dead to be dissected in his Academy. But another Monk, who aimed at promotion, refuted this book, and proved that Peter could not be Anti-christ, because the number 666 was not to be found in his name. The libeller was accordingly broke upon the wheel, and the author of the refutation was made Bishop of Rezan.

This reformer of Muscovy enacted in particular, a very salutary law, the want of which reflects disgrace on many civilized nations. This enacted that no man engaged in the service of the State, no citizen established in trade, and especially no minor, should retire into a convent.

Peter knew of what infinite consequence it was to prevent useful subjects from consecrating themselves to idleness, and to hinder young people from disposing of their liberty at an age when they were incapable of disposing of the least part of their patrimony. But this law, though calculated for the general interest of mankind, is daily eluded by the industry of the Monks; as if they were in fact gainers by peopling their convents at the expence of their country. . . .

The revenue of the Czar, when compared to the immense extent of his dominions, was indeed inconsiderable. It never amounted to four-and-twenty millions of livres, reckoning the mark at about fifty livres, as we do to-day, though we may not do so to-morrow. But he may always be accounted rich who has it in his power to accomplish great undertakings. It is not the scarcity of money that debilitates a State, it is the want of men, and of men of abilities. . . .

While the Czar was thus employed in changing the laws, the manners, the militia, and the very face of his country, he likewise resolved to encrease his greatness by encouraging commerce, which at once constitutes the riches of a particular State, and contributes to the interest of the world in general. He undertook to make Russia the center of trade between Asia and Europe. He determined to join the Duna, the Volga, and the Tanais, by canals, of which he drew the plans; and thus to open a new passage from the Baltick to the Euxine and Caspian seas, and from those seas to the Northern Ocean. The port of Archangel, frozen up nine months in the year, and which could not be entered without making a long and dangerous circuit, did not appear to him sufficiently commodious. So long ago, therefore, as the year 1700, he had formed a design of opening a sea-port on the Baltick that should become the magazine of the North, and of building a city that should prove the capital of his empire.

He had even then attempted the discovery of a northeast passage to China; and the manufactures of Pekin and Paris were intended to embellish his new city.

A road by land, 754 versts long, running through marshes that were to be drained, was to lead from Moscow to his new city. Most of these projects have been executed by himself; and the two Empresses, his successors, have even improved upon those of his schemes that were practicable, and abandoned only such as it was impossible to accomplish.

He always travelled through his dominions as much as his wars would permit; but he travelled like a legislator and a naturalist; examining Nature every where; endeavouring to correct or perfect her; taking himself the soundings of seas and rivers; ordering sluices, visiting docks, causing mines to be worked, assaying metals, and in directing accurate charts to be drawn; in the execution of which he himself assisted.

He built upon a desert spot the imperial city of Petersburgh, containing at present sixty thousand houses, the residence of a splendid court, whose amusements are of the most refined taste. He built the harbour of Cronstadt, on the Neva, and St. Croix, on the frontiers of Persia; he erected forts in the Ukraine, and in Siberia; established offices of admiralty at Archangel, Petersburgh, Astracan, and Asoph; founded arsenals, and built and endowed hospitals. All his own houses were mean, and executed in a bad taste; but he spared no expence in rendering the public buildings grand and magnificent.

The sciences, which in other countries have been the slow product of so many ages, were, by his care and industry, imported into Russia in full perfection. He established an Academy on the plan of the famous Societies of Paris and London. The Delisles, the Bulfingers, the Hermannus's, the Bernouilles, and the celebrated Wolf, a man who excelled in every branch of philosophy, were all invited and brought to Petersburgh at a great expence. This Academy still subsists; and the Muscovites, at length, have philosophers of their own nation.

He obliged the young nobility to travel for improvement, and to bring back into Russia the politeness of foreign countries. I have myself seen young Russians who were men of genius and science. It was thus that a single man hath reformed the greatest empire in the world. It is, however, shocking to reflect, that this reformer of mankind should have been deficient in that first of all virtues, the virtue of humanity. Brutality in his pleasures, ferocity in his manners, and barbarity in his revenges, sullied the lustre of his many virtues. He civilized his subjects, and yet remained a barbarian. He was conscious of this, and once said to a magistrate of Amsterdam, "I reform my country, but am not able to reform myself." He has executed his sentence upon criminals with his own hands, and at a debauch at table has shewn his address at cutting off heads.

In Africa, there are Princes who thus with their own hands shed the blood of their subjects; but these pass for barbarians. The death of a son, whom he ought to have corrected, or disinherited, would render the memory of Peter the object of universal hatred, were it not that the great and many blessings he bestowed upon his subjects, were almost sufficient to excuse his cruelty to his own offspring.

27. CONDORCET: SKETCH FOR A HISTORICAL PICTURE OF THE PROGRESS OF THE HUMAN MIND

Marie-Jean-Antoine-Nicolas de Caritat, Marquis de Condorcet (1743-1794), a French aristocrat who became an ardent revolutionist (he was president of the legislative assembly in 1792), but ended his life as a suicide in one of Robespierre's dungeons, was not primarily a historian. He established his reputation as a mathematician, economist, and statistician, contributed to the *Encyclopedie,* that massive summary of the knowledge and ideology of the Enlightenment, was elected to the French Academy of Sciences at 26, and to the French Academy at 39. He knew and was closely associated with virtually all the *philosophes,* from Diderot to Voltaire. His *Sketch,* designed as an outline of a massive universal social and intellectual history, was written when Condorcet, who had dared to express public opposition to the Jacobin constitution of 1793, was in hiding from the agents of the Committee of Public Safety.

To a certain extent the inclusion of Condorcet in this volume represents an exception to its general rule of drawing a line between history (narrative accounts of the past) and philosophy of history (speculation about historical meaning and purpose). This line is nowhere harder to maintain than for the historiography of the 18th century, with its tendency to use history so largely as a vehicle for the presentation of moral and philosophical theses. Condorcet merely represents the extreme of this trait. The *Sketch* outlines the history of mankind as a saga of progress, which had carried man through nine stages, each characterized by a particular central accomplishment (e.g., the formation of political communities, the invention of agriculture, of the alphabet, of printing), which progressively emancipated human reason from the forces of nature and of ignorance. A tenth stage, which would bring the human race to the apex of wisdom, virtue, equality, peace, and prosperity, lay just ahead. Condorcet, in his unbounded optimism and faith in reason and progress, went beyond the position of such thinkers as Voltaire. For him, the perfectibility of the human condition also implied the ultimate perfectibility of human nature, and the paradise of the future is not merely the reign of philosopher kings, acting for the good of mankind, but in the tenth stage of human development all men (and women) would achieve equality, in reason and virtue.

Despite this sweeping vision, in which facts and details virtually disappear, except as they domonstrate the laws and purposes of universal progress, Condorcet still shares with Gibbon and Voltaire one characteristic: While all of them recognize the role of historical environment and social forces, the importance of individual genius, and of human will, virtuous or otherwise, is writ very large in the historiography of this age. The dilemma of free will vs. determination, freedom vs. necessity, individuals vs. historical forces looms as large for the thinkers of the Enlightenment as it does for those of any other age. However, it is rarely recognized or dealt with.

The Eighth Stage

From the invention of printing to the time
when philosophy and the sciences shook off
the yoke of authority

To those who have not reflected much upon the progress of the human spirit in the sphere of scientific discovery or of artistic method, it might well seem amazing that such a long period of time should have elapsed between the discovery of the art of printing designs and the discovery of the art of printing characters. Doubtless some engravers had thought of such an application of their art; but the difficulties of its execution had weighed with them more than the benefits of success; and it is indeed fortunate that nobody had suspected the full extent of future success, for priests and kings would surely have united to smother at birth an enemy who was to unmask and dethrone them.

With printing the copies of any book can be multiplied indefinitely at little cost. Since its invention, it has been possible for anyone who could read to obtain any book that he wanted or needed; and this which made reading easier in turn increased the will to learn and the means of instruction.

With so many copies of a book in circulation at the same time, information about facts and discoveries reached a wider public, and also reached it more promptly. Knowledge became the subject of a brisk and universal trade.

Previously people had had to search for manuscripts just as today we search for rare books. What formerly only a few individuals had been able to read,

"Sketch for a Historical Picture of the Progress of the Human Mind," by Condorcet. By permission of Weidenfeld and Nicolson Publishers, London, England.

could now be read by a whole nation and could reach almost at the same moment everyone who understood the same language.

Men found themselves possessed of the means of communicating with people all over the world. A new sort of tribunal had come into existence in which less lively but deeper impressions were communicated; which no longer allowed the same tyrannical empire to be exercised over men's passions but ensured a more certain and more durable power over their minds; a situation in which the advantages are all on the side of truth, since what the art of communication loses in the power to seduce, it gains in the power to enlighten. The public opinion that was formed in this way was powerful by virtue of its size, and effective because the forces that created it operated with equal strength on all men at the same time; no matter what distances separated them. In a word, we have now a tribunal, independent of all human coercion, which favours reason and justice, a tribunal whose scrutiny it is difficult to elude, and whose verdict it is impossible to evade. . . .

Any new mistake is criticized as soon as it is made, and often attacked even before it has been propagated; and so it has no time to take root in men's minds. Those fallacies which are imbibed in infancy, becoming in some way identified with the reason of the individual, and which weaker characters cling to out of terror or hope, have now been eradicated for this reason alone—that it has become impossible to prevent their being openly discussed, to disguise the fact that they can be attacked and rejected, or to maintain them against the progress of truth which by argument must ultimately reveal them as absurd. . . .

Without this art, how would it be possible to produce in adequate numbers books suited to the different classes of men and to the different degrees of education? Prolonged discussion which alone can cast an unwavering light on doubtful questions and establish on an unshakable foundation truths that are too abstract, too subtle, too far-removed from the prejudices of the vulgar or the accepted opinion of the learned not to be soon forgotten and misunderstood; elementary books, dictionaries, works of reference containing a host of facts, observations and experiments in which all proofs are developed and all doubts discussed; valuable compilations containing all that has been observed, written or thought about one particular branch of the sciences, or setting out the work of all the scientists of one country in a given year; tables and diagrams of all kinds, some that show us conclusions that our minds would otherwise have grasped only after long struggle, some to which we can refer for some fact, observation, sum, formula, or object that we need, and others that give us in a convenient form, in a methodical arrangement, the materials from which genius can extract

new truths: all these means of accelerating, assisting, ensuring the forward
march of the human mind must be numbered amongst the blessings brought by
printing. . . .

Has not printing freed the education of the people from all political and
religious shackles? It would be vain for any despotism to invade all the schools;
vain for it to issue cruel edicts prescribing and dictating the errors with which
men's minds were to be infected, and the truths from which they were to be
safeguarded; vain for the chairs dedicated to the moral enlightenment of the
vulgar or the instruction of the young in philosophy and the sciences to be
obliged under duress to put forward nothing but opinions favourable to the
maintenance of this double tyranny: printing would still be able to diffuse a clear
and independent light. The instruction that every man is free to receive from
books in silence and solitude can never be completely corrupted. It is enough for
there to exist one corner of free earth from which the press can scatter its
leaves. . . .

So we shall see reason triumphing over all such vain attempts, and we shall
see it, in this ever recurrent and often cruel war, overcoming violence as well as
cunning, braving the executioners and resisting the tempters, crushing under its
all-powerful hand, first, religious hypocrisy which demands sincere adoration for
its dogmas and, then, the political hypocrisy which abjectly pleads that it may be
allowed to profit in peace from those errors in which, if we are to believe it, it is
profitable not only for itself but for mankind that mankind should be sunk for
ever.

Three great men have marked the transition from this stage of history to the
next: Bacon, Galileo, Descartes.

Bacon revealed the true method of studying nature and of using the three
instruments that she has given us for penetrating her secrets; observation,
experience and calculation. He asked that the philosopher, cast into the middle of
the universe, should begin by renouncing all the beliefs that he had received and
even all the notions he had formed, so that he might then recreate for himself, as
it were, a new understanding admitting only of precise ideas, accurate notions
and truths whose degree of certainty or probability had been strictly weighed.
But Bacon, who possessed the genius of philosophy in the highest degree, was
without the genius of science; and these methods for discovering truth, of which
he gave no examples, were admired by philosophers but in no way influenced the
course of science.

Galileo enriched the sciences by useful and brilliant discoveries. He showed by example how to arrive at a knowledge of the laws of nature by a sure and fruitful method, which did not necessitate sacrificing the hope of success to the fear of error. He founded the first school in which the sciences were studied without any admixture of superstition in favour of either popular prejudices or authority, and where all methods other than experiment and calculation were rejected with philosophical severity. But in limiting himself exclusively to the mathematical and physical sciences, he could not afford mankind that general guidance of which it seemed to stand in need.

This honour was reserved for Descartes, a bold and clever philosopher. Endowed with great genius for the sciences, he joined example to precept and gave a method for finding and recognizing truth. He showed how to apply this in his discovery of the laws of dioptrics and the laws of the collision of bodies and finally in the development of a new branch of mathematics which was to move forward the frontiers of the subject.

He wished to extend his method to all the subjects of human thought; God, man and the universe were in turn the objects of his meditations. If his progress in the physical sciences was less certain than Galileo's, if his philosophy was less wise than Bacon's, if he can be reproached with not having learnt sufficiently from the precepts of the one and the practice of the other, to distrust his imagination, to ask questions of nature only by experiment, to believe only in calculation and the observation of the universe instead of fashioning it, to study man instead of speculating about him, still the very audacity of his mistakes served to further the progress of the human race. He stimulated men's minds, and this all the wisdom of his rivals had never done. He commanded men to shake off the yoke of authority, to recognize none save that which was avowed by reason; and he was obeyed, because he won men by his boldness and led them by his enthusiasm.

The human mind was not yet free but it knew that it was formed to be so. Those who dared to insist that it should be kept in its old chains or to try and impose new ones upon it, were forced to show why it should submit to them; and from that day onwards it was certain that they would soon be broken.

SOURCE NOTES

1. From Edward Gibbon, *The History of the Decline and Fall of the Roman Empire,* ed. by J. B. Bury (London, 1925), pp. 81-98, *passim.*

2. From Voltaire, *The History of Charles XII, King of Sweden* (New York, 1803), pp. 37-45, *passim*.
3. From Marie-Jean-Antoine-Nicolas Caritat de Condorcet, *Sketch for a Historical Picture of the Progress of the Human Mind*, trans. by June Barraclough (London: Weidenfeld & Nicolson, 1955). Pp. 99-103, 121-123 reprinted by permission of George Weidenfeld & Nicolson, Ltd.

11.
THE
ROMANTIC
SPIRIT

As we approach the present, this anthology abandons the organizational framework hitherto followed. Instead of grandly summarizing centuries of historical writing in one chapter, we now deal with different schools and trends of historiography which flourished simultaneously, which in many cases still have their contemporary exponents, and none of which can claim to reflect fully the great variety of the intellectual environment of the 19th and 20th centuries.

Perhaps, in taking this approach, we are simply the victims of historical myopia. Historians looking back from a vantage point several centuries hence may have no difficulty discerning in the various manifestations of the culture, and thus also of the historiography, of the 19th and 20th centuries an underlying unity of tendency, as clearly apparent to them as the guiding intellectual principles of earlier periods appear to us.

On the other hand, it is possible that the greater variety of cultural and intellectual expression which appears to characterize our age and that of our immediate forebears, is an objective fact. In the largest context, it may be explainable by the dissolution of the general cultural consensus which shaped earlier periods of Western history, and by the full unfolding of the spirit of questioning, and of individualism, of which we have seen evidence in previous chapters.

In historiography, there is also the "quantum leap" that occurred in the 19th century in the amount of historical writing produced. History developed from a branch of literature into an academic discipline, with a defined methodology. Vast storehouses of documentary sources were published and made accessible, and ancillary fields of learning, from archeology to linguistics, greatly widened our perspectives of the human past.

History, moreover, became democratized. Where earlier historians had explained and extolled the works and purposes of the deity, then of kings and other great men, historians of our age must explain, celebrate, and censure the deeds of nations, of popular movements, and of parties.

In the following selections, this tendency is exemplified by Michelet and Lamartine. Carlyle, on the other hand, celebrates the Hero, the exceptional individual, as the prime mover of history; in his view of the French Revolution he differed markedly from Michelet and Lamartine, seeing in it primarily the deserved punishment of a corrupt age, rather than the dawning of a splendid future.

Despite such obvious differences, all three are representative of that same Romantic spirit which so powerfully influenced the intellectual and artistic atmosphere of the early nineteenth century. For, unlike most of the other "isms" that flourished in that period, Romanticism is not an intellectual position, an ideology, or a program. One cannot point to a Romantic "school" of historians, in the sense that it is possible to speak of liberal, nationalist, or conservative historians. The romantic attitude might be combined with any of these positions: Michelet and Lamartine, for example, wrote history from a liberal point of view, but their style and mood was that of Romanticism.

This Romantic mood or attitude was a reaction to the intellectual climate and style of the eighteenth century. While the Enlightenment and its historiography emphasized rationalism, determinism, and regularities in its view of human affairs as well as of the physical universe, the Romantic rebellion stressed the elements of human freedom and will—hence its worship of the genius and the rebel. Romantic writers of history, as well as of fiction, delight in the imponderable, the accidental, the asymmetrical, the unique. It is not surprising that the age of Romanticism saw historical studies and literature flourish: The study of history, of all the approaches to the understanding of man and society, must inevitably deal with the unique and the exceptional; it tends to create or reinforce scepticism about all systems and *a priori* generalizations. In this way the Romantic spirit contributed to the development of the new "scientific" approach to history which will be discussed in Chapter 12.

28. MICHELET: HISTORY OF THE FRENCH REVOLUTION

Jules Michelet (1798-1874) ranks among the most famous historians of the 19th century. His career was wholly devoted to the teaching and writing of history. An *Introduction to a Universal History,* a *Roman History,* and a 17-volume *History of France* were among his important works. His seven volume *History of the French Revolution,* first published between 1847 and 1853, was the most significant historiographical expression of the renewed strength of republican sentiment in France during the reign of Louis Philippe, which foreshadowed the revolution of 1848. (Earlier histories and memoirs of the revolution had condemned it outright, or had, like the works of the moderate monarchists F. A. Mignet and Adolphe Thiers, applauded the ''moderate'' revolution of 1789, while condemning the excesses of the republican revolution of 1792-93.)

The following selections from Michelet's preface, and from the first chapter, illustrate two central features of his work: His sweeping, subjective, rhetorical style, which is that of Romanticism, and which unabashedly interjects the historian, as teacher and exhorter, between the reader and the ''facts'' of history; and Michelet's conviction (also expressive of Romantic attitudes) that it is ideas and human will that direct history, and here create the Revolution, which Michelet personifies as the embodiment of Virtue and Reason.

Every year, when I descend from my chair, at the close of my academic labours, when I see the crowd disperse,—another generation that I shall behold no more,—my mind is lost in inward contemplation. . . .

I commune with my own mind. I interrogate myself as to my teaching, my history, and its all-powerful interpreter,—the spirit of the Revolution.

It possesses a knowledge of which others are ignorant. It contains the secret of all bygone times. In it alone France was conscious of herself. When, in a moment of weakness, we may appear forgetful of our own worth, it is to this point we should recur in order to seek and recover ourselves again. Here, the inextinguishable spark, the profound mystery of life, is ever glowing within us.

The Revolution lives in ourselves,—in our souls; it has no outward monument. Living spirit of France, where shall I seize thee, but within myself?— The governments that have succeeded each other, hostile in all other respects, appear at least agreed in this, to resuscitate, to awaken remote and departed ages. But thee they would have wished to bury. Yet why? Thou, thou alone dost live.

Thou livest! I feel this truth perpetually impressed upon me at the present period of the year, when my teaching is suspended,—when labour grows fatiguing, and the season becomes oppressive. Then I wander to the Champ de Mars, I sit me down on the parched grass, and inhale the strong breeze that is wafted across the arid plain.

The Champ de Mars! This is the only monument that the Revolution has left. The Empire has its Column, and engrosses almost exclusively the arch of Triumph; royalty has its Louvre, its Hospital of Invalids; the feudal church of the twelfth century is still enthroned at Notre Dame; nay, the very Romans have their Imperial Ruins, the Thermæ of the Cæsars!

And the Revolution has for her monument—empty space. . . .

Yes, though a forgetful generation dares to select this spot for the theatre of its vain amusements, borrowed from a foreign land,—though the English race-horse may gallop insolently over the plain, a mighty breath yet traverses it, such as you nowhere else perceive; a soul, and a spirit omnipotent.

And though that plain be arid, and the grass be withered, it will, one day, renew its verdure.

For in that soil is profoundly mingled the fruitful sweat of their brows who, on a sacred day, piled up those hills,—that day when, aroused by the cannon of the Bastille, France from the North and France from the South came forward and embraced; that day when three millions of heroes in arms rose with the unanimity of one man, and decreed eternal peace.

Alas! poor Revolution. How confidingly on thy first day didst thou invite the world to love and peace. "O my enemies," didst thou exclaim, "there are no longer any enemies!" Thou didst stretch forth thy hand to all, and offer them thy cup to drink to the peace of nations—But they would not.

And even when they advanced to inflict a treacherous wound, the sword drawn by France was the sword of peace. It was to deliver the nations, and give them true peace—liberty, that she struck the tyrants. Dante asserts Eternal Love to be the founder of the gates of hell. And thus the Revolution wrote *Peace* upon her flag of war.

Chapter I

The convocation of the States-General, in 1789, is the true era of the birth of the people. It called the whole nation to the exercise of their rights.

They could at least write their complaints, their wishes, and choose the electors.

Small republican states had already admitted all their members to a participation of political rights; but never had a great kingdom,—an empire like France. The thing was new, not only in French annals, but even in those of the world.

Accordingly, when, for the first time, in the course of ages, these words were heard: *All* shall assemble to elect, *all* shall send in their complaints, there was an immense, profound commotion, like an earthquake; the mass felt the shock even in obscure and mute regions, where movement would have been least expected.

All the towns elected, and not the *good* towns only, as in the ancient States-General; country districts also elected, and not the towns alone.

It is affirmed that five millions of men took part in the election.

Grand, strange, surprising scene! To see a whole people emerging, at once, from nonentity to existence, who, till then silent, suddenly found a voice.

The same appeal of equality was addressed to populations, prodigiously unequal, not only by position, but by worship, by their moral state and ideas. How would that people answer? That was a great question. The exchequer on one side, feudality on the other, seemed striving to brutalise them under the weight of miseries. Royalty had deprived them of their municipal rights,—of that education which they derived from business connected with the commune. The clergy, the teachers thrust upon them, had not taught them for a long time past. They seemed to have done everything to render them dull, dumb, speechless, and senseless, and then they said to them, "Arise now, walk, and speak!"

They had relied, too much relied, upon that incapacity; otherwise they would never have ventured to make this grand move. The first who pronounced the name of the States-General,—the parliaments which demanded them,—the ministers who promised them,—Necker who convoked them,—all, believed the people incapable of taking any serious part therein. They only thought, by this solemn convocation of a great lifeless mass, to frighten the privileged classes. The court, which was itself the privilege of privileges, the abuse of abuses, had no desire to make war on them. It merely hoped, by the forced contributions of the clergy and nobility, to fill the public coffers, from which they filled their own. . . .

This people, though wholly unprepared, showed a very sure instinct. When they were called to election and informed of their rights, it was found that little remained to be taught them. In that prodigious movement of five or six millions of men, there was some sort of hesitation, through their ignorance of forms, and especially, because the majority knew not how to read. But they knew how to speak; they knew how, in presence of their lords, without infringing upon their respectful habits, or laying aside their humble demeanour, to select worthy electors, who all nominated safe and certain deputies.

The admission of the country districts to election had the unexpected result of placing even among the deputies of the privileged orders a numerous democracy, of whom they had never thought, two hundred *curés* and more, very hostile to their bishops. In Brittany, and in the South, the peasant willingly nominated his *curé*, who, moreover, alone knowing how to write, received the votes, and directed all the election.

The people of the towns, rather better prepared, having been somewhat enlightened by the philosophy of the age, evinced an admirable eagerness, a lively consciousness of their rights. This appeared plain at the elections, by the rapidity, the certainty with which crowds of inexperienced men took this their first political step. It appeared evident in the uniformity of the memorials (*cahiers*) in which they recorded their complaints,—an unexpected, powerful combination, which imparted irresistible strength to the will of the people. How long had those complaints existed in every heart! It was but too easy to write them. Many a memorial of our districts, containing almost a code, was begun at midnight, and finished at three in the morning.

A movement so vast, so varied, so wholly unprepared, and yet so unanimous, is most wonderful! All took part in it, and (except an insignificant number) they all desired the same thing.

Unanimous! There was a complete and unreserved concord, a perfectly simple state of things,—the nation on one side and privilege on the other. Yet, there was no possible distinction then in the nation between the people and the citizens; only one distinction appeared,—the instructed and the ignorant; the educated alone spoke and wrote; but they wrote the thoughts of all. They drew up into a formula the general demands; and they were the demands of the mute masses as much as, and more than their own.

Oh! who would not be touched by the remembrance of that unrivalled moment, when we started into life? It was shortlived; but it remains for us the ideal whereunto we shall ever tend, the hope of the future! O sublime Concord, in which the rising liberties of classes, subsequently in opposition, embraced so tenderly, like brothers in the cradle—shall we never more see thee return upon our earth?

29. LAMARTINE: HISTORY OF THE GIRONDINS

Alphonse de Lamartine (1790-1869) practiced as well as wrote about politics. His background was aristocratic and royalist; he served the reactionary king Charles X as a diplomat, while he also established his fame as a romantic poet. In 1833, under the "bourgeois monarchy" of Louis Philippe, he was elected to the Chamber of Deputies as a champion of Legitimism. Unable to convince his fellow conservative royalists to link the cause of social justice for the lower classes with that of Bourbon restoration, Lamartine gradually moved towards republicanism. In the spring of 1848 he was at the zenith of popularity and power, functioning as the virtual head of the revolutionary Provisional Government. With the break between the socially conservative bourgeois republicans within that government and the exponents of radical social reform Lamartine's fortunes waned rapidly: As a candidate for President of the second French Republic in the fall of 1848, he polled a mere 20,000 votes. Louis Napoleon, while perhaps less sincere, was infinitely more successful at combining appeals for law and order with vague egalitarianism and slogans of social justice.

Lamartine's *History of the Girondins,* like Michelet's account of the French Revolution, appeared in 1847. It is similar in style, and in viewing the revolution as a moral movement of the whole nation. Lamartine, however, unlike Michelet, was a religious believer, a liberal Catholic, and he sought to link the ethics of Christianity with those of the Enlightenment as a common root cause of the revolution. His remarks about Louis XVI reflect Lamartine's own, ultimately unsuccessful, endeavors to guide and control a revolutionary movement by placing himself in its van. Like Michelet, Lamartine views the Revolution as an Idea that guides the imperfect human beings who realize it, but that must be considered apart from, and infinitely superior to them.

There are objects in nature, the forms of which can only be accurately ascertained when contemplated afar off. Too near, as well as too far off, prevents a correct view. Thus it is with great events. The hand of God is visible in human things, but this hand itself has a shadow which conceals what it accomplishes. All that could then be seen of the French Revolution announced all that was great in this world, the advent of a new idea in human kind, the democratic idea, and afterwards the democratic government.

This idea was an emanation of Christianity. Christianity finding men in serfage and degraded all over the earth, had arisen on the fall of the Roman Empire, like a mighty vengeance, though under the aspect of a resignation. It had proclaimed the three words which 2000 years afterwards was re-echoed by French philosophy—liberty, equality, fraternity—amongst mankind. But it had for a time hidden this idea in the recesses of the Christian heart. As yet too weak to attack civil laws, it had said to the powers—"I leave you still for a short space of time possession of the political world, confining myself to the moral world. Continue if you can to enchain, class, keep in bondage, degrade the people, I am engaged in the emancipation of souls. I shall occupy 2000 years, perchance, in renewing men's minds before I become apparent in human institutions. But the day will come when my doctrines will escape from the temple, and will enter into the councils of the people; on that day the social world will be renewed."

This day had now arrived; it had been prepared by an age of philosophy, sceptical in appearance but in reality replete with belief. The scepticism of the 18th century only affected exterior forms, and the supernatural dogmata of Christianity, whilst it adopted with enthusiasm, morality and the social sense. What Christianity called revelation, philosophy called reason. The words were different, the meaning identical. The emancipation of individuals, of castes, of people, were alike derived from it. Only the ancient world had been enfranchised in the name of Christ, whilst the modern world was freed in the name of the rights which every human creature has received from the hand of God; and from both flowed the enfranchisement of God or nature. The political philosophy of the Revolution could not have invented a word more true, more complete, more divine than Christianity, to reveal itself to Europe, and it had adopted the dogma and the word of *fraternity*. Only the French Revolution attacked the form of this ruling religion; because it was incrusted in the forms of government, monarchial, theocratic, or aristocratic, which they sought to destroy. It is the explanation of that apparent contradiction of the mind of the 18th century, which borrowed all from Christianity in policy, and denied, whilst it despoiled, it. . . .

Three things were then evident to reflecting minds from and after the month of April, 1791; the one, that the march of the revolutionary movement advanced from step to step to the complete restoration of all the rights of suffering humanity—from those of the people by their government, to those of citizens by castes, and of the workmen by the citizen; thus it assailed tyranny, privilege, inequality, selfishness: . . . the second—that this philosophic and social movement of democracy would seek its natural form in a form of government analogous to its principle, and its nature; that is to say, representing the sovereignty of the people; republic with one or two heads: and, finally, that the social and political emancipation would involve in it the intellectual and religious emancipation of the human mind; that the liberty of thought, of speaking and acting, should not pause before the liberty of belief; that the idea of God confined in the sanctuaries, should shine forth pouring into each free conscience the right of liberty itself; that this light, a revelation for some, and reason for others, would spread more and more with truth and justice, which emanate from God to overspread the earth.

Human thought, like God, makes the world in its own image.

Thought was revived by a philosophical age.

It had to transform the social world.

The French Revolution was therefore in its essence a sublime and impassioned spirituality. It had a divine and universal ideal. This is the reason why its passion spread beyond the frontiers of France. Those who limit, mutilate it. It was the accession of three moral sovereignties: —

The sovereignty of right over force;

The sovereignty of intelligence over prejudices;

The sovereignty of people over governments.

Revolution in rights; equality.

Revolution in ideas; reasoning substituted for authority.

Revolution in facts; the reign of the people.

A Gospel of social rights.

A Gospel of duties, a charter of humanity.

France declared itself the apostle of this creed. In this war of ideas France had allies every where, and even on thrones themselves.

Thus on the 1st of June, 1791, were parties situated, such the men and things in the midst of which the irresistible spirit of a vast social renovation advanced with occult and continuous impulse. What but contention, anarchy, crime, and death could emanate from such elements! No party had the reason, no mind had the genius, no soul had the virtue, no arm had the energy, to control this chaos, and extract from it justice, truth, and strength. Things will only produce what they contain. Louis XVI. was upright and devoted to well doing, but he had not understood, from the very first symptoms of the Revolution, that there was only one part for the leader of a people, and that was to place himself in the van of the newly born idea, to forbear any struggle for the past, and thus to combine in his own person the twofold power of chief of the nation, and chief of a party. The character of moderation is only possible on the condition of having already acquired the unreserved confidence of the party whom it is desired to control. Henri IV. assumed this character, but it was *after* victory; had he attempted it *before* Ivry, he would have lost, not only the kingdom of France, but also of Navarre.

The court was venal, selfish, corrupt; it only defended in the king's person the sources of its vanities,—profitable exactions. The clergy, with Christian virtues, had no public virtues: a state within a state, its life was apart from the life of the nation; its ecclesiastical establishment seemed to be wholly independent of the monarchical establishment. It had only rallied round the monarchy, on the day it had beheld its own fortune compromised; and then it had appealed to the faith of the people, in order to preserve its wealth; but the people now only saw in the monks mendicants, and in the bishops extortioners. The nobility, effeminate by lengthened peace, emigrated in masses, abandoning their king to his besetting perils, and fully trusting in the prompt and decisive intervention of foreign powers. The third estate, jealous and envious, fiercely demanded their place and their rights amongst the privileged castes; its justice appeared hatred. The Assembly comprised in its bosom all these weaknesses, all this egotism, all these vices. Mirabeau was venal, Barnave jealous, Robespierre fanatic, the Jacobin Club bloodthirsty, the National Guard selfish, La Fayette a waverer, the government a nullity. No one desired the Revolution but for his own purpose, and according to his own scheme; and it must have been wrecked on these shoals a hundred times, if there were not in human crises something even stronger than the men who appear to guide them—the will of the event itself.

The Revolution in all its comprehensive bearings was not understood at that period by any one except, perchance, Robespierre and the thorough going democrats. The King viewed it only as a vast reform, the Duc d'Orleans as a great faction, Mirabeau but in its political point of view, La Fayette only in its constitutional aspect, the Jacobins as a vengeance, the mob as the abasing of the higher orders, the nation as a display of patriotism. None ventured as yet to contemplate its ultimate consummation.

All was thus blind, except the Revolution itself. The virtue of the Revolution was in the idea which forced these men on to accomplish it, and not in those who actually accomplished it; all its instruments were vitiated, corrupt, or personal; but the idea was pure, incorruptible, divine. The vices, passions, selfishness of men were inevitably doomed to produce in the coming crises those shocks, those violences, those perversities, and those crimes which are to human passions what consequences are to principles.

If each of the parties or men, mixed up from the first day with these great events had taken their virtue, instead of their impulses as the rule of their actions, all these disasters which eventually crushed them, would have been saved to them and to their country. If the king had been firm and sagacious, if the clergy had been free from a longing for things temporal, and if the aristocracy had been good; if the people had been moderate, if Mirabeau had been honest, if La Fayette had been decided, if Robespierre had been humane, the Revolution would have progressed, majestic and calm as a heavenly thought, through France, and thence through Europe; and it would have been installed like a philosophy in facts, in laws, and in creeds. But it was otherwise decreed. The holiest most just and virtuous thought, when it passes through the medium of imperfect humanity, comes out in rags and in blood. Those very persons who conceived it, no longer recognise, disavow it. Yet it is not permitted, even to crime, to degrade the truth, that survives all, even its victims. The blood which sullies men does not stain its idea; and despite the selfishness which debases it, the infamies which trammel it, the crimes which pollute it, the blood-stained Revolution purifies itself, feels its own worth, triumphs, and will triumph.

30. CARLYLE: HISTORY OF FRIEDRICH II OF PRUSSIA

Thomas Carlyle (1795-1881), son of a Scottish farmer, became one of the most celebrated literary figures of his century. Educated at Edinburgh University, he first intended to be a minister, then a lawyer. Instead, he developed an interest in German literature, and began his career as an independent writer by translating several of the works of Goethe and Schiller, and with articles on German literature. His first historical work, on the French Revolution, was published in 1837 and established his reputation.

An extreme individualist, whose pronounced views on a variety of subjects seldom coincided for long with those of his contemporaries, occasionally morose and always a hypochondriac, Carlyle nevertheless was admired and befriended by such diverse figures as John Stuart Mill, Ralph Waldo Emerson, Giuseppe Mazzini, Charles Dickens, Lord Tennyson, and William Thackeray. His prodigious literary production included fiction, literary and political commentary, and several historical works, notably an account of the French Revolution, a life of Cromwell, and the *History of Friedrich II of Prussia,* his most ambitious endeavor in this field. Based on considerable primary research, it was begun in 1851 and furthered during two visits to Germany in 1852—Carlyle's first journey abroad—and in 1858. The first chapters were published in 1857; the final volume appeared in 1865. The work was acclaimed in Germany as well as in Britain. It was Carlyle's last major literary success. Full of honors, but in declining health and increasingly pessimistic about and alienated from his age, he spent the final years of his life in semi-seclusion.

The following passages, from the first and final chapters of the *History of Friedrich II of Prussia,* strikingly illustrate Carlyle's approach, idiosyncrasies, and prejudices. The spirit of Romanticism is exemplified in the grandeur, sweep, and individuality of Carlyle's style, which disregards all accepted rules and models, no less than in the theme of the work: The Great Man who, like Samson, upsets the Philistines and their puny world, who does not conform to the accepted rules and standards, and who triumphs over the odds. Carlyle explicitly states Romanticism's antipathy to the spirit of the eighteenth century, which is implicit throughout the work.

1. Friedrich then, and Friedrich now.

This was a man of infinite mark to his contemporaries; who had witnessed surprising feats from him in the world; very questionable notions and ways, which he had contrived to maintain against the world and its criticisms. As an original man has always to do; much more an original ruler of men. The world, in fact, had tried hard to put him down, as it does, unconsciously or consciously, with all such; and after the most conscious exertions, and at one time a dead-lift spasm of all its energies for Seven Years, had not been able. Principalities and powers, Imperial, Royal, Czarish, Papal, enemies innumerable as the sea-sand, had risen against him, only one helper left among the world's Potentates (and that one only while there should be help rendered in return); and he led them all such a dance as had astonished mankind and them.

No wonder they thought him worthy of notice. Every original man of any magnitude is;—nay, in the longrun, who or what else is? But how much more if your original man was a king over men; whose movements were polar, and carried from day to day those of the world along with them. The Samson Agonistes,—were his life passed like that of Samuel Johnson in dirty garrets, and the produce of it only some bits of written paper,—the Agonistes, and how he will comport himself in the Philistine mill; this is always a spectacle of truly epic and tragic nature. The rather, if your Samson, royal or other, is not yet blinded or subdued to the wheel; much more if he vanquish his enemies, *not* by suicidal methods, but march out at last flourishing his miraculous fighting implement, and leaving their mill and them in quite ruinous circumstances. As this King Friedrich fairly managed to do.

For he left the world all bankrupt, we may say; fallen into bottomless abysses of destruction; he still in a paying condition, and with footing capable to carry his affairs and him. When he died, in 1786, the enormous Phenomenon since called FRENCH REVOLUTION was already growling audibly in the depths of the world; meteoric-electric coruscations heralding it, all round the horizon. Strange enough to note, one of Friedrich's last visitors was Gabriel Honoré Riquetti, Comte de Mirabeau. These two saw one another; twice, for half-an-hour each time. The last of the old Gods and the first of the modern Titans;—before Pelion leapt on Ossa; and the foul Earth taking fire at last, its vile mephitic elements went up in volcanic thunder. This also is one of the peculiarities of Friedrich, that he is hitherto the last of the Kings; that he ushers in the French Revolution, and closes an Epoch of World-History. Finishing off forever the trade of King, think many; who have grown profoundly dark as to Kingship and him.

2. Eighteenth Century

One of the grand difficulties in a History of Friedrich is, all along, this same, That he lived in a Century which has no History and can have little or none. A Century so opulent in accumulated falsities,—sad opulence descending on it by inheritance, always at compound interest, and always largely increased by fresh acquirement on such immensity of standing capital;—opulent in that bad way as never Century before was! Which had no longer the consciousness of being false, so false had it grown; and was so steeped in falsity, and impregnated with it to the very bone, that—in fact the measure of the thing was full, and a French Revolution had to end it. To maintain much veracity in such an element, especially for a king, was no doubt doubly remarkable. But now, How extricate the man from his Century? How show the man, who is a Reality worthy of being seen, and yet keep his Century, as a Hypocrisy worthy of being hidden and forgotten, in the due abeyance?

To resuscitate the Eighteenth Century, or call into men's view, beyond what is necessary, the poor and sordid personages and transactions of an epoch so related to us, can be no purpose of mine on this occasion. The Eighteenth Century, it is well known, does not figure to me as a lovely one; needing to be kept in mind, or spoken of unnecessarily. To me the Eighteenth Century has nothing grand in it, except that grand universal Suicide, named French Revolution, by which it terminated its otherwise most worthless existence with at least one worthy act;—setting fire to its old home and self; and going up in flames and volcanic explosions, in a truly memorable and important manner. A very fit termination, as I thankfully feel, for such a Century. Century spendthrift, fraudulent-bankrupt; gone at length utterly insolvent, without real *money* of performance in its pocket, and the shops declining to take hypocrisies and speciosities any farther:—what could the poor Century do, but at length admit, "Well, it is so. I am a swindler-century, and have long been; having learned the trick of it from my father and grandfather; knowing hardly any trade but that in false bills, which I thought foolishly might last forever, and still bring at least beef and pudding to the favoured of mankind. And behold it ends; and I am a detected swindler, and have nothing even to eat. What remains but that I blow my brains out, and do at length one true action?" Which the poor Century did; many thanks to it, in the circumstances.

For there was need once more of a Divine Revelation to the torpid, frivolous children of men, if they were not to sink altogether into the ape condition. And in that whirlwind of the Universe,—lights obliterated, and the torn wrecks of Earth and Hell hurled aloft into the Empyrean; black whirlwind, which made even apes serious, and drove most of them mad,—there was, to men, a voice audible; voice from the heart of things once more, as if to say: "Lying is not permitted in this Universe. The wages of lying, you behold, are death. Lying means damnation in this Universe; and Beelzebub, never so elaborately decked in crowns and mitres, is *not* God!" This was a revelation truly to be named of the Eternal, in our poor Eighteenth Century; and has greatly altered the complexion of said Century to the Historian ever since. . . .

—"And yet it is the Century of our own Grandfathers?" cries the reader. Yes, reader; truly. It is the ground out of which we ourselves have sprung; whereon now we have our immediate footing, and first of all strike down our roots for nourishment:—and, alas, in large sections of the practical world,`it (what we specially mean by *it*) still continues flourishing all round us! To forget it quite is not yet possible, nor would be profitable. What to do with it, and its forgotten fooleries and 'Histories,' worthy only of forgetting?—Well: so much of it as by nature *adheres;* what of it cannot be disengaged from our Hero and his operations: approximately so much, and no more! Let that be our bargain in regard to it.

The Death of Friedrick

Tuesday, August 15th, 1786, Contrary to all wont, the King did not awaken till 11 o'clock. On first looking up, he seemed in a confused state, but soon recovered himself; called in his Generals and Secretaries, who had been in waiting so long, and gave, with his old precision, the Orders wanted,—one to Rohdich, Commandant of Potsdam, about a Review of the troops there next day; Order minutely perfect, in knowledge of the ground, in foresight of what and how the evolutions were to be; which was accordingly performed on the morrow. The Cabinet work he went through with the like possession of himself, giving, on every point, his Three Clerks their directions, in a weak voice, yet with the old power of spirit,—dictated to one of them, among other things, an 'Instruction' for some Ambassador just leaving; 'four quarto pages, which,' says Herzberg, 'would have done honour to the most experienced Minister;' and, in the evening, he signed his Missives as usual. This evening still,—but—no evening more. We are now at the last scene of all, which ends this strange eventful History.

Wednesday morning, General-Adjutants, Secretaries, Commandant, were there at their old hours; but word came out, "Secretaries are to wait:" King is in a kind of sleep, of stertorous ominous character, as if it were the death-sleep;

seems not to recollect himself, when he does at intervals open his eyes. After hours of this, on a ray of consciousness, the King bethought him of Rohdich, the Commandant; tried to give Rohdich the Parole as usual; tried twice, perhaps three times; but found he could not speak;—and with a glance of sorrow, which seemed to say, "It is impossible, then!" turned his head, and sank back into the corner of his chair. Rohdich burst into tears: the King again lay slumberous;—the rattle of death beginning soon after, which lasted at intervals all day. Selle, in Berlin, was sent for by express; he arrived about 3 of the afternoon: King seemed a little more conscious, knew those about him, 'his face red rather than pale, in his eyes 'still something of their old fire.' Towards evening the feverishness abated (to Selle, I suppose, a fatal symptom); the King fell into a soft sleep, with warm perspiration; but, on awakening, complained of cold, repeatedly of cold, demanding wrappage after wrappage ('*Kissen,*' soft *quilt* of the old fashion);—and on examining feet and legs, one of the Doctors made signs that they were in fact cold, up nearly to the knee. "What said he of the feet?" murmured the King some time afterwards, the Doctor having now stepped out of sight. "Much the same as before," answered some attendant. The King shook his head, incredulous.

He drank once, grasping the goblet with both hands, a draught of fennel-water, his customary drink; and seemed relieved by it;—his last refection in this world. Towards 9 in the evening, there had come on a continual short cough, and a rattling in the breast, breath more and more difficult. Why continue? Friedrich is making exit, on the common terms; you may hear the curtain rustling down. For most part he was unconscious, never more than half-conscous. As the wall-clock above his head struck 11, he asked: "What o'clock?" "Eleven," answered they. "At 4," murmured he, "I will rise." One of his dogs sat on its stool near him; about midnight he noticed it shivering for cold: "Throw a quilt over it," said or beckoned he; that, I think, was his last completely-conscious utterance. Afterwards, in a severe choking fit, getting at last rid of the phlegm, he said. "*La montagne est passée, nous irons mieux,* We are over the hill, we shall go better now."

Attendants, Herzberg, Selle and one or two others, were in the outer room; none in Friedrich's but Strützki, his Kammerhussar, one of Three who are his sole valets and nurses; a faithful ingenious man, as they all seem to be, and excellently chosen for the object. Strützki, to save the King from hustling down, as he always did, into the corner of his chair, where, with neck and chest bent forward, breathing was impossible,—at last took the King on his knee; kneeling on the ground with his other knee for the purpose,—King's right arm round

Strützki's neck, Strützki's left arm round the King's back, and supporting his other shoulder; in which posture the faithful creature, for above two hours, sat motionless, till the end came. Within doors, all is silence, except this breathing; around it the dark earth silent, above it the silent stars. At 20 minutes past 2, the breathing paused,—wavered; ceased. Friedrich's Life-battle is fought out; instead of suffering and sore labour, here is now rest. Thursday morning, 17th August 1786, at the dark hour just named. On the 31st of May last, this King had reigned 46 years. 'He has lived,' counts Rödenbeck, '74 years, 6 months and 24 days.'

His death seems very stern and lonely;—a man of such affectionate feelings, too; "a man with more sensibility than other men!" But so had his whole life been, stern and lonely; such the severe law laid on him. Nor was it inappropriate that he found his death in that poor Silesian Review; punctually doing, as usual, the work that had come in hand. Nor that he died now, rather than a few years later. In these final days of his, we have transiently noticed Arch-Cardinal de Rohan, Arch-Quack Cagliostro, and a most select Company of Person and of Actions, like an Elixir of the Nether World, miraculously emerging into daylight; and all Paris, and by degrees all Europe, getting loud with the *Diamond-Necklace* History. And to eyes of deeper speculation,—World-Poet Goethe's, for instance,—it is becoming evident that Chaos is again big. As has not she proved to be, and is still proving, in the most teeming way! Better for a Royal Hero, fallen old and feeble, to be hidden from such things.

Friedrich was not buried at Sans-Souci, in the Tomb which he had built for himself; why not, nobody clearly says. By his own express will, there was no embalming. Two Regiment-surgeons washed the Corpse, decently prepared it for interment: 'at 8 that same evening, Friedrich's Body, dressed in the uniform of the First Battalion of Guards, and laid in its coffin, was borne to Potsdam, in a hearse of eight horses, twelve Non-commissioned Officers of the Guard escorting. All Potsdam was in the streets; the soldiers, of their own accord, formed rank, and followed the hearse; many a rugged face unable to restrain tears: for the rest, universal silence as of midnight, nothing audible among the people but here and there a sob, and the murmur, *"Ach, der gute König!"*

'All next day, the Body lay in state in the Palace; thousands crowding, from Berlin and the other environs, to see that face for the last time. Wasted, worn; but beautiful in death, with the thin gray hair parted into locks, and slightly powdered. And at 8 in the evening' (Friday 18th), 'he was borne to the Garnison-Kirche of Potsdam; and laid beside his Father, in the vault behind the Pulpit there,'—where the two Coffins are still to be seen.

I define him to myself as hitherto the Last of the Kings;—when the Next will be, is a very long question! But it seems to me as if Nations, probably all Nations, by and by, in their despair,—blinded, swallowed like Jonah, in such a whale's-belly of things brutish, waste, abominable (for is not Anarchy, or the Rule of what is Baser over what is Nobler, the one life's-misery worth complaining of, and, in fact, the abomination of abominations, springing from and producing all others whatsoever?)—as if the Nations universally, and England too if it hold on, may more and more bethink themselves of such a Man and his Function and Performance, with feelings far other than are possible at present. Meanwhile, all I had to say of him is finished: that too, it seems, was a bit of work appointed to be done. Adieu, good readers; bad also, adieu.

SOURCE NOTES

1. From Jules Michelet, *Historical View of the French Revolution* (London: 1864), pp. 1-3, 73-74, 76-78.
2. From Alphonse M. L. de Lamartine, *History of the Girondins* (London: 1856), pp. 10-12, 39-41.
3. From Thomas Carlyle, *History of Friedrich II of Prussia, called Frederick the Great* (London: 1862, 1865), vol. I, pp. 7-8, 10-13; vol. II, pp. 693-698.

12.
"SCIENTIFIC" HISTORY

No society in history had so much reason for self-confident optimism as the Western world in the 19th century. Increasingly the forces of nature were being harnessed for the benefit of man, plague and famine overcome, the evils of slavery, cruel punishment, and mass ignorance abolished. Even war was subjected to the limitations of law as a new concern for humanity, born out of the spirit of the Enlightenment, fully blossomed. More people than ever before were freed from the deadening restrictions of environment and tradition, could exercise options, and participate to a previously unknown degree in their states and societies. Even the age-old iron law that had dictated poverty for the great majority in all times and places could now be questioned, as unheard-of wealth was brought into being by science and its technological applications.

The belief in the potential of science as a liberating force was central to the spirit of the age. Naturally it also found its expression in historiography. Along with the Romantic impulse, it can be seen as one of the roots of the modern view of history: The spirit of Romanticism led men to investigate the past for its own sake, for its treasures of human individuality, wisdom, color, and concrete experience, not merely to ransack history for evidence supporting particular views of the nature and destiny of mankind. The 19th century's optimistic faith in science as an unfailing guide to ever greater comprehension of all aspects of reality and, indeed, to ultimate truth, influenced the writing of history equally profoundly.

We have seen that this was already true of the historians of the 17th and 18th centuries. But the triumphs of early modern science were achieved primarily in the fields of physics and mathematics, and had thus influenced the general intellectual trends of that age towards definitions of reality in terms of static, abstract universal laws. 19th-century scientific

191

achievements, especially the work of Sir Charles Lyell in geology and of Lamarck and Darwin in biology, made time and change crucial dimensions of the scientific world view. The physical structure of the Earth and the characteristics of its inhabitants came to be described and explained in terms of evolution: 19th-century science was itself historically oriented.

This fact, and the growing prestige of and faith in science, influenced historiography in two major ways. In the first place, historians sought to imitate the natural scientists by turning their pursuit into a "discipline," with rigorous methodological rules analogous to those of science. This meant, first of all, the marshaling of available data: Hence the enormous activity devoted by 19th century historians to the collecting, organizing, and publishing of vast bodies of historical source material. Secondly, the new discipline insisted that these sources must be examined critically by trained experts as to their genuineness, dependability, and inherent bias; every historical account, moreover, must ideally be based on *all* the evidence available. These rules led to the development of a new manner of historical writing, the monograph. Far from the poetic flights and grand generalizations of earlier history, this form calls for the meticulous detailed investigation of all aspects of a limited period, event, or historical problem. The underlying assumption of the new breed of historical specialists was that from the data, and their organization and classification in monographic detail work, there might eventually be induced general laws of history—just as the theory of evolution was based on the work of countless collectors and classifiers of biological specimens.

Some historians, represented here by Henry Buckle, went beyond this conception of scientific history, to the attempt to demonstrate a direct connection between the historical development of human societies and their natural environment. In this view the method and laws of history were not only analogous, but reducible to those of natural science. Human action, no less than the behavior of minerals, vegetables, and animals, were seen as ultimately determined by the laws of nature.

The philosophy and historical view of Marxism also sprang from these intellectual tendencies: Materialism, faith in science, and history viewed as evolutionary process. Marx and Engels taught that human ideas and motivations, and hence historical actions, conflicts, and forms of social organization, are determined by economic factors, themselves shaped by the natural environment. Human activity in turn modifies this environment in an unending dialectical process, and thus there is change and progress toward "higher" forms of social organization and human consciousness. Marxist historians conceive of their task as the elucidation and illustration of the laws governing this process, in their own version of scientific history.

31. RANKE: HISTORY OF THE POPES
IN THE 16TH AND 17TH CENTURIES

Leopold von Ranke (1795-1886), more than anyone else, was responsible for the transformation of history from a branch of literature into an autonomous "scientific" discipline. As Professor of History at the University of Berlin (1825-1872) he initiated the methodical training of professional historians through the device of the historical seminar, which came to be imitated at universities throughout the world. He was instrumental in the founding of the Historical Commission of the Bavarian Academy of Sciences, and in the organization of such major projects as that Commission's massive editions of historical sources and the General German Biography series. An immensely prolific researcher and writer, Ranke produced political histories, biographies, and monographic studies spanning the history of Europe from the Renaissance to his century, which in the complete edition of his works encompass fifty-four volumes. His immense stature in the new historical profession was reflected in the remark of his contemporary, the British historian Lord Acton, who referred to Ranke as "almost the Columbus of modern history."

Ranke's famous dictum that the task of the historian is to record history "as it really happened" (*"wie es eigentlich gewesen"*) has been quoted *ad nauseam,* and is frequently misunderstood. Ranke was under no illusion that history could ever be value-free, and written from a neutral point of view, divorced from the historian's own beliefs and the concerns of his present. In the famous quote he merely cautions that the conscientious historian must be governed in his work by the facts, all the facts available to him, and must realize that the past was just as real to the people living then as our present is to us. "Each age," Ranke also said, "is immediate unto God": The lives, achievements, and struggles of the past must be described by the historian in their proper context, not in terms of their "end result," the conditions, values, and motivations of our own day.

Ranke, the prophet of "scientific history" in the methodological sense, was himself rooted in the intellectual soil of Romanticism, and he was a Christian. With most of the Romantics he shared a high view of the role of the individual as a shaper of history. His works focus primarily on the deeds of rulers and great men. Ranke's Christian morality is manifest in his belief in moral responsibility: Understanding all, to him, was not equivalent to excusing all.

Ranke moreover believed that a divine purpose manifested itself in the world of history. His personal relations with the philosopher G.W.F. Hegel, his great contemporary at the University of Berlin, were cool. The historian was suspicious of Hegel's speculative system. But Ranke, like Hegel, felt that there moved in history, underlying all human actions, a current of transcendant purpose. To Hegel, this was the emanation of the World Spirit; to Ranke, the will of God. In his eighties, deaf and blind, he began a vast universal history which, he hoped, would illustrate the direction of that current.

The following selection is taken from the first and second chapters of his *History of the Popes in the 16th and 17th Centuries*. Based on years of research in the archives of Italy and Vienna, and first published between 1834 and 1837, it established Ranke's towering reputation and remains perhaps his most impressive work.

Contrasts Between the Fourteenth and Fifteenth Centuries

There are periods in the history of the world which excite in us a peculiar and anxious curiosity to search into the plans of the divine government, to investigate the phases of the education of the human race.

However defective be the civilisation we have delineated, it was necessary to the complete naturalisation of Christianity in the west. It was no light thing to subdue the haughty spirits of the north, the nations under the dominion of ancestral superstitions, to the ideas of Christianity. It was necessary that the religious element should predominate for a time, in order that it might gain fast hold on the German mind. By this, at the same time, was effected the intimate blending of the Roman and Germanic elements. There is a community among the nations of modern times which has always been regarded as the main basis of the general civilisation; a community in church and state, in manners, customs, and literature. In order to produce this it was necessary that the western nations should, for a time, form, as it were, a single state, temporal and spiritual.

But this too was only one stage in the great progess of things. As soon as the change was accomplished, new consequences appeared.

The commencement of a new epoch was announced by the simultaneous and almost universal rise of national languages. With slow but unbroken course they forced their way into all the various branches of intellectual activity; the peculiar idiom of the church receded before them step by step. Universality gave place to a new and nobler kind of individuality. Hitherto the ecclesiastical element had overpowered all national peculiarities: under a new character and aspect, but once more distinct, they now entered upon a new career.

It seems as though all human designs and actions were subject to the silent and often imperceptible, but mighty and resistless march of events. The previous state of the world had been favourable to the papal domination; that of the moment we are considering was directly hostile to it. The nations no longer stood in their former need of the impulse given by the ecclesiastical power; they arose in opposition to it. They felt their own capacity for independence.

It is worth while to recall to our recollection the more important events in which this tendency manifested itself.

It was, as is well known, the French who made the first decisive stand against the pretensions of the popes. The nation unanimously resisted the bulls of excommunication issued by Boniface VIII. In several hundred acts of adhesion, all the popular authorities expressed their assent to the measures of Philip the Fair.

The Germans followed. When the popes attacked the empire with their old animosity, although it had lost much of its former importance, the electors, determined to secure it from foreign influence, assembled on the banks of the Rhine, in the field of Rense, to deliberate in their chairs of stone on some common measure for the maintenance "of the honour and dignity of the empire."

Their purpose was to establish its independence against all aggressions of the popes, by a solemn resolution. Shortly after, this was simultaneously proclaimed, with all due forms, by the whole body of potentates; emperor, princes, and electors. They made a common stand against the principles of papal policy.

Nor did England long remain behind. Nowhere had the popes enjoyed greater influence, nor disposed more arbitrarily of benefices; till at length, when Edward III would no longer pay the tribute which his predecessors had engaged to pay, his parliament united with him and promised to support him in his resistance. The king took measures to prevent any further encroachments of the papal power.

We see one nation after another awaken to a consciousness of its own independence and unity.

The civil power will no longer acknowledge any higher authority. The popes no longer find allies in the middle classes; their interference is resolutely repelled by princes and legislative bodies.

It happened at the same time that the papacy itself fell into a weakness and confusion which enabled the civil power, hitherto only acting on the defensive, to retaliate aggressions.

Schism broke out. We must mark its consequences. For a long time it rested with princes to attach themselves, according to their political convenience, to this or that pope: the spiritual power found within itself no means of putting an end to the division; the secular power alone could do this. When a council assembled for this purpose in Constance the members no longer voted, as formerly, ly, by individuals, but by the four nations. Each nation was allowed to hold preliminary meetings to deliberate on the vote it was to give. They deposed a pope by common consent: the newly elected pontiff was compelled to sign with them, severally, concordats, which were, at least by the precedent they afforded, very important. During the council of Basle and the new schism, some states remained neutral; and this second division in the church could only be healed by the immediate intervention of the princes. Nothing could possibly have a stronger tendency to increase the preponderance of the secular power, and the independence of individual states.

And now the pope was once more the object of the highest reverence and of universal obedience. The emperor still continued to lead his palfrey. There were bishops, not only in Hungary but in Germany, who subscribed themselves, ''by the grace of the apostolic see.'' In the north the Peter's penny was regularly levied. At the jubilee of the year 1450, countless pilgrims from all lands sought the steps of the apostles. An eye-witness describes them as coming like swarms of bees or flights of migratory birds.

Yet, spite of all these appearances, the old relations no longer existed. In proof of this we need only call to mind the fervent zeal which characterised the early crusades, and compare it with the lukewarmness with which in the fifteenth century, every exhortation to a general combined resistance to the Turks was received. How much more urgent was it to defend their own borders against a danger which was imminent on every side, than to know that the holy sepulchre was in Christian hands! Æneas Sylvius in the diet, and the Minorite Capistrano in the marketplaces of cities, used all their eloquence, and we are told much of the impression they made; but we do not find that anybody took up arms in consequence. What efforts were made by the popes! One fitted out a fleet; another, Pius II. (the same Æneas Sylvius), repaired, feeble and sick as he was, to the port where the princes most immediately menaced by the Turks—if no others—were to meet. He insisted on being there, ''that he might, like Moses, raise his hands to God during the battle, as he alone had authority to do.'' But neither exhortations, nor prayers, nor examples, could move his contemporaries. The youthful ardour of chivalrous Christianity was extinct; it was not in the power of any pope to rekindle it.

Other interests agitated the world. It was the period at which the kingdoms of Europe acquired compactness and solidity. The central power succeeded in subduing the factions which had threatened the security of the throne, and in uniting all classes of its subjects in fresh bonds of obedience. The papacy, which aspired to govern all and to interfere with all, soon came also to be regarded in a political point of view. The pretensions of kings were infinitely higher than they had been at any preceding period. It is common to represent the papal authority as nearly unlimited up to the time of the reformation; but the fact is, that the civil governments had possessed themselves of no small share of ecclesiastical rights and privileges as early as the beginning of the sixteenth, or even the latter part of the fifteenth century. . . .

In short, throughout all Christendom, in the south as well as in the north, a general struggle was made to curtail the rights of the pope. It was more especially to a share of the ecclesiastical revenues and the nomination to ecclesiastical benefices and offices, that the several governments laid claim. The popes made no serious resistance. They tried to preserve all they could; on other points they gave way. Lorenzo de' Medici, speaking of Ferdinand king of Naples, and of a dispute which he had with the see of Rome, says, "He will make no difficulty about promising; as to the fulfilment of his promises, he will experience the indulgence at last which all popes have had for all kings." For this spirit of opposition had found its way even into Italy. We are informed by Lorenzo de' Medici, that in this he followed the example of greater potentates; he obeyed the pope's commands just so far as he had a mind, and no further.

It were an error to see in these facts only manifestations of a contemporaneous caprice and wilfulness. The ecclesiastical spirit had ceased to pervade and direct the whole existence of the nations of Europe, as it had done in earlier times.

The development of national character and national institutions, the progress of civilisation, now exercised a mighty and conspicuous influence. The relation between the spiritual and temporal powers necessarily underwent a complete revolution; nor was the change in the popes themselves less remarkable.

Extension of the States of the Church

Whatever may be the opinion we form of the popes of the earlier ages of the church, we must admit that they had always great interests in view; the guardianship of an oppressed religion, the conflict with paganism, the diffusion of Christianity over the nations of the North, the foundation of an independent hierarchical power. The ability to conceive, to will and to accomplish some great object, is among the qualities which confer the greatest dignity on man; and this it was that sustained the popes in their lofty course. But these tendencies had passed away with the times to which they belonged. Schism was at an end; the attempt to stir men to a general rising against the Turks was evidently hopeless. It followed that the head of the church pursued the interests of his temporal sovereignty with greater ardour and pertinacity than heretofore, and devoted all his activity to their advancement.

For some time things had strongly tended this way. "Formerly," said an orator in the council of Basle, "I was of opinion that it would be well to separate the temporal entirely from the spiritual power; but I have learned that virtue without force is ludicrous—that the pope of Rome, without the hereditary possessions of the Church, is only the servant of kings and princes." This orator, who had sufficient influence in the council to determine the election of Pope Felix, does not think it so much amiss that a pope should have sons to take his part against tyrants.

This matter was, at a later period, viewed in a different light in Italy. It was thought in the regular order of things that a pope should promote and provide for his family; people would have despised one who did not. "Others," writes Lorenzo de' Medici to Innocent VIII., "have not so long deferred their endeavour to be popes, and have troubled themselves little about the decorum and modesty which your holiness has for so long a time observed. Your holiness is now not only excused in the sight of God and man, but men may perhaps even censure this reserved demeanour, and ascribe it to other motives. My zeal and duty render it a matter of conscience with me to remind your holiness that no man is immortal; that a pope is of the importance which he chooses to give himself; he cannot make his dignity hereditary; the honours and the benefits he confers on those belonging to him are all that he can call his own." Such was the advice of him who was regarded as the wisest man in Italy. It is true, he had an interest in the matter, for his daughter was married to a son of the pope. But he would never have ventured to express himself so unreservedly, had not these views been notoriously prevalent among the higher classes.

Two facts here engage our attention, between which there exists a profound but not obvious connexion; the governments of Europe were stripping the pope of a portion of his privileges, while at the same time the latter began to occupy himself exclusively with worldly concerns. He felt himself, above all, an Italian prince. It was not long since the Florentines had defeated their neighbours, and the Medici had established their power over both. The power of the Sforzas in Milan, of the house of Aragon in Naples, of the Venetians in Lombardy, had all been acquired and established within the memory of man. Might not the pope reasonably hope to found, in the domains which were regarded as the hereditary property of the Church, but which were actually governed by a number of independent rulers, a still mightier personal domination?

The first who, with deliberate purpose and permanent effect, acted upon this idea was Sixtus IV. Alexander VI. pursued it with the utmost vigour and with singular success. Julius II. gave it an unexpected turn, which it retained.

Sixtus IV. (1471-1484) conceived the plan of founding a principality for his nephew Girolamo Riario in the rich and beautiful plains of Romagna. The other powers of Italy were already contending for possession, or for ascendancy, in these territories, and, if there was any question of right, the pope had manifestly a better right than any other. But he was not nearly their equal in force, or in the resources of war. He was restrained by no scruple from rendering his spiritual power (elevated by its nature and purpose above all earthly interests) subservient to his worldly views, or from debasing it by a mixture with those temporary intrigues in which his ambition had involved him. The Medici being peculiarly in his way, he took part in the Florentine troubles; and, as is notorious, brought upon himself the suspicion of being privy to the conspiracy of the Pazzi, and to the assassination which they perpetrated on the steps of the altar of the cathedral; the suspicion that he, the father of the faithful, was an accomplice of such acts!

When the Venetians ceased to favour the schemes of his nephew, as they had done for a considerable time, the pope was not satisfied with deserting them in a war into which he himself had driven them; he went so far as to excommunicate them for persisting in it. He acted with no less violence in Rome: he persecuted the opponents of Riario, the Colonnas, with savage ferocity: he seized Marino from them; he caused the prothonotary Colonna to be attacked, arrested, and executed in his own house. The mother of Colonna came to San Celso in Banchi, where the body lay—she lifted the severed head by the hair, and cried, "Behold the head of my son! Such is the faith of the pope. He promised that if we would give up Marino to him, he would set my son at liberty; he has Marino: and my son is in our hands—but dead! Behold, thus does the pope keep his word!"

So much was necessary to enable Sixtus IV. to obtain the victory over his enemies, at home and abroad, He succeeded in making his nephew lord of Imola and Forli; but it is certain that if his temporal dignity was much augmented, his spiritual suffered infinitely more. An attempt was made to assemble a council against him.

Meanwhile Sixtus was destined soon to be far outdone. Alexander VI. ascended the papal throne shortly after him (1492). . . .

32. BUCKLE: HISTORY OF CIVILIZATION IN ENGLAND

Henry Thomas Buckle (1821-1862) was a somewhat eccentric, self-educated genius. Among his attainments were mastery of nineteen languages and of chess at the championship level. Politically he was a radical of the school of John Stuart Mill, religiously a "free-thinker." His fame rests solely on the *History of Civilization in England* of which, due to Buckle's early death, only the first two introductory volumes were ever completed. Published in 1857 and 1861, they achieved instant success, assailed by traditionalists and applauded by believers in the faith of Science. Buckle's was the first major attempt to write a history from the viewpoint of Positivist materialism. This philosophy, whose outstanding proponent was Auguste Comte, reached the height of its influence and popularity in the 1850's and 60's. As illustrated in the following selections, Buckle's view of history was predicated upon a rigid belief in material determinism: Geography, meteorology, biology, and psychology are the sciences that basically explain all historical development. Buckle planned and wrote most of his work before the appearance of Charles Darwin's *Origin of the Species,* whose implications might have provided him with a more systematic scientific framework. Later historians of his persuasion were to seek the motive force of history in the biological process of selection through competition for survival.

The "analytical table of contents" reproduced below indicates how systematically and relentlessly Buckle pursued his major theme: All history is explainable in terms of "general causes". The passage from the first chapter of his second volume illustrates the particular importance ascribed to the physical environment in shaping the values and character of nations.

Analytical Table of Contents.

CHAPTER I

**Outlines of the History of the Spanish Intellect from the Fifth
to the Middle of the Nineteenth Century.**

Chapter I

Outline of the History of the Spanish Intellect from the Fifth
to the Middle of the Nineteenth Century

In the preceding volume, I have endeavoured to establish four leading propositions, which, according to my view, are to be deemed the basis of the history of civilization. They are: 1st, That the progress of mankind depends on the success with which the laws of phenomena are investigated, and on the extent to which a knowledge of those laws is diffused. 2d, That before such investigation can begin, a spirit of scepticism must arise, which, at first aiding the investigation, is afterwards aided by it. 3d, That the discoveries thus made, increase the influence of intellectual truths, and diminish, relatively, not absolutely, the influence of moral truths; moral truths being more stationary than intellectual truths, and receiving fewer additions. 4th, That the great enemy of this movement, and therefore the great enemy of civilization, is the protective spirit; by which I mean the notion that society cannot prosper, unless the affairs of life are watched over and protected at nearly every turn by the state and the church; the state teaching men what they are to do, and the church teaching them what they are to believe. Such are the propositions which I hold to be the most essential for a right understanding of history, and which I have defended in the only two ways any proposition can be defended; namely, inductively and deductively. The inductive defence comprises a collection of historical and scientific facts, which suggest and authorize the conclusions drawn from them; while the deductive defence consists of a verification of those conclusions, by showing how they explain the history of different countries and their various fortunes. To the former, or inductive method of defence, I am at present unable to add any thing new; but the deductive defence I hope to strengthen considerably in this volume, and by its aid confirm not only the four cardinal propositions just stated, but also several minor propositions, which, though strictly speaking flowing from them, will require separate verification. According to the plan already sketched, the remaining part of the Introduction will contain an examination of the history of Spain, of Scotland, of Germany, and of the United States of America, with the object of elucidating principles on which the history of England supplies inadequate information. And as Spain is the country where what I conceive to be the fundamental conditions of national improvement have been most flagrantly violated, so also shall we find that it is the country where the penalty paid for the violation has been most heavy, and where, therefore, it is most instructive to ascertain how the prevalence of certain opinions causes the decay of the people among whom they predominate.

We have seen that the old tropical civilizations were accompanied by remarkable features which I have termed Aspects of Nature, and which, by inflaming the imagination, encouraged superstition, and prevented men from daring to analyze such threatening physical phenomena; in other words, prevented the creation of the physical sciences. Now, it is an interesting fact that, in these respects, no European country is so analogous to the tropics as Spain. No other part of Europe is so clearly designated by nature as the seat and refuge of superstition. Recurring to what has been already proved, it will be remembered that among the most important physical causes of superstition are famines, epidemics, earthquakes, and that general unhealthiness of climate, which, by shortening the average duration of life, increases the frequency and earnestness with which supernatural aid is invoked. These peculiarities, taken together, are more prominent in Spain than any where else in Europe; it will therefore be useful to give such a summary of them as will exhibit the mischievous effects they have produced in shaping the national character.

If we except the northern extremity of Spain, we may say that the two principal characteristics of the climate are heat and dryness, both of which are favoured by the extreme difficulty which nature has interposed in regard to irrigation. For, the rivers which intersect the land, run mostly in beds too deep to be made available for watering the soil, which consequently is, and always has been, remarkably arid. Owing to this, and the infrequency of rain, there is no European country as richly endowed in other respects, where droughts and therefore famines have been so frequent and serious. At the same time the vicissitudes of climate, particulary in the central parts, make Spain habitually unhealthy; and this general tendency being strengthened in the middle ages by the constant occurrence of famine, caused the ravages of pestilence to be unusually fatal. When we moreover add that in the Peninsula, including Portugal, earthquakes have been extremely disastrous, and have excited all those superstitious feelings which they naturally provoke, we may form some idea of the insecurity of life, and of the ease with which an artful and ambitious priesthood could turn such insecurity into an engine for the advancement of their own power.

Another feature of this singular country is the prevalence of a pastoral life, mainly caused by the difficulty of establishing regular habits of agricultural industry. In most parts of Spain, the climate renders it impossible for the labourer to work the whole of the day; and this forced interruption encourages among the people an irregularity and instability of purpose, which makes them choose the wandering avocations of a shepherd, rather than the more fixed pursuits of agriculture. And during the long and arduous war which they waged against their Mohammedan invaders, they were subject to such incessant surprises and forays on the part of the enemy, as to make it advisable that their means of subsistence should be easily removed; hence they preferred the produce of their flocks to that of their lands, and were shepherds instead of agriculturists, simply because by that means they would suffer less in case of an unfavourable issue. Even after the capture of Toledo, late in the eleventh century, the inhabitants of the frontier in Estramadura, La Mancha, and New Castile, were almost entirely herdsmen, and their cattle were pastured not in private meadows but in the open fields. All this increased the uncertainty of life, and strengthened that love of adventure, and that spirit of romance, which, at a later period, gave a tone to the popular literature. Under such circumstances, every thing grew precarious, restless, and unsettled; thought and inquiry were impossible; doubt was unknown; and the way was prepared for those superstitious habits, and for that deep-rooted and tenacious belief, which have always formed a principal feature in the history of the Spanish nation.

To what extent these circumstances would, if they stood by themselves, have affected the ultimate destiny of Spain, is a question hardly possible to answer; but there can be no doubt that their effects must always have been important, though, from the paucity of evidence, we are unable to measure them with precision. In regard, however, to the actual result, this point is of little moment, because a long chain of other and still more influential events became interwoven with those just mentioned, and, tending in precisely the same direction, produced a combination which nothing could resist, and from which we may trace with unerring certainty the steps by which the nation subsequently declined. The history of the causes of the degradation of Spain will indeed become too clear to be mistaken, if studied in reference to those general principles which I have enunciated, and which will themselves be confirmed by the light they throw on this instructive though melancholy subject.

After the subversion of the Roman Empire, the first leading fact in the history of Spain is the settlement of the Visigoths, and the establishment of their opinions in the Peninsula. They, as well as the Suevi, who immediately preceded them, were Arians, and Spain during a hundred and fifty years became the rallying point of that famous heresy, to which indeed most of the Gothic tribes then adhered. But, at the end of the fifth century, the Franks, on their conversion from Paganism, adopted the opposite and orthodox creed, and were encouraged by their clergy to make war upon their heretical neighbours. Clovis, who was then king of the Franks, was regarded by the church as the champion of the faith, in whose behalf he attacked the unbelieving Visigoths. His successors, moved by the same motives, pursued the same policy; and, during nearly a century, there was a war of opinions between France and Spain, by which the Visigothic empire was seriously endangered, and was more than once on the verge of dissolution. Hence, in Spain, a war for national independence became also a war for national religon, and an intimate alliance was formed between the Arian kings and the Arian clergy. The latter class were, in those ages of ignorance, sure to gain by such a compact, and they received considerable temporal advantages in return for the prayers which they offered up against the enemy, as also for the miracles which they occasionally performed. Thus early, a foundation was laid for the immense influence which the Spanish priesthood have possessed ever since, and which was strengthened by subsequent events. For, late in the sixth century, the Latin clergy converted their Visigothic masters, and the Spanish government, becoming orthodox, naturally conferred upon its teachers an authority equal to that wielded by the Arian hierarchy. Indeed, the rulers of Spain, grateful to those who had shown them the error of their ways, were willing rather to increase the power of the church than to diminish it. The clergy took advantage of this disposition; and the result was, that before the middle of the seventh century the spiritual classes possessed more influence in Spain than in any other part of Europe. The ecclesiastical synods became not only councils of the church, but also parliaments of the realm. At Toledo, which was then the capital of Spain, the power of the clergy was immense, and was so ostentatiously displayed, that in a council they held there in the year 633, we find the king literally prostrating himself on the ground before the bishops; and half a century later, the ecclesiastical historian mentions that this humiliating practice was repeated by another king, having become, he says, an established custom. That this was not a mere meaningless ceremony, is moreover evident from other and analogous facts. Exactly the same tendency is seen in their jurisprudence; since, by the Visigothic code, any layman, whether plaintiff or defendant, might insist on his cause being tried not by the temporal magistrate, but by the bishop of the diocese. Nay, even if both parties to the suit were agreed in preferring the civil tribunal, the bishop still retained the power of revoking the decision, if in his opinion it was incorrect; and it was his especial business to watch over the administration of justice, and to instruct the magistrates how to perform their duty. Another, and more painful proof of the ascendency of the clergy is that the laws against heretics were harsher in Spain than in any other country; the Jews in particular being persecuted with unrelenting rigour. Indeed, the desire of upholding the faith was strong enough to produce a formal declaration that no sovereign should be acknowledged, unless he promised to preserve its purity; the judges of the purity being of course the bishops themselves, to whose suffrage the king owed his throne.

Such were the circumstances which, in and before the seventh century, secured to the Spanish Church an influence unequalled in any other part of Europe. Early in the eighth century, an event occurred which apparently broke up and dispersed the hierarchy, but which, in reality, was extremely favourable to them. In 711 the Mohammedans sailed from Africa, landed in the south of Spain, and in the space of three years conquered the whole country, except the almost inaccessible regions of the north-west. The Spaniards, secure in their native mountains, soon recovered heart, rallied their forces, and began in their turn to assail the invaders. A desperate struggle ensued, which lasted nearly eight centuries, and in which, a second time in the history of Spain, a war for independence was also a war for religion; the contest between Arabian Infidels and Spanish Christians, succeeding that formerly carried on between the Trinitarians of France and the Arians of Spain. Slowly, and with infinite difficulty, the Christians fought their way. By the middle of the ninth century, they reached the line of the Douro. Before the close of the eleventh century, they conquered as far as the Tagus, and Toledo, their ancient capital, fell into their hands in 1085. Even then much remained to be done. In the south, the struggle assumed its deadliest form, and there it was prolonged with such obstinacy, that it was not until the capture of Malaga in 1487, and of Granada in 1492, that the Christian empire was re-established, and the old Spanish monarch finally restored.

The effect of all this on the Spanish character was most remarkable. During eight successive centuries, the whole country was engaged in a religious crusade; and those holy wars which other nations occasionally waged, were, in Spain, prolonged and continued for more than twenty generations. The object being not only to regain a territory, but also to re-establish a creed, it naturally happened that the expounders of that creed assumed a prominent and important position. In the camp, and in the council-chamber, the voice of ecclesiastics was heard and obeyed; for as the war aimed at the propagation of Christianity, it seemed right that her ministers should play a conspicuous part in a matter which particularly concerned them. The danger to which the country was exposed being moreover very imminent, those superstitious feelings were excited which danger is apt to provoke, and to which, as I have elsewhere shown, the tropical civilizations owed some of their leading peculiarities. Scarcely were the Spanish Christians driven from their homes and forced to take refuge in the north, when this great principle began to operate. In their mountainous retreat, they preserved a chest filled with relics of the saints, the possession of which they valued as their greatest security. This was to them a national standard, round which they rallied, and by the aid of which they gained miraculous victories over their Infidel opponents. Looking upon themselves as soldiers of the cross, their minds became habituated to supernatural considerations to an extent which we can now hardly believe, and which distinguished them in this respect from every other European nation. Their young men saw visions, and their old men dreamed dreams. Strange sights were vouchsafed to them from heaven; on the eve of the battle mysterious portents appeared; and it was observed, that whenever the Mohammedans violated the tomb of a Christian saint, thunder and lightning were sent to rebuke the misbelievers, and, if need be, to punish their audacious invasion.

Under circumstances like these, the clergy could not fail to extend their influence; or, we may rather say, the course of events extended it for them. The Spanish Christians, pent up for a considerable time in the mountains of Asturias, and deprived of their former resources, quickly degenerated, and soon lost the scanty civilization to which they had attained. Stripped of all their wealth, and confined to what was comparatively a barren region, they relapsed into barbarism, and remained, for at least a century, without arts, or commerce, or literature. As their ignorance increased, so also did their superstition; while this last, in its turn, strengthened the authority of their priests. The order of affairs, therefore, was very natural. The Mohammedan invasion made the Christians poor; poverty caused ignorance; ignorance caused credulity; and credulity, depriving men both of the power and of the desire to investigate for themselves, encouraged a reverential spirit, and confirmed those submissive habits, and that blind obedience to the Church, which form the leading and most unfortunate peculiarity of Spanish history.

From this it appears, that there were three ways in which the Mohammedan invasion strengthened the devotional feelings of the Spanish people. The first way was by promoting a long and obstinate religious war; the second was by the presence of constant and imminent dangers; and the third way was by the poverty, and therefore the ignorance, which it produced among the Christians.

33. ENGELS: THE PEASANTS' WAR IN GERMANY

Friedrich Engels (1820-1895) was born in Barmen, Germany, the son of a textile manufacturer. After completing secondary school, he went to Britain in 1842, to manage family business interests in Manchester. Most of the rest of his life was spent in England. Confronted with the social dislocation and misery produced by the early industrial revolution, he wrote *The Condition of the Working Class in England in 1844,* a meticulously documented indictment of early capitalism and its results. In 1844 he met Karl Marx in Brussels, beginning an association that is one of history's greatest and most significant examples of cooperation between two individuals. Engels virtually devoted his life to Marx, assisting him financially, aiding and advising him in his literary and organizational work, editing and publishing his writings, and continuing to expound and interpret his doctrines after Marx's death in 1883.

Nevertheless, "Marx and Engels" were not Siamese twins. While fundamentally in agreement with Marx's thought and objectives, and yielding first place to him in their partnership, Engels' background, personality, temperament, and intellectual bent set individual accents on his own work. Marx's world outlook had been profoundly shaped by Hegelian philosophy during his university years. Even after he "turned Hegel upside down" by substituting material factors for ideas as the prime motive forces of historical development, his thought retained a tendency towards quasi-metaphysical abstractions: Marx, the prophet, was more interested in the ends towards which history inexorably moved than in the historical process itself.

Engels was more fascinated by the specific manifestations of the historical dialectic, the *process* of evolution from one stage of human organization and consciousness to another. While not a professional historian, he read a great deal of history and had obvious respect for historical research. *The Peasants' War in Germany,* a long essay first published in Marx's and Engels' *New Rhenish Review* in 1850, was an attempt to analyze that event in German 16th-century history from the position of dialectical materialism. In the introduction, Engels stressed that it was not based on any original research. He hoped some day to be able to repair this shortcoming and to produce a more substantial account; but this was never to be.

Our selection from this first "Marxist" historical work illustrates how Engels' engaged view of the events of his present dominated his historical consciousness. He is determined to show how the great timeless moving force of human events, the conflict between economic classes, had shaped the developments of the past, no less than those of his own day. The rather contentious tone of the essay (and of much Marxist history ever since) stems from this fact: Engels' thesis is a statement not only about events in the 16th century, but about all human history, including that of the present. It is engaged and demands engagement. Non-Marxists, of course, those who doubt that the understanding of history can be reduced to universal principles, as well as those who see different principles as its mainspring, will see Engels' work as fundamentally unhistorical. Nevertheless, it represents a tradition of viewing the past that became tremendously influential and that today, around the world, has more followers than any other school of historiography.

The merging of the estates, then so variegated, into larger entities, was made almost impossible by decentralization, industrial and commercial isolation of the provinces, and poor communications. Such mergers begin to develop only with the general spread of revolutionary religious-political ideas during the Reformation. The various estates which embrace or oppose these ideas consolidate the nation—only with great effort and imperfectly, to be sure—into three camps: the Catholic or reactionary, the Lutheran-bourgeois-reforming, and the revolutionary. If we discover little logic in these great divisions of the nation, if we sometimes find the same elements in different camps, this is evidence of the conditions of fragmentation which characterized most of the official estates surviving from the Middle Ages, and of decentralization, which might lead members of some groups temporarily into opposing directions, depending on their location. Over the past few years we have frequently had occasion to observe very similar situations in Germany, so that we should not be surprised by such a seeming confusion of estates and classes in the much more complicated conditions of the 16th century.

German ideology, despite the most recent experiences, continues to see in the struggles to which the Middle Ages succumbed nothing but virulent theological quarrels. If only the folk of that time had been able to agree about heavenly affairs, then, according to our coryphees of history and affairs of state, there would have been no reason to dispute about the condition of this world. These ideologues are credulous enough to accept every illusion which an epoch holds about itself, or which the ideologies of a period held about that period. The same sort of folk see, for example, in the revolution of 1789 only a somewhat heated debate about the advantages of constitutional over absolute monarchy, and in the July Revolution [of 1830] a . . . controversy over the untenability of rule "by the grace of God. . . ." Even today, our ideologues have scarcely an idea of the *class struggles* which are fought out in these convulsions, struggles of which the political slogan inscribed upon the banners is merely a symbol, though evidence of them may be gleaned not only from abroad, but from the murmurings and rumblings of thousands of indigenous proletarians which rise from below.

In the so-called religious wars of the 16th century, too, the issues primarily at stake were very definite material class interests, and these wars were class wars, as were the later internal collisions in England and France. If the class wars of that time had their religious shibboleths, if the interests, needs, and demands of the several classes were hidden by a religious cover, this does not change the situation, and can easily be explained by the conditions of the time.

The Middle Ages had developed wholly out of the primitive. They had made a clean break with the old civilization, the old philosophy, politics, and law, so as to start everything anew. The only things which they had taken over from the doomed world of antiquity were Christianity and a number of half-ruined towns, bared of all civilization. The consequence was, as always in primitive stages of social evolution, that priests gained a monopoly of intellectual education, and education itself thus acquired an essentially theological character. In the hands of the priests, politics and law, like all other branches of learning, remained mere adjuncts of theology and were dealt with according to the principles prevailing in the latter. The dogmas of the church were at the same time political axioms, and passages from the Bible had the force of law in every court. Even long after a separate legal profession developed, jurisprudence remained under the tutelage of theology. And this suzerainty of theology over all areas of intellectual activity was at the same time the necessary result of the character of the Church as the most general coordinating force and sanction of the existing feudal structure.

It is therefore obvious that every general attack upon feudalism, especially attacks upon the Church, and all revolutionary social and political doctrines had to become, at the same time and primarily, theological heresies. In order to change the existing social conditions, they had to be deprived of the aura of sanctity.

Revolutionary opposition to feudalism exists throughout the Middle Ages. It appears, depending on the conditions of the period, as mysticism, as open heresy, or as armed rebellion. As for mysticism, it is well known how important it was for the 16th-century reformers; even M;untzer owed much to it. The heresies were partly an expression of the reaction of patriarchal Alpine herdsmen against the encroaching feudal system (the Waldensians); partly of opposition against feudalism by cities that had outgrown it (the Albigensians, Arnold of Brescia, etc.); and partly direct peasant insurrections (John Ball, the Hungarian Master, Picardy, etc.). We can disregard the patriarchal heresy of the Waldensians, and the Swiss uprising as an attempt, reactionary in form and content, at isolation from the movement of history, and as of only local importance. In the two other forms of medieval heresy we find, as early as the 12th century, the precursors of the great contradiction between bourgeois and peasant-plebeian oppositions which was later to cause the failure of the Peasants' War.

The heresy of the cities—and it is really the official heresy of the Middle Ages—was directed mainly against the clergy, whose riches and political position it attacked. Just as today's bourgeoisie calls for a . . . cheap government, so the medieval bourgeois demanded first of all a . . . cheap church. Reactionary in form, like all heresies, which can see in the development of the Church and its dogmas only a degeneration, bourgeois heresy demanded the restoration of the simple state of the Church of primitive Christianity, and the abolition of an exclusive priestly estate. This economical arrangement did away with monks, prelates, the Roman court, in short, everything that was expensive about the Church. The towns, themselves republics, though under the protection of monarchs, express for the first time, in their attacks on the papacy, the general proposition that the normal form of the rule of the bourgeoisie is the republic. Their hostility towards a number of dogmas and ecclesiastical laws may be explained partly by these factors, and partly by other conditions. . . . Why, for example, they took such a strong position against celibacy is nowhere better explained than by Bocaccio. Arnold of Brescia in Italy and Germany, the Albigensians in southern France, John Wycliffe in England, Hus and the Calixtines in Bohemia, these were the main representatives of this opposition. That the opposition against feudalism appears here only as opposition to *spiritual* feudalism is simply explained by the fact that cities everywhere were already a recognized estate, and thus could combat lay feudalism and its privileges adequately by force of arms or in the assemblies of estates.

Here, as in southern France, England, and Bohemia, we find the larger part of the lower nobility joining the cities in the battle against the priests, and thus in heresy—a phenomenon explainable by the dependence of the lower nobility upon the towns and by the commonality of interests of both estates, vis-a-vis the princes and prelates; we will find it again in the Peasants' War.

34. KAUTSKY: COMMUNISM IN CENTRAL
EUROPE AT THE TIME OF THE REFORMATION

Karl Johann Kautsky (1854-1938) succeeded his friend Engels as the leading intellectual spokesman and theoretician of Western European Marxism. In his journal *Die Neue Zeit* he opposed Lenin and his Bolshevik followers, who stressed the role of the activist cadre party in revolutionary strategy. Kautsky, whose education at the University of Vienna had been strongly influenced by Darwinist evolutionary thought, tended to see the proletarian revolution as a necessary and inevitable development that must grow out of historical development, and whose coming could not be hurried along. This essentially became the position of the social democratic parties of Western Europe, especially of Germany's. His left-wing opponents accused Kautsky, with some justice, of being no revolutionary at all. To him the historical process itself had, as it were, replaced revolutionary will and consciousness as the active principle of social and political change.

Our selection from the introductory chapter of Kautsky's *Communism in Central Europe at the Time of the Reformation* demonstrates this impersonal, evolutionary view of the historical process. His work represents a more sophisticated analysis of the relationship between material factors and ideas in the historical process than Engels'. While Kautsky is in conformity with orthodox Marxist philosophy in considering the former to be decisive, ideas are not, as they seem in Engels, simply considered "camouflage" of the real motives of social groups. Instead ideas, themselves the reflection and product of previous historical conditions and development, significantly influence the manner in which class antagonism manifests itself. Thus they give to each age its own unique historical characteristics. Struggle between social classes, economically motivated, may be a universal factor in all history; but Kautsky's version of Marxism holds that the circumstances and goals of the struggle, as well as the nature of the classes themselves, are wholly different in different periods.

II. The Antagonism between Rich and Poor in the Middle Ages

The distinctions between rich and poor, though more openly and aggres-
sively displayed, were not nearly so great during the Middle Ages and Reformation period as they have become in the present capitalised state of society. Then,
as now, these distinctions were chiefly found in towns; but, whereas modern
towns count their millions of inhabitants, and the districts of the poor lie far
removed from those of the wealthy, in the times of which we are treating a population of from 10,000 to 20,000 constituted a large city, and men were drawn
more closely together. Moreover, life was carried on to a far greater extent in
public—work as well as pleasure—and the joys and sorrows of one class
remained no secret to the others. Political life and festal life went on chiefly in
open places—in the markets and squares, in churches and halls. The marketplaces were the scenes of trade, but, when possible, the work of the handicrafts
was pursued in the streets, or, at least, with open doors.

One feature of those times, however, stands out in marked contrast to our
own. In these days the chief object which the capitalist sets before himself is
the accumulation of wealth. Your modern capitalist can never have enough
money. His great desire is to employ his whole income in amassing capital,
expanding his business, undertaking fresh enterprises, or ruining his competi-
tors. . . . The capitalist never employs his whole income for his personal
consumption unless, indeed, he is a fool or a spendthrift, or unless his income is
insufficient for his wants.

A very different state of things existed under the system of natural production and petty manufacture. The incomes of the rich and powerful, whether
in natural products or money, could not be invested in shares or government bonds. The only use to which they could put their revenues was that of
consumption, or—so far as they consisted in money—in the accumulation of
valuable and imperishable things—precious metals and precious stones. The
larger the incomes of temporal and spiritual princes and nobles, of patricians and
merchants, the greater their luxury. Being by no means able to expend their
wealth on themselves, they employed it in keeping up large establishments of
servants, in the purchase of fine horses and dogs, in clothing themselves and their
dependents in sumptuous apparel, in building lordly palaces and furnishing them
as magnificently as possible. The craving for amassing treasure contributed only
to the increase of luxury. The haughty lord of the Middle Ages did not, like the

timorous Hindoo, bury his treasure in the ground; nor did he deem it necessary to shield it from the sight of thieves and tax-collectors, as do our modern capitalists. His wealth was the sign and source of his power, and he displayed it proudly and ostentatiously in the sight of all men; his garments, his equipages, his houses, glittering with gold and silver, with precious stones and pearls. That was indeed a golden age; and a golden age for art as well.

The misery of those times, however, made itself quite as conspicuous as the widespread opulence. The proletariat was only in the first stage of development; though it was powerful enough to spur deep-thinking and sensitive men to meditate upon the ways and means by which want could be banished from the world, it was not sufficiently strong to count as a danger to state and society.

Thus the primitive Christian doctrine which had found its chief supporters among a tatterdemalian proletariat, now fell on fertile soil; the doctrine that poverty is no crime, but rather a providential, God-given condition, demanding earnest consideration. According to the teaching of the gospel the poor man was a representative of Christ who had said: "Inasmuch as ye have done it unto one of the least of these my brethren, ye have done it unto Me" (Matt. xxv. 40). In practice the proletarian did not benefit to any great extent by this precept, for "the representative of Christ" was sometimes treated in a most unchristian manner. But society was still far from possessing those contrivances of the modern police system which are intended to sweep all social as well as other rubbish from the path of the rich, not for the purpose of preventing misery, but merely to hide it out of sight. During the Middle Ages the poor were not shut up in almshouses, workhouses, reformatories, and the like. Begging was an acknowledged right; every church service, and especially every church festival, united the greatest splendour and the most abject want under the same roof—the roof of the Church.

At that time, as at the present, society could be defined by the Platonic description, "the two nations." In the decline of the Middle Ages however, the "two nations" of the rich and the poor still remained, at least, two neighbourly ones, understanding and knowing each other. In these latter days they have become such complete strangers, that when the "nation" of the wealthy desires to learn something about that of the proletarians a special expedition is required, as if it were a question of exploring the interior of Africa.

In the Middle Ages the rich had no need to study the proletariat in order to understand it. Unvailed misery met the observer everywhere, in glaring contrast with wanton and excessive luxury. It is not surprising, therefore, that this contrast, besides arousing the anger of the lower classes, should have excited the nobler spirits of the higher ranks against it and in favour of tendencies towards the re-establishment of equality.

III. The Influence of Christian Tradition

The transmission by tradition of ideas originating in earlier conditions of society has an important influence on the march of events. It often retards the progress of new social tendencies, by increasing the difficulty of arriving at an apprehension of their true nature and requirements. At the close of the Middle Ages, on the contrary, it favoured their development.

After the violent disturbances which took place during the general migrations of nations and the barbarism that followed it, and from the time of the Crusades, the peoples of occidental Christendom began to rise to a scale of civilisation which, in spite of its peculiar characteristics, accorded in many respects with the highest point attained by Attic and Roman society just before the decline. Literature, that treasury of thought bequeathed by this society to succeeding generations, harmonised fully with the needs of the newly rising classes at the close of the Middle Ages.

The revival of ancient literature and learning fostered to an extraordinary degree the self-consciousness and self-knowledge of these classes, and in consequence became a powerful motive force in social progress. Under such circumstances tradition, usually conservative in its influence, became a revolutionary factor.

It was natural that each class should appropriate to itself from the treasury of tradition whatever best accorded with its condition. Burgesses and princes appealed to the Roman law, because it appeared to them well adapted to the needs of simple production, trade, and the despotic power of the State. They rejoiced in pagan literature—a literature of the pleasures of life and even of wantonness.

Neither the Roman law nor classic literature could please the proletariat and its sympathisers; they found what they were seeking in another product of Roman society—the *Gospels*. The traditional communism of primitive Christianity was well suited to their own necessities. As the foundations of a higher order of communistic production were not yet laid, theirs could only be an equalising communism; which meant the division and distribution of the rich man's superfluity among the poor who were destitute of the necessaries of life.

The communistic doctrines of the *Gospels* and *Acts of the Apostles,* did not create the analogous tendencies of the Middle Ages, but they favoured the growth and dissemination of the latter quite as much as the Roman law aided the development of absolutism and the bourgeoisie.

Hence the Christian and religious basis of the communistic tendencies. Conflicts were inevitable with the Church, the richest among the rich, which had indeed for a long time denounced the demands of the prevailing communism as a devilish heresy, and had sought by all kinds of sophistries to distort and obscure the communistic purport of primitive Christian writings.

If, however, the effort to establish a communistic order of society necessarily conduced to heresy, so, on the other hand, the struggle with the Church favoured the growth of communistic ideas. The time had not yet come when men could harbour the thought of dispensing with the Church. It is true that during the declining period of the Middle Ages there existed in the towns a culture far above that represented by the hierarchy. The newly rising classes—the princes with their courtiers, the merchants, the Roman jurists—were at that time far from being Christian-minded, and were, indeed, still less so the nearer to Rome they resided. The metropolis of Christendom was itself the headquarters of unbelief. Any new form of government or secular bureaucracy which could step into the place of the spiritual organisation had scarcely begun to be fashioned, and the Church as a supreme governing power remained indispensable for the ruling, *i.e.,* for the unbelieving classes. The task of the revolutionary portions of society was not to destroy the Church, but to conquer it, and, by its means, to govern the community and advance their own interests, just as, in the present day, it is the work of the proletarians to conquer the state and make it subservient to their own ends.

The increase of unbelief among the upper classes led them to concern themselves more than hitherto about the orthodoxy of the lower orders, and to use every means in their power to withhold from the latter every form of culture which could raise their views above the horizon of the Christian doctrines; no very difficult task certainly, for the social condition of the peasants, handicraftsmen, and proletarians was such that it was impossible for them to attain to a higher culture.

Nevertheless, the Papal Church gained very little by this circumstance; for it did not prevent the development of great popular movements against the money-making hierarchy. Its only effect was to enable the participants in these movements to appeal with greater weight to religious arguments in confirmation of the reasonableness of their efforts.

The literary productions of primitive Christianity offered an arsenal full of weapons to all those who, on any grounds whatsoever, might wish to confiscate the wealth of the Church; for it was fairly evident from these writings that Jesus and His disciples were poor, and that they required voluntary poverty in their followers; but the wealth of the Church belonged not to the priesthood. but to the community.

The return to primitive Christianity, the restoration of "the pure Word of God" which the Papal Church had falsified and interpreted in a sense opposed to the true one—these were the objects striven for by all parties and classes who were enemies to the papacy. It must be confessed that each of these parties construed the "pure Word of God" differently and in a manner consonant with its own interests. Only on one point were they unanimous—the despoliation of the Church. It is true that the various Protestant parties diverged from each other widely with regard to the question whether that "pure Word" demanded the reorganisation of the Church government or the introduction of the community of goods. As, however, according to the evidence of tradition, democratic organisation and community of goods had existed in primitive Christianity, any one who reverenced that form of Christianity must have had very large interests in the opposite state of things to enable him to find anything in the "pure Word of God" upholding different views. Hence every candid member of the propertied classes who took part in a heretical movement, and was in a position to raise himself mentally above the interests and prejudices of his particular faction, could with comparative ease be won over to democratic communism. This was especially the case so long as the Papal government was regarded by the wealthy classes opposing it as an overpowerful enemy, while at the same time communism seemed to be the harmless toy of eccentric idealists. Their partisanship of the communistic doctrine would, however, cease when they were confronted with the necessity of uniting all antagonistic elements in one phalanx. At first heretical communism showed itself to be dangerous only to the accumulation of wealth by the papacy, and hence easily acquired the tolerance of the upper classes, where these were heretically minded.

Taking all these circumstances into consideration, it is comprehensible that, at the period when heretical movements had as their object the overthrow of the Papal power, communistic tendencies were able to acquire a force and vogue out of all proportion to the strength, extent, and self-consciousness of the proletariat.

But directly they made any attempt to assail the whole existing order of society, instead of uniting their efforts with those of the wealthy class against the papacy only, the collapse of heretical communistic movements was, as a rule, sudden and inevitable, apparently leaving no trace behind it.

The class-character of these movements from the twelfth and thirteenth centuries to the era of the Reformation was much more effectually concealed by the veil of religion, under whose guise they first made their appearance, than was the case with the other popular agitations of that period. This resulted from the circumstances already enumerated, viz., the lack of class-feeling among the poor, a proportionately greater interest in communistic strivings among the wealthy (merchants, nobles, and particularly the ecclesiastics), and the powerful literary influence of the communistic records of primitive Christianity.

Nevertheless, the spirit of the proletariat had already impressed itself upon communistic movements. The proletariat of the Middle Ages differed from the proletariat of Rome in the days of her degeneration, and also from that of modern times. Moreover, the communism which it upheld differed from that of primitive Christianity and from that of the nineteenth century. It constituted a transitional stage between the two.

SOURCE NOTES

1. From Leopold von Ranke, *The Popes of Rome* (London: 1866), vol. I, pp. 22-32, *passim*.
2. From Henry Thomas Buckle, *History of Civilization in England* (New York: 1872), vol. II, pp. VII-IX, 1-14.
3. From Friedrich Engels, "Der Bauernkrieg in Deutschland," in Karl Marx, Friedrich Engels, *Werke,* (Berlin: Dietz Verlag, 1964), vol. VII, pp. 342-345. Translation by Wolfe W. Schmokel.
4. From Karl Kautsky, *Communism in Central Europe in the Time of the Reformation,* trans. by J. L. and E. G. Milliken (1897) (New York: Russell & Russell, 1959), pp. 5-12.

13.

NATIONALISM

Like Romanticism, Nationalism cuts across other intellectual, ideological, and political categories. In its origins it was closely linked to the spirit of the French Revolution. In transforming the "subject" of a dynastic ruler into a "citizen", and in abolishing the corporate divisions of society (hereditary orders, guilds, special regional laws and local privileges) that characterized the "Old Regime," the Revolution gave Frenchmen a new common identity, and demanded that their *primary loyalty* be given to the "one and indivisible" nation. (Michelet's work expresses this spirit.) Since then nationalism has appeared in liberal and conservative, socialist and fascist, Romanticist and materialist, religious and "scientific" guises. More than any other doctrine or historical force, it has shaped the destinies of the world over the past century and a half. More and more peoples, first in Europe and North America, then in Asia and Africa, discovered or created national identities and claimed the right of sovereign "self-determination" for their communities.

History and historians have played a central role in this movement. The discovery and celebration of a common past, real or mythical, has been one of the basic preconditions of the development of national consciousness everywhere. In the 12th century the French Abbot Suger praised the distinctive glories of "sweet" or "gentle" France; in our time African historians stress the achievements of African empires of past ages, thus vindicating a claim to national historical identity and greatness for their new nations. Whatever other criteria may be used to define what is a nation—language, culture, customs, religion—the vision of a common, unifying past, however remote or recent, is central to all national self-definition.

The following selections illustrate two kinds of nationalist history, the liberal or Whig, and the integral or organic version. Macauley sees the development of England, Bancroft that of America, centered about a national *mission,* leading to the establishment of common institutions based on liberty and concepts of individual rights. The nation is "justified" and its history celebrated in the universal moral category of human freedom. This kind of nationalism could, at least in principle, be generous, open, and pluralistic. Treitschke and Seeley set a different accent. Here the nation is seen as an organic whole, personified as a timeless, changeless, exclusive entity. It has its own purposes and values, independent of and superior to those of the individuals who compose it, striving for survival, power, and expansion. It was this version of nationalism (in Seeley with Social Darwinist overtones) that manifested itself in the aggressiveness and imperialism of the 19th and early 20th centuries.

35. MACAULEY: HISTORY OF ENGLAND

Thomas Babington Macauley (1800-1859) was the son of a wealthy West India merchant. Essayist, poet, Whig politician and statesman, he was one of the most celebrated Englishmen of his age. The first two volumes of his *History of England from the Ascension of James II* appeared in 1848, volumes III and IV in 1855, and an unfinished fifth volume posthumously in 1861. The work was unanimously acclaimed and enormously popular, its author heaped with honors: Elected Lord Rector of Glasgow University in 1849, raised to the peerage in 1857 as Baron Macauley, buried among England's great in Westminster Abbey.

In part at least, the success of Macauley's work must be ascribed to the fact that it was precisely in tune with the confident and self-congratulatory mood of the upper and middle classes of England. When it appeared in 1848 the continent of Europe was in revolutionary turmoil, England at peace. Macauley's picture of her history as a majestic progress towards ordered liberty, unmarred, with the notable exception of the 17th century civil war, by extremes of violent upheaval and bloodshed, seemed to account for this contrast: Over the past two centuries Englishmen had understood how to achieve change and reform, and to extend the realm of freedom of the individual, without abandoning the traditions and institutional forms of their history, or falling into the traps of utopianism, radicalism, or violence.

Latter-day critics have attacked this Whiggish view of history on two related grounds: They consider it unhistorical because it passes judgments on the basis of end results. The motives of English gentlemen and merchants, whose opposition to royal absolutism sprang as much from narrow group interest as from abstract principle, are exalted and identified with Liberty, that is, moral good. Those of the Stuart kings and their ministers, who were concerned with the strength and well-being of the state as a whole, as well as with personal power, are depicted as unmitigated lust for tyranny. English 17th-century Protestantism, not noted for its tolerance, especially towards Catholics, is too easily equated with the principle of liberty of conscience. Whig history thus became a morality play in which Good unfailingly triumphed over Evil.

Linked to this trait there was a tendency to see the past as *instrumental*, designed, as it were, to create the perfection of the present. The implication was that there was no further need for change and evolution.

Thus Macauley, the historian and celebrant of British liberty, opposed extension of the franchise to the lower classes and reforms in Ireland.

For all of this, Macauley's account, with its sweeping, colorful panoramas of the life of the past, its masterful style and wealth of fascinating detail, remains a great work of history. The following passage is excerpted from the early part of the first volume.

[In 1625] James died. Charles the First succeeded to the throne. He had received from nature a far better understanding, a far stronger will, and a far keener and firmer temper than his father's. He had inherited his father's political theories, and was much more disposed than his father to carry them into practice. He was, like his father, a zealous Episcopalian. He was, moreover, what his father had never been, a zealous Arminian, and, though no papist, liked a papist much better than a Puritan. It would be unjust to deny that Charles had some of the qualities of a good, and even of a great prince. He wrote and spoke, not, like his father, with the exactness of a professor, but after the fashion of intelligent and well-educated gentlemen. His taste in literature and art was excellent, his manner dignified though not gracious, his domestic life without blemish. Faithlessness was the chief cause of his disasters, and is the chief stain on his memory. He was, in truth, impelled by an incurable propensity to dark and crooked ways. It may seem strange that his conscience, which, on occasions of little moment, was sufficiently sensitive, should never have reproached him with this great vice. But there is reason to believe that he was perfidious, not only from constitution and from habit, but also on principle. He seems to have learned from the theologians whom he most esteemed, that between him and his subjects there could be nothing of the nature of mutual contract; that he could not, even if he would, divest himself of his despotic authority; and that, in every promise which he made, there was an implied reservation that such promise might be broken in case of necessity, and that of the necessity he was the sole judge.

And now began that hazardous game on which were staked the destinies of the English people. It was played on the side of the House of Commons with keenness, but with admirable dexterity, coolness, and perseverance. Great statesmen, who looked far behind them and far before them, were at the head of that assembly. They were resolved to place the king in such a situation that he must either conduct the administration in conformity with the wishes of his Parliament, or make outrageous attacks on the most sacred principles of the Constitution. They accordingly doled out supplies to him very sparingly. He found that he must govern either in harmony with the House of Commons, or in defiance of all law. His choice was soon made. He dissolved his first Parliament, and levied taxes by his own authority. He convoked a second Parliament, and found it more intractable than the first. He again resorted to the expedient of dissolution, raised fresh taxes without any show of legal right, and threw the chiefs of the Opposition into prison. At the same time, a new grievance, which the peculiar feelings and habits of the English nation made insupportably painful, and which seemed to all discerning men to be of fearful augury, excited general discontent and alarm. Companies of soldiers were billeted on the people, and martial law was, in some places, substituted for the ancient jurisprudence of the realm.

The king called a third Parliament, and soon perceived that the opposition was stronger and fiercer than ever. He now determined on a change of tactics. Instead of opposing an inflexible resistance to the demands of the Commons, he, after much altercation and many evasions, agreed to a compromise, which, if he had faithfully adhered to it, would have averted a long series of calamities. The Parliament granted an ample supply. The king ratified, in the most solemn manner, that celebrated law which is known by the name of the Petition of Right, and which is the second Great Charter of the Liberties of England. By ratifying that law, he bound himself never again to raise money without the consent of the houses, never again to imprison any person except in due course of law, and never again to subject his people to the jurisdiction of courts martial.

The day on which the royal sanction was, after many delays, solemnly given to this great act, was a day of joy and hope. The Commons, who crowded the bar of the House of Lords, broke forth into loud acclamations as soon as the clerk had pronounced the ancient form of words by which our princes have, during many ages, signified their assent to the wishes of the estates of the realm. Those acclamations were re-echoed by the voice of the capital and of the nation; but within three weeks it became manifest that Charles had no intention of observing the compact into which he had entered. The supply given by the representatives of the nation was collected. The promise by which that supply had been obtained was broken. A violent contest followed. The Parliament was dissolved with every mark of royal displeasure. Some of the most distinguished members were imprisoned; and one of them, Sir John Eliot, after years of suffering, died in confinement.

Charles, however, could not venture to raise, by his own authority, taxes sufficient for carrying on war. He accordingly hastened to make peace with his neighbors, and thenceforth gave his whole mind to British politics.

Now commenced a new era. Many English kings had occasionally committed unconstitutional acts, but none had ever systematically attempted to make himself a despot, and to reduce the Parliament to a nullity. Such was the end which Charles distinctly proposed to himself. From March, 1629, to April, 1640, the houses were not convoked. Never in our history had there been an interval of eleven years between Parliament and Parliament. Only once had there been an interval of even half that length. This fact alone is sufficient to refute those who represent Charles as having merely trodden in the footsteps of the Plantagenets and Tudors.

It is proved by the testimony of the king's most strenuous supporters, that, during this part of his reign, the provisions of the Petition of Right was violated by him, not occasionally, but constantly, and on system; that a large part of the revenue was raised without any legal authority; and that persons obnoxious to the government languished for years in prison, without being ever called upon to plead before any tribunal.

For these things history must hold the king himself chiefly responsible.

The government of England was now, in all points but one, as despotic as that of France. But that one point was all important. There was still no standing army. There was, therefore, no security that the whole fabric of tyranny might not be subverted in a single day. And, if taxes were imposed by the royal authority for the support of an army, it was possible that there would be an immediate and irresistible explosion. This was the difficulty which more than any other perplexed Wentworth. The Lord-keeper Finch, in concert with other lawyers who were employed by the government, recommended an expedient, which was eagerly adopted. The ancient princes of England, as they called on the inhabitants of the counties near Scotland to arm and array themselves for the defense of the border, had sometimes called on the maritime counties to furnish ships for the defense of the coast. In the room of ships money had sometimes been accepted. This old practice it was now determined, after a long interval, not only to revive, but to extend. Former princes had raised ship-money only in time of war; it was now exacted in a time of profound peace. Former princes, even in the most perilous wars, had raised ship-money only along the coasts; it was now exacted from the inland shires. Former princes had raised ship-money only for the maritime defense of the country; it was now exacted, by the admission of the Royalists themselves, with the object, not of maintaining a navy, but of furnishing the king with supplies, which might be increased at his discretion to any amount, and expended at his discretion for any purpose.

The whole nation was alarmed and incensed. John Hampden, an opulent and well-born gentleman of Buckinghamshire, highly considered in his own neighborhood, but as yet little known to the kingdom generally, had the courage to step forward to confront the whole power of the government, and take on himself the cost and the risk of disputing the prerogative to which the king laid claim. The case was argued before the judges in the Exchequer Chamber. So strong were the arguments against the pretensions of the crown, that, dependent and servile as the judges were, the majority against Hampden was the smallest possible. Still there was a majority. The interpreters of the law had pronounced that one great and productive tax might be imposed by the royal authority. Wentworth justly observed that it was impossible to vindicate their judgment except by reasons directly leading to a conclusion which they had not ventured to draw. If money might legally be raised without the consent of Parliament for the support of a fleet, it was not easy to deny that money might, without consent of Parliament, be legally raised for the support of an army.

The decision of the judges increased the irritation of the people. A century earlier, irritation less serious would have produced a general rising. But discontent did not now so readily, as in former ages, take the form of rebellion. The nation had been long steadily advancing in wealth and in civilization. Since the great northern earls took up arms against Elizabeth, seventy years had elapsed; and during those seventy years there had been no civil war. Never, during the whole existence of the English nation, had so long a period passed without intestine hostilities. Men had become accustomed to the pursuits of peaceful industry, and, exasperated as they were, hesitated long before they drew the sword.

This was the conjuncture at which the liberties of our country were in the greatest peril. The opponents of the government began to despair of the destiny of their country; and many looked to the American wilderness as the only asylum in which they could enjoy civil and spiritual freedom. There a few resolute Puritans, who, in the cause of their religion, feared neither the rage of the ocean nor the hardships of uncivilized life, neither the fangs of savage beasts nor the tomahawks of more savage men, had built, amid the primeval forest, villages which are now great and opulent cities, but which have, through every change, retained some trace of the character derived from their founders. The government regarded these infant colonies with aversion, and attempted violently to stop the stream of emigration, but could not prevent the population of New England from being largely recruited by stout-hearted and God-fearing men from every part of the old England. And now Wentworth exulted in the near prospect of Thorough. A few years might probably suffice for the execution of his great design. If strict economy were observed—if all collisions with foreign powers were carefully avoided, the debts of the crown would be cleared off: there would be funds available for the support of a large military force, and that force would soon break the refractory spirit of the nation.

36. BANCROFT: HISTORY OF THE UNITED STATES OF AMERICA

George Bancroft (1800-1891) was the greatest American historian of his century and the first to gain international fame. After receiving his undergraduate education at Harvard, Bancroft studied at the German universities of Göttingen (where he obtained his Ph.D. at 20) and Berlin. The philosophers Schleiermacher and Hegel were among his professors. The young Brahmin also made the acquaintance of the naturalist Alexander von Humboldt and his brother Wilhelm, the great educational reformer of the Prussian Reform Era. Throughout his life he maintained close ties with the intellectual life of Germany.

Like his great contemporary Macauley, Bancroft made history in the political and diplomatic arenas, as well as writing about it. A strong supporter of Jacksonian Democracy, he wrote speeches and state papers for several Presidents, ran for governor of Massachusetts, and was Collector of the Port of Boston. As Secretary of the Navy (1845-1846), Bancroft established the U.S. Naval Academy. Later he became Minister to London (1846-1849), and to Berlin (1867-1874). During the London years Bancroft became personally acquainted with many leading British and French historians, including Macauley, Guizot, and Thiers; in Berlin his circle included Ranke and the classical historian Theodor Mommsen, as well as Bismarck and Moltke. Richly honored in his lifetime, in Germany as well as at home, upon his death he was given the singular distinction (for a historian) of a state funeral in Washington.

Bancroft's *History of the United States of America,* which deals with the colonial and revolutionary periods, through the adoption of the Constitution, was written in the intervals of his busy public life. The first of its 12 volumes was published in 1837, the last in 1882. Their reception was generally enthusiastic. Like Macauley for England, Bancroft wrote a history for the United States that exactly reflected the patriotism, pride, and love of liberty of the young Republic. To a considerable extent criticisms of Macauley's Whig view of history also apply to Bancroft's work.

Ranke called it "the best book ever written from the democratic point of view"—offending Bancroft, who felt he had written an "objective" history. Ranke, no doubt, was the better judge. What Bancroft produced was an epic of liberty, of freedom being realized by her chosen people, to radiate into the world. The influence of Hegel's philosophy, in which the end and purpose of the world spirit that moves history is the ever fuller realization of the idea of freedom, is clearly reflected in Bancroft's work. In the period of which he writes, and especially in the American Revolution, he sees Americans as the chosen instrument of that universal spirit of liberty, which had prepared and led them up to their world historical moment.

The resolution of congress changed the old thirteen British colonies into free and independent states. It remained to set forth the reason for this act, and the principles which the new people would own as their guides. Of the committee appointed for that duty, Thomas Jefferson of Virginia had received the largest number of votes, and was in that manner singled out to draft the confession of faith of the rising empire. He owed this distinction to respect for the colony which he represented, to the consummate ability of the state papers which he had already written, and to that general favor which follows merit, modesty, and a sweet disposition; but the quality which specially fitted him for the task was the sympathetic character of his nature, by which he was able with instinctive perception to read the soul of the nation, and, having collected its best thoughts and noblest feelings, to give them out in clear and bold words, mixed with so little of himself that his country, as it went along with him, found nothing but what it recognised as its own. Born to an independent fortune, he had from his youth been an indefatigable student. "The glow of one warm thought was worth more to him than money." Of a hopeful temperament and a tranquil, philosophic cast of mind, always temperate in his mode of life and decorous in his manners, he was a perfect master of his passions. He was of a delicate organization, and fond of elegance; his tastes were refined; laborious in his application to business or the pursuit of knowledge, music, the most spiritual of all pleasures of the senses, was his favorite recreation; and he took a never-failing delight in the varied beauty of rural life, building himself a home in the loveliest region of his native state. He was a skilful horseman, and with elastic step would roam the mountains on foot. The range of his studies was very wide; he was not unfamiliar with the literature of Greece and Rome; had an aptitude for mathematics and mechanics, and loved especially the natural sciences; scorning nothing but metaphysics. British governors and officials had introduced into Williamsburg the prevalent free-thinking of Englishmen of that century, and Jefferson had grown up in its atmosphere; he was not only a hater of priestcraft and superstition and bigotry and intolerance, he was thought to be indifferent to religion; yet his instincts all inclined him to trace every fact to a general law, and to put faith in ideal truth;

the world of the senses did not bound his aspirations, and he believed more than he himself was aware of. He was an idealist in his habits of thought and life, and he was kept so, in spite of circumstances, by the irresistible bent of his character. He had great power in mastering details as well as in searching for general principles. His profession was that of the law, in which he was methodical, painstaking, and successful; at the same time he pursued it as a science, and was well read in the law of nature and of nations. Whatever he had to do, it was his custom to prepare himself for it carefully; and in public life, when others were at fault, they often found that he had already hewed out the way; so that in council men willingly gave him the lead, which he never appeared to claim, and was always able to undertake. But he rarely spoke in public, and was less fit to engage in the war of debate than calmly to sum up its conclusions. It was a beautiful trait in his character that he was free from envy; he is the constant and best witness to the greatness of John Adams as the advocate and defender of independence. A common object now riveted the two statesmen together. At that period Jefferson, by the general consent of Virginia, stood first among her civilians. Just thirty-three years old, married, and happy in his family, affluent, with a bright career before him, he was no rash innovator by his character or his position; if his convictions drove him to demand independence, it was only because he could no longer live with honor under the British "constitution, which he still acknowledged to be better than all that had preceded it." His enunciation of general principles was fearless, but he was no visionary devotee of abstract theories; the nursling of his country, the offspring of his time, he set about the work of a practical statesman, and the principles which he set forth grew so naturally out of previous law and the facts of the past that they struck deep root and have endured.

The Dutch manifesto of the twenty-sixth of June 1581, renounced Spanish sovereignty "according to the rights of nature." "Every man knows," it said, "that subjects are not created by God for princes, but princes for the sake of their subjects. If a prince endeavors to take from his subjects their old liberties, privileges, and customs, he must be considered not as a prince, but as a tyrant;" adding, "and another prince may of right be chosen in his place as the head."

From the fulness of his own mind, without consulting one single book, yet having in memory the example of the Swiss and the manifesto of the United Provinces of the Netherlands, Jefferson drafted the declaration, in which, after citing the primal principles of government, he presented the complaints of the United States against England in the three classes of the iniquitous use of the royal prerogative, the usurpation of legislative power over America by the king in parliament, and the measures for enforcing the acts of the British parliament. He submitted the paper separately to Franklin and to John Adams, accepted from each of them one or two verbal, unimportant corrections, and on the twenty-eighth of June reported it to congress, which, on the second of July, immediately after adopting the resolution of independence, entered upon its consideration. During the remainder of that day, and the next two, the language, the statements, and the principles of the paper were closely scanned.

[Most] changes and omissions in Jefferson's paper were either insignificant or much for the better, rendering its language more terse, more dispassionate, and more exact; and, in the evening of the fourth day of July, New York still abstaining from the vote, twelve states, without one negative, agreed to this "Declaration by the Representatives of the United States of America in Congress assembled. . . .

[The Declaration of Independence] paper was "the genuine effusion of the soul of the country at that time," the revelation of its mind, when, in its youth, its enthusiasm, its sublime confronting of danger, it rose to the highest creative powers of which man is capable. The bill of rights which it promulgates is of rights that are older than human institutions, and spring from the eternal justice. Two political theories divided the world: one founded the commonwealth on the advantage of the state, the policy of expediency, the other on the immutable principles of morals; the new republic, as it took its place among the powers of the world, proclaimed its faith in the truth and reality and unchangeableness of freedom, virtue, and right. The heart of Jefferson in writing the declaration, and of congress in adopting it, beat for all humanity; the assertion of right was made for the entire world of mankind and all coming generations, without any exception whatever; for the proposition which admits of exceptions can never be self-evident. As it was put forth in the name of the ascendent people of that time, it was sure to make the circuit of the world, passing everywhere through the despotic countries of Europe; and the astonished nations, as they read that all men are created equal, started out of their lethargy, like those who have been exiles from childhood, when they suddenly hear the dimly remembered accents of their mother tongue.

In the next place, the declaration, avoiding specious and vague generalities, grounds itself with anxious care upon the past and reconciles right and fact. Of universal principles enough is repeated to prove that America chose for her own that system of politics which recognises the rule of eternal justice; and independence is vindicated by the application of that rule to the grievous instructions, laws, and acts, proceeding from the king, in the exercise of his prerogative, or in concurrence with the lords and commons of Great Britain. The colonies professed to drive back innovations, and not, with roving zeal, to overturn all traditional inequalities; they were no rebels against the past, of which they knew the present to be the child; with all the glad anticipations of greatness that broke forth from the prophetic soul of the youthful nation; they took their point of departure from the world as it was. They did not declare against monarchy itself; they sought no general overthrow of all kings, no universal system of republics; nor did they cherish in their hearts a lurking hatred against princes. Till within a few years or months, loyalty to the house of Hanover had been to them another name for the love of civil and religious liberty; the British constitution, the best system that had ever been devised for the security of liberty and property by a representative government. Neither Franklin, nor Washington, nor John Adams, nor Jefferson, nor Jay, had ever expressed a preference for a republic. The voices that rose for independence spoke also for alliances with kings. The sovereignty of George III. was renounced, not because he was a king, but because he was deemed to be "a tyrant."

The insurgents, as they took up self-government, manifested no impatience at the recollection of having been ruled by a royal line, no eagerness to blot out memorials of their former state; they sent forth no Hugh Peter to recommend to the mother country the abolition of monarchy, which no one seems to have proposed or to have wished; in the moment of revolution in America, they did not counsel the English to undertake a revolution. The republic was to America a godsend; it came, though unsought, because society contained the elements of no other organization. Here, and in that century here only, was a people which, by its education and large and long experience, was prepared to act as the depositary and carrier of all political power. America developed her choice from within herself; and therefore it is that, conscious of following an inner law, she never made herself a propagandist of her system, where the conditions of success were wanting.

Finally, the declaration was not only the announcement of the birth of a people, but the establishment of a national government; a most imperfect one, it is true, but still a government, in conformity with the limited constituent powers which each colony had conferred upon its delegates in congress. The war was no longer a civil war; Britain was become to the United States a foreign country. Every former subject of the British king in the thirteen colonies now owed primary allegiance to the dynasty of the people, and became a citizen of the new republic; except in this, everything remained as before; every man retained his rights; the colonies did not dissolve into a state of nature, nor did the new people undertake a social revolution. The management of the internal police and government was carefully reserved to the separate states, which could, each for itself, enter upon the career of domestic reforms. But the states which were henceforth independent of Britain were not independent of one another: the United States of America, presenting themselves to mankind as one people, assumed powers over war, peace, foreign alliances, and commerce.

The declaration was not signed by the members of congress on the day on which it was agreed to, but it was duly authenticated by the president and secretary, and published to the world. The nation, when it made the choice of its great anniversary, selected not the day of the resolution of independence when it closed the past, but that of the declaration of the principles on which it opened its new career.

37. TREITSCHKE: HISTORY OF GERMANY

Heinrich von Treitschke (1834-1896) received his academic training at the universities of Bonn, Leipzig, Tübingen, and Heidelberg. He taught at the latter, as well as in Freiburg and Kiel, before coming to the University of Berlin in 1874. Here he succeeded Ranke as editor of the *Preussische Jahrbücher (Prussian Annals),* a historical-political journal of conservative orientation, and, in 1886, as Prussia's official Historiographer. An active supporter and admirer of Bismarck, Treitschke served in the German *Reichstag* from 1871 until 1888, first as a National Liberal, later as a Conservative.

As a member of the post-1848 generation, Treitschke shared the disillusionment of his contemporaries over the failure of the German revolution, which had sought to establish a united Germany on the basis of popular sovereignty and liberal ideology. Like many of them, he became an uncritical admirer of Bismarck, who succeeded in founding a German national state through "blood and iron" (and a good deal of rather unscrupulous diplomacy). Even in his National Liberal period Treitschke, like many of his middle-class contemporaries, confined his liberalism largely to a belief in freedom of economic opportunity, that is, opposition to socialism and governmental interference in the economy, and to antipathy against the Catholic Church. Having seen Bismarck and Prussian arms succeed where democrats and parliaments failed, he became an ardent believer in German strength and the necessity of war to achieve and maintain it. The need for a strong state—which he considered the central lesson of Germany history—overrode for him the claims of individual rights and liberties.

The *History of Germany in the Nineteenth Century* was Treitschke's major work. Enhanced by his gift for colorful description, and by the power of his historical style, it found many enthusiastic readers. Treitschke, too, touched just the right cord in his audience and told his countrymen in the newly united, powerful German Empire exactly what they wanted to hear: Germany, long divided and in bondage to foreign forces, had finally mustered her united strength and thus achieved her rightful place in the world. The nation is personified, cultural and intellectual developments are explained in terms of unchanging national characteristics inherent in the *Volk:* Thus Protestantism is an expression of Germandom, Catholicism its enemy. Aside from these national-racial stereotypes, there is here, again, a teleological tendency: History was *directed* towards the unification of Germany through Prussia. Everything in history that furthered the growth of Prussian power was thus "good," everything that hindered it, "bad."

Treitschke had an enormous impact upon a generation of young Germans, not only through his published work, but also as the most popular lecturer at the University of Berlin. Among his disciples were Heinrich Class, the founder of the Pan-German League, Wilhelm II, and the father of the German version of the world power-through-sea power doctrine, Admiral von Tirpitz. In this way Treitschke exercised a significant, baleful influence upon the events of our century.

Germany after the Peace of Westphalia

I. The Imperial Constitution

Despite the antiquity of her history, Germany is the youngest of the great nations of Europe. Twice has she been granted a period of youth, twice has she been through the struggle for the principles of national power and free civilisation. It is a thousand years since she created for herself the glorious kingdom of the Germans; eight hundred years later she found it necessary to re-establish the state upon an entirely new foundation; first in our own days did she as a unified power resume her place in the ranks of the nations.

Long ago, forced by the overwhelming power of events, she united with her own the imperial crown of Christendom, she adorned her life with all the charms of knightly art and culture, she shrank from neither risk nor sacrifice in order to maintain the leadership of the western world. In the world-wide campaigns of her great emperors the power of the German monarchy passed away. Upon the ruins of the old kingdom there immediately grew up a new structure of territorial dominions: spiritual and temporal princes, free cities, counts and knights—a formless medley of inchoate state-structures, but full of marvellous vital energy. Amid the decline of the imperial glory, the princes of Lower Saxony, the knights of the Teutonic Order, and the burghers of the Hanseatic League, completed with sword and plough the greatest work of colonisation which the world had seen since the days of the Romans. The lands between the Elbe and the Niemen were conquered and settled; for centuries to come the Scandinavian and Slav peoples were subordinated to German commerce and to German culture. But princes and nobles, burghers and peasants, went their separate ways; the reciprocal hatred of the estates rendered nugatory every attempt to effect the political organisation of the nation's superabundant creative energy, to restore in federal form the lost unity of the state.

Then came Martin Luther, to unite once more for great ends talented men drawn from all sections of our divided people. Through the earnestness of the German spirit, the secularised Church was led back into the lofty simplicity of Protestant Christianity, and in that spirit there burgeoned the idea of freeing the State from the dominion of the Church. For the second time our people attained to one of the summits of its civilisation and entered straightway upon the most venturesome revolution ever attempted. In other Teutonic lands, the universal work of Protestantism was to strengthen the authority of the national state, to put an end to the multiplex dominion of the Middle Ages. In the land of its birth it effected merely the dissolution of the old order. During those days of joyful expectation, a foreigner wore our crown, and this was decisive in its influence upon the whole future of the German monarchy; for the nation hailed the Monk of Wittenberg with shouts of exultation, and, moved to the depths of its being, awaited an entire transformation of the empire. The imperial power, which should have been the leader of the Germans in their struggle with the Papacy, renounced at once ecclesiastical and political reform. The empire of the Hapsburgs chose the Catholic side, led the Latin peoples of Southern Europe into the field against the German heretics, and remained henceforward, until its inglorious fall, the enemy of all that was truly German.

Protestantism turned for help to the temporal rulers. These territorial princes justified their right to existence by their work as protectors of the German faith. But the nation was unable to secure the universal victory on German soil of its own especial work, the Reformation, and was likewise unable to rejuvenate its own national state in accordance with the temporal ideas of the new time. The German spirit, inclined, as always, to excessive idealism, was alienated from the struggles of political life by the profundities of the new theology; impassioned Lutheranism did not understand how to avail itself of the fortunate hour for the work of liberation. Germany so powerful in arms, was ignominiously beaten in the Schmalkaldian War, and had for the first time to submit to a foreign yoke. Then came the wild uprising of Maurice of Saxony to rescue German Protestantism and to destroy the Spanish dominion, but to destroy also the ultimate bonds of monarchical order which still served to unite Germany, and the freedom of the estates of the realm assumed henceforward the form of boundless licence. After a rapid succession of partial victories and partial defeats, the wearied factions concluded the premature religious peace of Augsburg. Thereupon ensued the most deplorable period of German history. The empire voluntarily quitted the circle of the great powers and renounced all share in European politics. The amorphous mass of Catholic, Lutheran, and Calvinistic principalities, immobile and yet unreconciled, passed two generations in idle dreams, whilst at our very gates the armies of the Catholic world-empire were fighting to rob the heretics of the Netherlands of the freedom of belief, and its navies were disputing the command of the sea.

Then at length the last and decisive war of the epoch, the war of the religions, broke out. The home of Protestantism became also its battle-ground. All the powers of Europe took part in the war. The scum of all nations was heaped up on German soil. In a disturbance without parallel, the old Germany passed away. Those who had once aimed at world-dominion were now, by the pitiless justice of history, placed under the feet of the stranger. The Rhine and the Ems, the Elbe and the Weser, the Oder and the Vistula, all the ways to the sea, became "captives of foreign nations"; on the Upper Rhine were established the outposts of French rule, while the south-east became subject to the dominion of the Hapsburgs and of the Jesuits. Two-thirds of the entire nation were involved in this dreadful war; the people, degenerating into savagery, carrying on a burdened life amid dirt and poverty, no longer displayed the old greatness of the German character, were no longer animated by the free-spirited and serene heroism of their ancestors. The dominion of an ancient civilisation, that civilisation which alone adorns and ennobles existence, had disappeared into oblivion; forgotten were even the craft-secrets of the guilds. The nation, which once had sung of Kriemhild's revenge, and which had fortified its heart by the heroic strains of Luther's hymns, now embellished its impoverished speech with foreign tinsel, and those who still remained capable of profound thought wrote French or Latin. The entire life of Germany lay open without defence to the influence of the superior civilisation of the foreigner. Under the urgency of the Swedish distresses, amid the petty sorrows of poverty-stricken everyday life, the very memory of the glories of the wonderful centuries of old disappeared from the minds of the masses; in the transformed world, the ancient cathedrals, witnesses to the former magnificence of German burghership, seemed strange and unfriendly. Not till a century and a half had elapsed were the treasures of ancient German poetry recovered by the laborious research of learned investigators, so that all were astonished at the wealth of the former treasure-house. Never was any other nation so forcibly estranged from itself and from its own past; not even modern France is separated by so profound a chasm from the days of the old regime.

This horrible confusion seemed to foreshadow the destruction of the German name, and yet it proved the beginning of a new life. In those days of misery, in the time of the Peace of Westphalia, our new history begins. It is to two forces that we owe the restoration of our declining nation, which since those days has transformed its life politically and economically, in faith, in art, and in science, to make that life ever richer and ever wider in its scope: the force of religious freedom, and the force of the Prussian state.

Through the sorrows and struggles of the Thirty Years' War, Germany secured the future of Protestantism in the western world, and at the same time established upon an indestructible basis the characteristics of her own civilisation. The extreme south adhered to the Catholic world of the Romans; the northern marches touched the hard Lutheranism of Scandinavia; but the central regions of Germany remained the common ground of three confessions. Of all the great nations, Germany was the only one in which these different creeds competed on equal terms, and Germany was therefore compelled to establish in her homes and her schools, throughout her political and social life, that ecclesiastical peace which had been attained through a long, fierce, and bloody struggle. In earlier days, when the Roman Church was still the Church Universal, bearing in its bosom no more than the germs of Protestantism, it was Catholicism which had trained our people for civilisation, and which had provided the abundant groundwork of art and science. But when Catholicism expelled from herself these powers of freedom, and when, with the assistance of the Latin peoples, she became transformed into a closely knit ecclesiastical party, she was enabled, it is true, through the talent for dominion of the House of Hapsburg, to reconquer for herself a portion of Germany; but the spirit of our people remained ever hostile to the Jesuitic faith. The rich spiritual forces of the Neo-Roman Church flourished in their Latin homelands; but they could strike no root upon this foreign German soil, in this nation of born heretics. Here sang no Tasso or Calderon, here painted no Rubens or Murillo. Hardly one among the slothful German monks was found to compete in zeal for learning with the diligent fathers of the Maurist Congregation. Among the Germans, the Society of Jesus educated many pious priests and many able statesmen. . . . But the entire culture of the Society of Jesus was the work of Roman brains, and Roman also were the stultifying educational methods of the Jesuits. In Germany, the new Catholicism worked only to hinder and confuse; the spiritual possessions of Catholicism contrasted with the thought-world of Protestantism much as the barren scholasticism of our first Jesuit, Canisius, contrasted with the straightforward wisdom of the works of

Luther. Despite all the wholesale conversions of the Counter-Reformation, Germany remained, as Rome well knew, the citadel of heresy. The central fibre of our spirit was Protestant. . . .

Simultaneously there awakened the state-constructive powers of the nation. Amid the disintegration of outworn imperial forms and undeveloped territories, the young Prussian state raised its head; and in Prussia, henceforward, centered the political life of Germany. . . .With the rise of Prussia there began the long and bloody task of the liberation of Germany from foreign dominion. Despoiled by its neighbours for centuries past, the empire now saw for the first time the foreign powers yielding back a few fragments of German ground. In this single state of Prussia there reawakened, though still but half-conscious and as if drunken from prolonged slumber, the ancient stout-hearted pride in the fatherland. The faithful landsfolk of the County Mark began the little war against the French; the peasants of East Prussia put the Swedes to headlong flight. When the peasant Landwehr of the Altmark, guarding the Elbe-dike against the Swedes, wrote upon their flags, "We are peasants of little wealth, and serve our gracious elector and prince with goods and blood," the disjointed words breathed the same heroic spirit as that which of old, in days of greater freedom, was voiced by the warcry, "With God for King and Fatherland." . . .

The House of Hapsburg recognised, even earlier than the Hohenzollerns themselves, how dangerous to the ancient constitution of the Holy Empire was the growth of this modern North German state. Although electoral Saxony still bore the title of *Director Corporis Evangelicorum,* Prussia was the real leader of German Protestantism; its monarchical order threatened the whole structure of feudal and theocratic institutions which supported the imperial crown; its powerful army and its independent appearance in the community of states, threatened the traditional system of imperial domestic policy. In Silesia, in Pomerania, in the dispute about the Jülich-Cleves inheritance—everywhere, filled with misgivings, Austria encountered this dangerous rival. All the imperial princes regarded with as much suspicion as was felt by the court of Vienna, this restless state which threatened to embrace the whole of the German north. . . .

Thus the nation regarded the rise of the state of the Hohenzollerns with a hatred and alarm similar to that which had of old been inspired in the Italian tribes by the conquests of Rome. The free spirits of the time were already beginning to turn towards the ideas of modern absolutism; but the mass of the people still cleaved to the ancient and traditional feudal forms which it was the mission of the House of Brandenburg to abolish. . . .

The people mocked the poverty of the "sandbox" of a Holy Empire, mocked the Brandenburg despotism; the burghers of Stettin fought desperately to preserve for their good town the advantages of Swedish freedom, and to protect it from the yoke of the men of blood from the Mark. The particularism of all the estates and of all the provinces learned with horror that the Great Elector forced his subjects to live as "members of one body," that he imposed upon the dispersed dominion of the diets the commands of the supreme central authority, and that he based his throne upon the two pillars of monarchical dominion, the *miles perpetuus* and permanent taxation. In the popular view, troops and taxes still seemed extraordinary burdens, for days of special need. Frederick William made the army a permanent institution, and weakened the power of the separate estates of his realm by the introduction of two taxes of general application: a general land tax in the country and an excise in the towns, a manifold system of small direct and indirect contributions, adapted to the poverty of the exhausted national economy, and impinging upon the taxable capacity to the widest possible extent. Throughout the empire there was one common voice of disapprobation against these first beginnings of the modern military and fiscal systems. From the first days of its independent history, Prussia was the best-hated of all the German states; the imperial lands which passed under the control of this princely house entered the new community of states in almost every case amid loud complaints and violent resistance, and yet all of them soon congratulated themselves on their new lot.

The terrible and hopeless confusion of German conditions, the hereditary respect of the Hohenzollerns for the imperial house, and the domestic needs of their own state surrounded as it was by powerful enemies, made it impossible for many decades for the old and the new Germany to come into open conflict each with the other. Frederick William lived and worked in the hope of imperial reform. With all the fiery impetuosity of his heroic nature, at the first Reichstag after the Peace of Westphalia, he pressed for that redrafting of the imperial constitution which had been promised at Osnabrück. When this plan came to nothing, George Frederick of Waldeck conceived the venturesome idea, that the Hohenzollern himself should impose a new order upon the empire. He suggested that there should be constituted a league of German princes under the hegemony of the enlarged Brandenburg state. The times, however, were not yet ripe. The Elector left his bold adviser in the lurch, for he was forced to meet a more immediate need, and to form an alliance with the emperor against the Swedes; subsequently he even abandoned the long-cherished plan of the conquest of Silesia because he needed the help of Austria in his struggle with France. Yet the way had been disclosed, and every new disturbance of German life led the Prussian state back to the twofold idea of the enlargement of its own dominion and of a federal hegemony.

Frederick William's successor brought to his house with the kingly crown a worthy place in the society of the European powers, and he gave to his people the common name of Prussians. It was only the need and the hope of Prussia's armed help that decided the imperial court to accede the new honour to its rival. . . . To the grandson of Frederick I, the possession of a kingly crown, with all the claims necessarily attaching to this position, seemed a serious warning of the need for increasing the power and independence of his state. But the weak spirit of the first king knew little of such pride. A loyal imperial prince, he served the imperial house, and fought in knightly fashion on the Rhine, in the artless hope that the emperor would recover the fortress of Strasburg; he helped the Hapsburgs to beat the Turks, allowed his army for a scanty pay to fight as an accessory force of Austria, and permitted his naval forces to take part in the war of the Spanish succession. It was then that the French first learned to dread the Prussian infantry as the nucleus of the German army; but the Berlin court played no part in the political conduct of the war. While the brave soldiers of Prussia were gaining fruitless renown in the campaigns of Hungary, the Netherlands, High Germany, and Italy, Sweden was carrying on a struggle of despair against the powers of the north; but Prussia failed to take advantage of its central position, and thus to bring the northern war to a decisive conclusion by a bold diversion of its forces from the Rhine to the Oder. Laboriously must Frederick William I subsequently pay for his father's mistakes in order, out of the shipwreck of the Swedish empire, to save for Germany at least the mouths of the Oder.

From of old the Hohenzollerns, in accordance with the sound custom of the German princes, had paid careful attention to the ideal aims of the life of the state; it was they who founded the universities of Frankfort and Königsberg, and re-established that of Duisburg. And now, under the tolerant rule of the free-handed Frederick and his philosophical queen, it seemed as if the reawakening art and science of Germany were finding their home in rude Brandenburg. The four great reforming thinkers of the age, Leibnitz, Puffendorf, Thomasius, and Spener turned towards the Prussian state. The new university at Halle became the centre of free investigation, assuming for several decades the leadership of Protestant science, and filling the gap which had been left by the destruction of the old university of Heidelberg. The poverty-stricken capital became adorned with the gorgeous architectural work of Schlüter; the court, greedy of fame as a patron of the arts, endeavoured to outshine the hated Bourbons. Yet the frivolous self-glorification of courtly despotism remained ever foreign to the House of Hohenzollern; the luxury of Frederick I lagged far behind the reckless extravagance of the Saxon Augustus. . . .

38. SEELEY: THE EXPANSION OF ENGLAND

Sir John Edward Seeley (1834-1895) was educated at Cambridge. His historical interests were far-ranging: In 1865, he established his reputation by a popular and controversial biography of Jesus Christ, *Ecce Homo*. Appointed Professor at Cambridge University in 1869, he produced, five years later, a well-received study of the leader of the Prussian reform movement of the early 19th century, *The Life and Times of Stein*, which reflected his interest in German history and intellectual developments. (Seeley was strongly influenced by Hegelian philosophy.) *The Expansion of England* was first prepared as a series of university lectures, and published in 1883. It was hugely successful in a Britain about to enter upon the apogee of its imperial adventure.

As with the other historians presented in this chapter, this success raises the basic question of historical cause and effect: Were Macauley, Bancroft, Treitschke, and Seeley so widely read because they expressed the values and ideas current in their time and place, or did they create, or at least help to create, that climate? The same question can be asked about most major intellectual figures, and it touches upon that most basic conundrum in the philosophy of history—free will versus determination.

Seeley, at any rate, became one of the intellectual patron saints of late Victorian imperialism, and his view that Britain's history and greatness was bound up with her imperial destiny fueled the enthusiasm of that last wave of British expansion. Our excerpt, from the concluding chapter of the book, sums up Seeley's argument. There is an interesting parallel to his German contemporary Treitschke: England, too, in this view appears as a personified entity acting throughout the centuries to accomplish her purposes, which are independent of and superior to the purposes of individual Englishmen.

Altogether I hope that our long course of meditation upon the expansion of England may have led you to feel that there is something fantastic in all those notions of abandoning the colonies or abandoning India, which are so freely broached among us. Have we really so much power over the march of events as we suppose? Can we cancel the growth of centuries for a whim, or because, when we throw a hasty glance at it, it does not suit our fancies? The lapse of time and the force of life, 'which working strongly binds,' limit our freedom more than we know, and even when we are not conscious of it at all. It is true that we in

England have never accustomed our imaginations to the thought of Greater Britain. Our politicians, our historians still think of England not of Greater Britain as their country; they still think only that England *has* colonies, and they allow themselves to talk as if she could easily whistle them off, and become again with perfect comfort to herself the old solitary island of Queen Elizabeth's time, 'in a great pool a swan's nest.' But the fancy is but a chimera produced by inattention, one of those monsters, for such monsters there are, which are created not by imagination but by the want of imagination!

But though this is a conclusion to which I am led, it is not the conclusion which I wish to leave most strongly impressed on your minds. What I desire here is not so much to impart to you a just view of practical politics as a just view of the object and method of historical study. My chief aim in these lectures has been to show in what light the more recent history of England ought to be regarded by the student. It seems to me that most of our historians, when they come to these modern periods, lose the clue, betray embarrassment in the choice of topics, and end by producing a story without a moral. I have argued in the first place that history is concerned, not mainly with the interesting things which may have been done by Englishmen or in England, but with England herself considered as a nation and a state. To make this more plain I have narrated nothing, told no thrilling stories, drawn no heroic portraits, I have kept always before you England as a great whole. In her story there is little that is dramatic, for she can scarcely die, and in this period at least has not suffered or been in danger of suffering much. What great changes has she undergone in this period? Considerable political changes no doubt, but none that have been so memorable as those she underwent in the seventeenth century. Then she made one of the greatest political discoveries, and taught all the world how liberty might be adapted to the conditions of a nation-state. On the other hand the modern political movement, that of Reform or Liberalism, began not in England but on the Continent, from whence we borrowed it. The peculiarly English movement, I have urged, in this period has been an unparalleled expansion. Grasp this fact, and you have the clue both to the eighteenth and the nineteenth centuries. The wars with France from Louis XIV. to Napoleon fall into an intelligible series. The American Revolution and the conquest of India cease to seem mere digressions, and take their proper places in the main line of English history. The growth of wealth, commerce and manufacture, the fall of the old colonial system and the gradual growth of a new one, are all easily included under the same formula. Lastly this formula binds together the past of England and her future, and leaves us, when we close the history of our country, not with minds fatigued and bewildered as though from reading a story that has been too much spun out, but enlightened and more deeply interested than ever, because partly prepared for what is to come next.

I am often told by those who, like myself, study the question how history should be taught, Oh, you must before all things make it interesting! I agree with them in a certain sense, but I give a different sense to the word interesting, a sense which after all is the original and proper one. By interesting they mean romantic, poetical, surprising; I do not try to make history interesting in this sense, because I have found that it cannot be done without adulterating history and mixing it with falsehood. But the word interesting does not properly mean romantic. That is interesting in the proper sense which affects our interests, which closely concerns us and is deeply important to us. I have tried to show you that the history of modern England from the beginning of the eighteenth century is interesting in this sense, because it is pregnant with great results which will affect the lives of ourselves and our children and the future greatness of our country. Make history interesting indeed! I cannot make history more interesting than it is, except by falsifying it. And therefore when I meet a person who does not find history interesting, it does not occur to me to alter history,—I try to alter *him*.

SOURCE NOTES

1. From Thomas Babington Macauley, *The History of England From the Ascension of James II* (New York: 1894), vol. I, pp. 78-81, 84-86.
2. From George Bancroft, *History of the United States of America* (New York: 1884), vol. IV, pp. 442-446, 450-452.
3. From Heinrich von Treitschke, *History of Germany in the Nineteenth Century* (New York: 1915), vol. I, pp. 3-8, 38-42.
4. From J. R. Seeley, M.A., *The Expansion of England* (London: 1883), pp. 306-308.

14.
THE
TWENTIETH
CENTURY

Unlike its predecessor, our century has not produced any new, widely accepted ideological systems claiming to elucidate the nature and purpose of man and society. The only exceptions that might be cited are fascism—essentially an amalgam of Romantic attitude, scientific (biological) determinism, and nationalism—and Existentialism, which rejects all systems and categories, and thus could hardly give rise to a school of historiography. By and large, our century has continued to analyze and attempt to solve the problems of our vastly complex societies in terms of earlier world views. Historical works, too, continue to be written from the positions of liberal rationalism, of Marxism, nationalism, materialist determinism, and the Judaeo-Christian ethos.

Above all, perhaps, the tradition of formal-"scientific," academic history has dominated the historiography of our age. With the huge expansion of education at all levels and thus of the historical profession and the historically interested public, the great bulk of history produced has been the fruit of careful, painstaking research into particular periods, events, or problems of the past. In many cases, no doubt, this professional, specialized historiography has yielded dry and dusty writing on insignificant subjects, far from the colorful, sweeping prose works of the 19th century, or has merely provided minute documentation and elucidation of the obvious (and promotion for assistant professors).

In some instances, however, detailed investigation (or reinvestigation) of historical evidence, particularly when motivated by engagement in concerns and controversies of the present, has caused significant changes, not only in our view of the past, but of present policies and possibilities. The "revisionist" historians of the Twenties and Thirties, through their researches and conclusions on the origins of World War I, contributed significantly to the repudiation of the moral validity of the Treaty of Versailles (which had imputed sole responsibility for the war to Germany and her allies)—and thus, alas, to the policy of appeasing Hitler's Germany. Revisionist historians of the Cold War began in the late 1950s to reexamine the origins of that conflict in the relations of the Allied powers during and immediately after World War II. Their work contributed to changing the governing assumptions of United States policy, which in the Fifties and early Sixties had been dominated by the belief in a Soviet-Communist design for world domination that had produced the Cold War and necessitated its continuation.

We present here an example of revisionism in another sphere, that of religious history. Erwin Iserloh, a German Catholic priest and historian, is motivated by his involvement in today's ecumenical movement in his challenge to a centuries-old view of the Reformation, based on close reexamination of the validity of one, seemingly minor, anecdote.

Aside from the continuation of the monographic tradition of academic history which, coupled with present-oriented engagement, has also produced various "revisionisms," the historiography of our age has been profoundly influenced by two major tendencies. The methodology and concerns of the social science disciplines have stimulated modern historians to investigate a broad variety of subjects rarely considered by their politics–and idea-oriented predecessors. They have also led them to examine evidence quite different from the archival documentary sources of the 19th century craft. At the same time, a new global, internationalist trend has produced analyses of historical developments transcending the narrow traditional framework of the nation-state. Several of our excerpts demonstrate how these two tendencies are mutually interrelated.

In the selection from Charles A. Beard we see that emphasis on economic aspects of historical motivation is no longer a Marxist monopoly. Goubert's chapter on the demography of 17th century France is an example of the attention given by many contemporary historians to the social conditions and everyday life of the anonymous masses of the population, a topic related to the concerns of the modern discipline of Sociology. Loewenberg's article brings insights derived from psychoanalysis to bear on a significant question of modern social and intellectual history. In his utilization of nonliterary sources, Ian Vansina illustrates the debt of historians dealing with the history of the non-Western world to Anthropology and other disciplines. Curtin demonstrates how quantification and the methods of statistics can enhance our understanding of an important aspect of the social history of three continents; and R.R. Palmer's analysis of intellectual and political trends of the 18th century integrates the researches of many national historians into an intercontinental context.

Most of these historians deal primarily with aspects of history other than their own national traditions. They demonstrate a new global outlook, born of worldwide communications and the interdependence of our world civilization. Perhaps this widening of perspectives, beyond national and disciplinary boundaries, foreshadows history's breakout from the prison of sterile academic specialization and a renascence of its centrality to the humanistic concern: The deepening of our appreciation of human potentiality, and of our understanding of the nature and destiny of man in his world.

39. ISERLOH: THE THESES WERE NOT POSTED

Erwin Iserloh (1915-) studied philosophy, history, and theology at the University of Münster. A Roman Catholic priest, he taught at the West German universities of Bonn and Trier before being called to Münster, where he is Professor of Church History. All of his published work deals with the Lutheran Reformation and its background.

It is difficult to present a meaningful excerpt from a monograph: The essence of this kind of work lies in its closely reasoned detailed examination of evidence, from the totality of which a conclusion is drawn, in this instance the one stated in the title, *The Theses Were Not Posted*. Any condensation of such a work must leave out important parts of the total argument. Nevertheless, we hope that the following passages illustrate Iserloh's method, thesis, and *concern*. They show that this kind of "scientific" (i.e., methodologically rigorous, specialized) history need not be value-free and sterile. The author is informed by the ecumenical spirit of the 1960s, which pervaded Roman Catholicism in the wake of the Second Vatican Council; the burden of his argument is that Luther was not a wilful heretic, determined to bring on revolution and the breakup of Western Christianity, but a sincere Christian driven to desperation by the frivolity and neglect of the church hierarchy. That argument clearly has present-day relevance to Catholics and Protestants, just as, for example, the revisionist history of Harry Elmer Barnes or Sidney B. Fay was relevant to international policy decisions in the 1930s, and the Cold War revisionism of Gabriel Kolko, William A. Williams, and others, to American policy in the 1960s and 1970s.

II Origin of the Controversy of 1517

On April 4, 1506, Pope Julius II laid the cornerstone of the new St. Peter's basilica. To finance this mammoth project he granted a plenary indulgence in 1507, which his successor Leo X renewed upon becoming pope in 1513. . . .

Special circumstances under Leo X . . . led to the introduction of the St. Peter's indulgence in roughly half of Germany, i.e., in the ecclesiastical provinces of Mainz and Magdeburg, in the civil territories of the bishop of these two cities, of the bishop of Halberstadt, and of the margrave of Brandenburg. Albrecht, the twenty-three-year-old younger brother of Prince-elector Joachim I of Brandenburg, had become archbishop of Magdeburg and administrator of the diocese of Halberstadt in 1513. Less than a year later, the cathedral chapter of Mainz nominated this easygoing Hohenzollern prince as archbishop and prince-elector of Mainz. Albrecht was the third prince-bishop to be named in Mainz within a decade, and the diocese was not able to pay once again the nomination taxes and the pallium fee; Albrecht therefore agreed to pay the needed 14,000 ducats himself. Since young Albrecht wanted to continue ruling the dioceses of Magdeburg and Halberstadt, there was the further question of 10,000 ducats for a dispensation from the law against the cumulation of benefices. As the humanist Konrad Mutian wrote cynically to a friend, "Is there anything that one cannot purchase in Rome?" The curia agreed to grant Albrecht's request for this dispensation, which was an extraordinary one both for the times and for so young a man. The dispensation fee of 10,000 ducats was applied to the building of St. Peter's. Albrecht did not have funds on hand to pay the 24,000 ducats, and he was already in debt to the Fuggers of Augsburg for the papal confirmation of his nomination in Magdeburg. But he was able to contract a further loan from them of 29,000 gold florins. The curia indicated the way Albrecht could pay his debts. If he were to allow the St. Peter's indulgence to be preached in his territories for eight years, he could keep half of the income. If we include the 2,143 ducats the emperor demanded from Albrecht, his total debt was 26,143 ducats. Therefore, if the indulgence were to be successful, it had to bring in a grand total of 52,286 ducats. . . .

The only real reason this indulgence came to be preached in Germany was the desire of Albrecht to pay the debts he accrued in buying himself a series of episcopal sees. The indulgence became thereby a "bartering piece in a business transaction." Whether this was formally simony or not is a purely speculative question. "The whole affair was," as we must with shame agree, "a notorious scandal."

As commissioner for the indulgence, Albrecht published the usual extensive instructions for his subcommissioners, for the preachers, and for confessors. The document is not an original composition but follows earlier instructions and in its main lines is identical with the instructions on the St. Peter's indulgence written by Giovannangelo Arcimboldi in 1515.

It may have been that the doctrine contained in the "*Instructio summaria*" was technically within the somewhat sketchy limits of official church teaching on indulgences. In practice the *instructio* lent support to various abuses and misunderstandings, and its frequent use of pious superlatives led to a highly commercialized extolling of indulgences. The *instructio* was unabashedly directed toward the highest possible financial return from the St. Peter's indulgences.

The preachers were to make it clear to their hearers "how necessary the indulgence graces were for a man desirous of eternal life." The preachers were to point out "the boundless and inestimable benefits of indulgences" and to warn people against neglecting or despising the unprecedented apostolic powers of the present indulgence because of earlier indulgences and their benefits. The *instructio* mentioned more than once the unprecedented powers of the indulgence to grant an extraordinary release from punishment. It is noteworthy that the parallel texts in Arcimboldi's instruction did not use the deceptive exaggerations (such as "unprecedented") and the superlatives of Albrecht's text. The faithful who already possessed confessional letters from earlier indulgences were to be urged nonetheless to purchase a new letter, because of the new graces granted now, which previous letters had not given.

IV Luther Writes to the Bishops

Luther thought for a time that the ideas about indulgences which he found objectionable were private opinions held and disseminated by the preachers. He thought the abuses of the indulgences arose from commercialized preaching. He had stressed that the papal bull was itself quite correct and had even cited the bull in support of his own delimitation of the power of the keys. He related that he knew nothing at first about Albrecht's negotiations with the curia and that he had not seen the *"Instructio summaria."* When however a copy of the *instructio* came into his hands it became clear that Tetzel's preaching was to some extent based on official instructions.

Let us hear Luther's own narrative of 1541 from *Wider Hans Worst*:

> Thus the bishop devised this scheme, hoping to pay the Fuggers (for they had advanced the money for the pallium) from the purse of the common man. And he sent this great fleecer of men's pockets into the provinces; he fleeced them so thoroughly that a pile of money began to come clinking and clattering into the boxes. He did not forget himself in this either. And in addition the pope had a finger in the pie as well,

because one-half was to go toward building St. Peter's Church in Rome. Thus these fellows went about their work joyfully and full of hope, rattling their boxes under men's purses and fleecing them. But, as I say, I did not know that at the time.

Then I wrote a letter with the *Theses* to the bishop of Magdeburg, admonishing and beseeching him to stop Tetzel and prevent this stupid thing from being preached, lest it give rise to public discontent—that was the proper thing for him to do as archbishop. I can still lay my hands on that letter.

This letter, of which Luther could produce a copy in 1541, was first printed in the first volume of his Latin works in Wittenberg in 1545. The original of the letter is extant in the Swedish royal archives in Stockholm. This letter to Archbishop Albrecht bears the date of October 31, 1517, and is important enough to be quoted in full.

Jesus. Grace and mercy from God and my complete devotion. Most Reverend Father in Christ, Most Illustrious Sovereign:

Forgive me that I, the least of all men, have the temerity to consider writing to Your Highness. The Lord Jesus is my witness that I have long hesitated doing this on account of my insignificance and unworthiness, of which I am well aware. I do it now impudently, and I am motivated solely by the obligation of my loyalty, which I know I owe you, Most Reverend Father in Christ. May Your Highness therefore deign to glance at what is but a grain of dust and, for the sake of your episcopal kindness, listen to my request.

Under your most distinguished name, papal indulgences are offered all across the land for the construction of St. Peter. Now, I do not so much complain about the quacking of the preachers, which I haven't heard; but I bewail the gross misunderstanding among the people which comes from these preachers and which they spread everywhere among common men. Evidently the poor souls believe that when they have bought indulgence letters they are then assured of their salvation. They are likewise convinced that souls escape from purgatory as soon as they have placed a contribution into the chest. Further, they assume that the grace obtained through these indulgences is so completely effective that there is no sin of such magnitude that it cannot be forgiven—even if (as they say) someone should rape the Mother of God, were this possible. Finally they also believe that man is freed from every penalty and guilt by these indulgences.

What can I do, excellent Bishop and Most Illustrious Sovereign? I can only beg you, Most Reverend Father, through the Lord Jesus Christ, to deign to give this matter your fatherly attention and totally withdraw that little book and command the preachers of indulgences to preach in another way. If this is not done, someone may rise and, by means of publications, silence those preachers and refute your little book. This would be the greatest disgrace for Your Most Illustrious Highness. I certainly shudder at this possibility, yet I am afraid it will happen if things are not quickly remedied.

I beg your Most Illustrious Grace to accept this faithful service of my humble self in a princely and episcopal—that is, in the most kind—way, just as I am rendering it with a most honest heart, and in absolute loyalty to you, Most Reverend Father. For I too am a part of your flock. May the Lord Jesus protect you, Most Reverend Father, forever. Amen.

From Wittenberg, 1517. All Saints' Eve.

Were it agreeable to your Most Reverend Father, you could examine my disputation theses, so that you may see how dubious is this belief concerning indulgences, which these preachers propagate as if it were the surest thing in the whole world.

> Your unworthy son
> *Martin Luther,*
> Augustinian,
> called Doctor of Sacred Theology

Thus Luther begged the archbishop to withdraw the *"Instructio summaria"* and to issue new directives to the preachers. His complaint is not based directly upon the words of Tetzel or of other preachers. He admits that he had not heard them. Instead, he begins from the erroneous ideas and hopes stirred up in those who heard the sermons.

Specifically, there were four popular misunderstandings that Luther brought to the archbishop's attention:

1. An indulgence makes salvation certain.
2. With the gift of money, a soul goes immediately to heaven.
3. Through the grace of this indulgence, the worst imaginable sins can be forgiven.
4. An indulgence frees from all guilt and punishment.

Luther asserts that he wrote to different bishops, and specifically wrote to Archbishop Albrecht on October 31, 1517, at a time when none of his closest friends knew that he planned a disputation and before he issued his theses. It was only when the archbishop did not answer, and when the other bishops gave indecisive and evasive answers, that Luther issued his sheets of theses and invited scholars to dispute them with him. This, however, rules out a posting of the theses on the door of the castle church on October 31, 1517. For if Luther did post his theses then, he gave the bishops no time to react as he repeatedly claims to have done. If Luther posted his theses on All Saints' Eve then in the course of the year 1518 he deceived both the pope and Prince-elector Frederick, his own sovereign. For so soon after the event a slip of the memory was impossible. Finally, if Luther posted his theses on October 31, 1517, then he maintained a falsified version of these events even at the end of his life, when he had no need for diplomatically underplaying his own role by stressing the inertia of the bishops.

. . . [then] what makes us assume that Luther posted his theses on October 31, 1517, and thus left the bishops no time to react to his letters? What historical evidence is there of a posting of the theses on October 31, 1517?

V Luther and his Contemporaries on the Outbreak of the Indulgence Controversy

We must first ask whether there is any contemporary testimony witnessing to Luther's posting of his theses. There appears to be no dearth of reports about Luther's entry onto the public scene and about the indulgence controversy. As authority for the posting of the theses on October 31, 1517, writers on Luther have up to now ordinarily assumed Luther's servant, Johannes Agricola (born Schneider), to have been an eyewitness. The otherwise quite reliable book of Heinrich Boehmer, *Martin Luther: Road to Reformation,* gives this account:

. . . he [Luther] said nothing of his project to any of his friends and colleagues; nor did he show anyone the placard containing the ninety-five theses on the power and efficacy of indulgences. Thus no one in Wittenberg suspected what he had in mind until, on the eve of All Saints (October 31) 1517, shortly before twelve o'clock noon, accompanied only by his famulus, Johannes Schneider of Eisleben, called Agricola, he walked from the Black Cloister to the castle church, about fifteen minutes away, and there on the door of the north entrance, which had often been used as a bulletin board before the great festivals, he nailed the placard with the ninety-five theses.

However, Boehmer's description is based on a mistaken translation of an autobiographical note attributed to Agricola. There the supposed text reads, "Anno 1517 proposuit Lutherus Witenbergae, quae urbs est ad Albim sita, pro veteri scholarum more themata quaedam disputanda, me teste quidem citra ullius hominis aut notam aut iniuriam." In translation: "In the year 1517 Luther presented in Wittenberg on the Elbe some theses for disputation according to the custom of scholars. His purpose, as I can testify, was in no way to insult or injure anyone." This source gives no date, nor does it mention a posting on the door of the castle church. And the *"me teste"* does not mean "as I witnessed," referring to the event itself, as Boehmer inferred, but refers to Luther's intention and motivation. Furthermore, *"me teste"* was not just misunderstood, the phrase was itself the product of a false reading. As Hans Volz has reported, the *"me teste"* stems from a misreading of Agricola's jottings, where the reading *"modeste"* (i.e., "modestly," modifying *proposuit*) is clearly to be preferred. This removes the last ground for considering Agricola as an eye witness of a theses posting.

From Luther himself, besides the statements we gave in the previous chapter which add up to a clear case against a posting of the theses on October 31, 1517, there are two other pieces of evidence to be considered.

1. In 1527 Luther wrote to Nicolas Amsdorf, a former canon of the All Saints' Church in Wittenberg, and dated his letter thus: "Wittenberg, All Saints' Day, 1527, ten years after indulgences were destroyed. Let us both drink to their memory—consoled in this hour."

Here Luther indicates that he struck the decisive blow against indulgences on All Saints' Day, which can just as well mean the afternoon of October 31 as November 1 itself. However, we do full justice to this evidence by supposing that Luther sent his theses to the competent church authorities on October 31.

2. Between January and March, 1532, Luther made a remark at table that agrees with what we have seen: "In the year 1517 I began on the feast of All Saints to write against the pope and against indulgences."

Luther spoke on other occasions about writing against the pope or against indulgences and about issuing or submitting his theses, but never did he mention a posting of the theses on the door of the castle church. The phrasing ''began . . . to write'' in the last citation does not allow us to conclude that a unique event like a posting of the theses occurred, but rather places the events of October 31, 1517, in a series with Luther's later writings.

Among the numerous other sources that up to the time of Luther's death speak of the indulgence theses and Luther's action against Tetzel's preaching and Albrecht's *instructio* there is not one word about a posting of the theses, to say nothing about such an event on October 31, or November 1, 1517.

I see . . . the genuine possibility of keeping Luther within the church. But for this to have happened the bishops who were involved, and the pope himself, would have to have matched Luther in religious substance and in pastoral earnestness. It was not just a cheap evasion when Luther repeated again and again in 1517 and 1518 that he felt bound only by teachings of the church and not by theological opinions, even if these came from St. Thomas or St. Bonaventure. The binding declaration Luther sought from the church came in Leo X's doctrinal constitution on indulgences, *''Cum postquam''*, on November 9, 1518. This was based on a text prepared by Cardinal Cajetan, and was published by him on December 13, 1518, in Linz on the Danube in what is now Austria.

The papal constitution declares that the pope by reason of the power of the keys can through indulgences remit punishments for sin by applying the merits of Christ and the saints. The living receive this remission as an absolution and the departed by way of intercession. The constitution was quite reticent and sparing in laying down binding doctrine. This contrasts notably with the manner of the indulgence preachers and Luther's attackers. Cajetan himself felt compelled in a treatise on indulgences on November 20, 1519, to criticize preachers who were publicizing their private opinions as the doctrine of the church.

Tetzel's disputation in Frankfurt on the Oder in January 1518 gives a good example of the extent of this thoughtless indentification of personal theological opinion with dogma, and the consequent branding of an opponent as a heretic. Tetzel's thesis 42 asserts that it is ''Christian dogma'' that one need not be in the state of grace to gain a plenary indulgence for the departed—a thesis Luther found repulsive and which Catholic theologians today unanimously reject.

This arbitrary proclamation of dogma in open theological questions was surely one of the most dangerous forms of the ''theological confusion'' of the time. Added to this was the shocking lack of religious earnestness evident in the first responses to Luther's intervention.

In his thirty-fourth thesis Tetzel lightly defended the conception that under-lay the sardonic couplet, "When the coin in the basket clings, then the soul from the fire springs." In fact Tetzel maintained that the soul would be freed even more quickly, since a spirit needed no time to move from purgatory to heaven, while the coin needed time for falling into the basket.

Silvester Prierias, the papal court theologian, exceeded his fellow Domini-can Tetzel in frivolity. For him, a preacher maintaining the doctrines attacked by Luther is much like a cook adding seasoning to make a dish more appealing. Here we see the same lack of religious earnestness and pastoral awareness that marked the bishops' reaction to the theses.

This lack of theological competence and of apostolic concern was all the more freighted with consequences, in the face of Martin Luther's zeal for the glory of God and the salvation of souls in 1517–18. There was a real chance to channel his zeal toward renewal of the church from within.

In this context it does seem important whether Luther actually posted his theses for the benefit of the crowds streaming into the Church of All Saints in Wittenberg. It is important whether he made such a scene or whether he simply presented his ninety-five theses to the bishops and to some learned friends. From the former he sought the suppression of practical abuses, and from the latter the clarification of open theological questions.

I, for one, feel compelled to judge Luther's posting of the ninety-five theses a legend. With this legend removed it is much clearer to what a great extent the theological and pastoral failures of the bishops set the scene for Luther to begin the divisive Reformation we know, instead of bringing reform from within the church.

40.BEARD: ECONOMIC ORIGINS
OF JEFFERSONIAN DEMOCRACY

Charles A. Beard (1874–1948) was educated at Depauw University and at Columbia, where he received his Ph.D. in 1904. Subsequently he also studied in England. He taught at Columbia until 1917, when he resigned in protest against infringements of academic freedom. Later he served as president of the American Historical Association and the American Political Science Association. Both his early works on English and European history and his later ones on American history stressed economic themes. In *The Economic Basis of Politics,* published in 1922, he summarized his essential position: While he did not accept the rigid class analysis of Marxism, and without espousing economic determinism as the explanation of all historical phenomena, he considered economic interest, not ideology, as the fundamental cause of political groupings (parties) and group action. Beard, a former Progressive, became an anti-Roosevelt isolationist in the 1930's; his later works dealt in a critical vein with U.S. foreign policy before and during World War II.

Economic Origins of Jeffersonian Democracy, published in 1915, is one of Beard's most important works. In the following passage from the introductory chapter of the book we have a clear illustration of Beard's controversial views, which flew in the face of much patriotic mythology about the founding fathers of the Republic, but have gained wide acceptance among American historians.

Chapter I

The Federalist-Republican Antagonism and the Conflict over the Constitution

An examination into the origins of Jeffersonian Democracy naturally opens with an inquiry whether there was any connection between that party and the large body of citizens who opposed the establishment of the Constitution of the United States. In the struggle over the adoption of that instrument, there appeared, it is well known, a sharp antagonism throughout almost the entire country. The views of competent contemporary observers and of modern students of the period are in accord on that point. Of this there can be no doubt. Chief Justice Marshall, a member of the Virginia ratifying convention and a Federalist of high standing, who combined with his unusual opportunities for personal observation his mastery of President Washington's private correspondence, informs us that the parties to the conflict over the Constitution were in some states evenly balanced, that in many instances the majority in favor of the new system was so small that its intrinsic merits alone would not have carried the day, that in some of the adopting states a majority of the people were in the opposition, and that in all of them the new government was accepted with reluctance only because a dread of dismemberment of the union overcame hostility to the proposed fundamental law.

A half a century after Marshall thus described the contest over the ratification of the Constitution, Hildreth, a patient and discriminating student of the Federalist period, on turning over the sources in a fresh light, came to the same conclusion. . . . Bancroft, whose devotion to the traditions of the Constitution is never to be questioned, was no less emphatic than Hildreth in his characterization of the contest for the new political order as a hard-fought battle ending in victory snatched from the very jaws of defeat. From the day of Hildreth and Bancroft to this, no serious student of the eighteenth century has doubted at least the severity and even balance of the conflict over the Constitution. Only those publicists concerned with the instant need of political controversies have been bold enough to deny that the fundamental law of the land was itself the product of one of the sharpest partisan contests in the history of the country.

This stubbornly fought battle over the Constitution was in the main economic in character, because the scheme of government contemplated was designed to effect, along with a more adequate national defence, several commercial and financial reforms of high significance, and at the same time to afford an efficient check upon state legislatures that had shown themselves prone to assault acquired property rights, particularly of personalty, by means of paper money and other agrarian measures. To speak more precisely, the contest over the Constitution was not primarily a war over abstract political ideals, such as state's rights and centralization, but over concrete economic issues, and the political division which accompanied it was substantially along the lines of the interests affected—the financiers, public creditors, traders, commercial men, manufacturers, and allied groups, centering mainly in the larger seaboard towns, being chief among the advocates of the Constitution, and the farmers, particularly in the inland regions, and the debtors being chief among its opponents. That other considerations, such as the necessity for stronger national defence, entered into the campaign is, of course, admitted, but with all due allowances, it may be truly said that the Constitution was a product of a struggle between capitalistic and agrarian interests.

This removal of the Constitution from the realm of pure political ethics and its establishment in the dusty way of earthly strife and common economic endeavor is not, as some would have us believe, the work of profane hands. It has come about through the gathering of the testimony of contemporary witnesses of undoubted competency and through the researches of many scholars. Although in the minds of some, the extent of the economic forces may be exaggerated and the motives of many leaders in the formation and adoption of the Constitution may be incorrectly interpreted, the significant fact stands out with increasing boldness that the conflict over the new system of government was chiefly between the capitalistic and agrarian classes.

Occupying an influential position in the former of these classes were the holders of the state and continental debt amounting to more than all the rest of the fluid capital in the United States. No less an important person than Washington assigned the satisfaction of the claims of the public creditors as the chief reason for the adoption of the Constitution, for he held that unless provisions were made for the payment of the debt, the country might as well continue under the old order of the Articles of Confederation. . . .

Without doubting the fact that the standard of honor which Washington here set up was a consideration in the minds of many, it is no less a fact that the numerous holders of the public debt themselves formed a considerable centre corps in the political army waging the campaign for the adoption of the Constitution. For instance, a prominent Federalist of Connecticut, Chauncey Goodrich, a man placed by his connections and experience in a position to observe closely the politics of that and surrounding states, wrote, in 1790, that "perhaps without the active influence of the creditors, the government could not have been formed, and any well-grounded dissatisfaction on their part will make its movements dull and languid, if not worse." The willingness of a number of Northern men to break up the Union before the new government was fairly launched because they could not secure a satisfactory settlement of the debt is proof that Goodrich had correctly gauged the weight of the public creditors in the battle for the Constitution.

To the testimony of Virginia and Connecticut in this matter of the influence of public creditors and allied interests in the formation and ratification of the Constitution we may add that of New York, then as now one of the first financial centres, speaking through a witness of such high authority that the most incredulous would hardly question it,—Alexander Hamilton, the first Secretary of the Treasury under the new system. He had been a member of the Convention which drafted the Constitution. He was intimately associated with the leaders in the movement for ratification. He shared in the preparation of that magnificent polemic, *The Federalist*. But above all, he was, as Secretary of the Treasury, in full possession of the names of those who funded continental and state securities after the Constitution was adopted. No one in all the United States, therefore, had such excellent opportunities to know the real forces which determined the constitutional conflict. What Goodrich could surmise, Hamilton could test by reference to the Treasury ledgers at his elbow. That the public creditors were "very influential" and the allied property interests, that is, in the main, capitalistic interests, were "very weighty" in securing the adoption of the Constitution, he distinctly avowed, although he wisely refrained from estimating exactly their respective values in the contest. . . .

Other contemporaries stressed other features in the conflict, but nevertheless agreed that it had been primarily economic in character. For instance, Fisher Ames, of Massachusetts, who had been a member of the state ratifying convention, laid emphasis upon the commercial rather than the financial aspects of the constitutional battle. Speaking in the House of Representatives, on March 28, 1789, he said: "I conceive, sir, that the present Constitution was dictated by commercial necessity more than any other cause. The want of an efficient government to secure the manufacturing interests and to advance our commerce, was long seen by men of judgement and pointed out by patriots solicitous to promote our general welfare." The inevitable inference from this remark is that, in Ames's opinion, men of commercial and manufacturing interests must have seen the possibilities of economic advantage in the adoption of the Constitution, and naturally arrayed themselves on its side.

41. GOUBERT: LOUIS XIV AND
TWENTY MILLION FRENCHMEN

Pierre Goubert (1915-   ) has had a distinguished academic career in French secondary education and as a member of the prestigious Centre National de la Recherche Scientifique. Presently he is Professor of Letters at the University of Paris-Nanterre. All of his publications, from *Merchant Families under the Old Regime* (1959) to *Louis XIV and Twenty Million Frenchmen* (published in French in 1966), deal with aspects of 17th and 18th century social history. Nowhere has interest in social history, that is, in the question *"wie es eigentlich gewesen"* for the ordinary men and women of the past, been cultivated as extensively and successfully as in France. The labors of a group of historians associated with the journal *Les Annales,* established in 1929 by the Medievalist Marc Bloch and the Renaissance scholar Lucien Febvre, have produced a wealth of informative detail studies about the life styles, living standards, social values and assumptions of various social groups in all periods of French and European history. In the whole, the work of this "Annales School," of which Goubert is an exponent, is characterized by devotion to exactitude in research and suspicion of ideological *a priori* assumptions and generalizations. It simply seeks to recover knowledge about the life of the past, as it was lived.

I

Demography

In 1969, the average expectation of life is something over seventy years. In 1661 it was probably under twenty-five. These brutal figures show how, in those days, death was at the centre of life, just as the graveyard was at the centre of the village. Out of every hundred children born, twenty-five died before they were one year old, another twenty-five never reached twenty and a further twenty-five perished between the ages of twenty and forty-five. Only about ten ever made their sixties. The triumphant octogenarian, surrounded by an aura of legend that made him seem at least a hundred, was regarded with the superstitious awe spontaneously accorded to champions. His sons and daughters, nephews and nieces long dead, as well as a good half of his grandchildren, the sage lived on to become an oracle for his entire village. His death was a major event for the whole region.

In normal times other deaths were part of the ordinary fabric of existence. New-born babies died, followed or preceded by their young mothers, the victims, as like as not, of an ignorant midwife or incompetent surgeon. The widower consoled himself quickly, remarried – anything from a few months to two years after – and forgot. At certain times, in August and September especially, parish priests, dominies and grave-diggers would perform cut-price funerals for the 'small corpses' of children. The family was not unduly concerned and the lost infant would be replaced within a year or two. These were day to day events, of less moment than a bad storm, a freak tempest or the death of a horse.

There were certain places – marshy or low-lying areas, coastal regions and even the industrial outskirts of some towns or cities – where death struck with a peculiar relish, but this did not prevent the people flocking there because there was rarely any shortage of work for their distaffs, spinning wheels or looms, and because land, wood and water were plentiful and, if not actually free, at least available.

At certain times of the year, and in some years more than others, the familiar face of the countryside underwent an appalling transformation. At such times the apocalyptic figure of Death took on three terrible faces, sometimes distinct but more often confused. The three immemorial scourges of mankind, war, pestilence and famine fell upon King Louis' subjects. From war, which had claimed countless German victims in the second quarter of the century, the people of Picardy and Champagne had learned to protect themselves to some extent by retreating into walled towns, taking with them their cattle and their goods, by fleeing into the interior of the country, or by taking refuge in the astonishing networks of caves and underground tunnels which lay behind many of their villages. But the armies, which ravaged more than they killed, often left hunger and disease in their wake. France in those days was still a prey to that most dreaded of all disease, bubonic plague. Its symptoms, all too familiar to doctors, seemed, in the past thirty years or so, to have developed an even more virulent strain. One summer or the next, towns or provinces in every part of Europe might lose a quarter or a third of their entire populations within the space of a few weeks in a single, devastating outbreak. Then the disease would seem to lie dormant for a while, only to break out again without warning to the north, south or west. Its appearance was followed by panic, the wholesale flight of all who could afford it, isolation and quarantine. In 1661 mild outbreaks occurred in one or two places, although these may have been due to some other disease since every epidemic of any magnitude was invariably ascribed to the plague. The

French were to suffer further visitations before long, and so, on an even worse scale, were the English.

Periods of scarcity or famine, *cherté* as it was euphemistically and accurately called, occurred with fair regularity. They were the inevitable result of persistent bad weather, an economy relying too heavily on cereal crops and of a particular type of society and attitude of mind. Except in the mountains and the south, the huge majority of the French people subsisted chiefly, if not entirely, on porridge, soup, and bread and dripping. Cereals – in this case rye with a leavening of wheat – were far and away the cheapest and most traditional form of nourishment. But it was also a fact that the varieties of grain used for making flour came from the Near East and did not adapt easily to a maritime climate with the cold wet summers so common in France and its rarer bitter winters. Over at least half the country, therefore, harvests were no longer sufficient to meet the immediate needs of the population. News and transport moved so slowly that swift relief was impossible. Rumours of famine spread quickly and made the situation worse. By May or June the price of grain would have risen sharply in the numerous markets, most of which were very small.

Society was organized in such a way that more than half the people of France, peasants included, were in the habit of buying their corn. Prices at twice or even three times their normal level put it out of their reach and sent half of them in search of other sources of food, much of it unfit for human consumption. People put their children to beg by the wayside, or fell back on private charity or theft, and tempers rose to the point where hoarders were threatened or actually beaten up.

Very soon infection appeared, spread by swarms of vermin and the constant movement of beggars, troops and pedlars. Much of the sickness was due to malnutrition, various deficiency diseases and in many cases to starvation. People in 1661 had not yet forgotten the famines of the 1630s, still less the horrors of the years 1649-52: four years of rotten summers and bad harvests, four years of mounting famine made worse by bands of vagabond soldiers, rebels or not, and by the insecurity of the roads. Cases of cannibalism are known to have occurred and letters addressed to Monsieur Vincent at this time reveal still greater wretchedness. All this was still fresh in men's minds, even down to the names of the victims, one or two in every family over and above the normal toll. And ever since 1658, the times were out of joint again and the price of corn was rising steadily. By March 1661 the time for surmise was past, leaving only fear of the imminent reality. The major event of this year was to be not the death of the Italian cardinal, but one of the worst famines of the century. We shall have more to say about this.

Struggling to combat this obsession with death there was an extraordinary force of sheer, undisciplined animal life. The cult of Our Lady, the holy mother of God, was in many places simply a perpetuation of the cults of countless, half-forgotten goddesses of fertility. Mankind reproduced itself fast enough to keep pace with the appetite of death and still preserve the race. Except among courtesans and a sprinkling of great ladies, notably the burghers' wives of Geneva, nature was given free rein to produce all the births biologically possible –a child every twenty-five to thirty months was the regular pattern in regions where prolonged breast-feeding was the custom. Forty babies were born each year for every thousand or so of the population.

This natural fecundity was somewhat curtailed by custom and religious observance. There were not many illegitimate births, not nearly as many as in the twentieth century, and very few children arrived too promptly after the wedding. On the whole, people married late: boys marrying for the first time seem to have been from twenty-six to twenty-eight and girls from twenty-three to twenty-five on average. Numbers of bachelors and widowers who did not remarry were no greater than they are today. Contrary to popular belief, very large families were rare. Girls married too late in life and death soon undid too many marriages. The average was not more than five children for each household, only two or three of whom might reach maturity. No historian of the period has unearthed a family of more than twenty children among the rural population and even twelve was rare enough.

Nevertheless, in the never-ending battle marked by advances and withdrawals of the plague, by sudden attacks of famine, followed by equally sudden retreats, the forces of life and fertility tended on the whole to combat death in all its aspects. Such reliable information as we have, though this concerns only a very few parishes, suggests that in the first half of the seventeenth century, in spite of terrible but short-lived plagues and famines, the forces of life were almost uniformly victorious. It is possible that France in 1640 had reached an exceptionally high level of population. There is little doubt that the natural, political and economic disasters which occurred during the period of the Fronde dealt a severe blow to the kingdom's population everywhere except in the south; but after a few years, as always after a period of crisis, the time of multiple deaths had passed, to be followed by a spate of marriages and a triumphant increase in the number of christenings. Not all mourning was yet a thing of the past, and the generation which had suffered remained inevitably much reduced, but there were masses of young children to pave the way for future generations twice the size of any that had gone before. Even so, no one in March 1661 could have said for sure whether the forces of life and growth would carry the day and mark the real beginning of the reign of Louis XIV.

42. LOEWENBERG: THE PSYCHOHISTORICAL ORIGINS OF THE NAZI YOUTH COHORT

Peter Loewenberg (1933–   ) was born in Hamburg, Germany, and educated at the University of California at Santa Barbara, and Berkeley, where he received his Ph.D. in History in 1966. In 1967–1968 he was a Resident Fellow at the Southern California Psychoanalytical Institute. His areas of academic interest include modern Germany, modern European cultural and intellectual history, and the relationship of history to other disciplines.

His article on the Nazi youth cohort, which appeared in the *American Historical Review* in 1971, is one of the most successful attempts to apply the insights of psychiatry into human motivation to a historical problem. Previous attempts to do this (among the best known are Erik Erikson's *Young Man Luther,* the controversial study of President Wilson by William C. Bullitt and Sigmund Freud, and Walter C. Langer's wartime investigation into *The Mind of Adolf Hitler)* generally dealt with individuals. They were open to criticism because the authors lacked sufficient first hand psychological evidence (it is difficult to put a dead man or the leader of an enemy nation on a psychiatrist's couch), and because they tended towards monocausal views, isolating the mind of the subject of their investigation from its environment, historical circumstances, and the social and psychological patterns of its time and society.

Loewenberg's article does not fall into these traps. In carefully documenting the factors that shaped the personality development of young Germans of the 1920s and early 30s, he does not claim to present a total explanation of Nazism, and thus to elevate psychoanalysis to a historical system: The political weaknesses of the Weimar Republic and the economic collapse of 1929–1930 are real factors; along with many other things they must be taken into account in explaining Hitler's success. The experiences and personality inclinations of Loewenberg's "youth cohort" are to be considered as no more than one significant contributory cause of this development. Loewenberg successfully bridges the often yawning gap between history of ideas (and of ideological movements) and the behavioral school of social science research that emphasizes environmental factors in the determination of human action.

The historical relationship between the events of World War I and its catastrophic aftermath in Central Europe and the rise of National Socialism has often been postulated. The causal relationship is usually drawn from the savagery of trench warfare on the western front, the bitterness of defeat and revolution, to the spectacular series of National Socialist electoral victories beginning in 1930, as if such a relationship were historically self-evident. It is the thesis of this paper that the relationship between the period from 1914 to 1920 and the rise and triumph of National Socialism from 1929 to 1935 is specifically generational. The war and postwar experiences of the small children and youth of World War I explicitly conditioned the nature and success of National Socialism. The new adults who became politically effective after 1929 and who filled the ranks of the SA and other paramilitary party organizations such as the Hitler-Jugend and the Bund-Deutscher-Madel were the children socialized in the First World War. . . .

Most explanations for the rise of National Socialism stress elements of continuity in German history. These explanations point to political, intellectual, social, diplomatic, military, and economic factors, all of which are important and none of which should be ignored. The historian and social scientist studying nazism should be conversant with and well versed in these categories of explanation. The study of political leadership is also of unquestioned importance for the understanding of the dynamics of totalitarianism, and it should be intensively developed by historians as an approach to that understanding.

This essay, however, will focus not on the leader but on the followers, not on the charismatic figure but rather on the masses who endow him with special superhuman qualities. It will apply psychoanalytic perceptions to the problem of National Socialism in German history in order to consider the issues of change rather than continuity in history, to deal with social groups rather than individual biography, and to focus on the ego-psychological processes of adaptation to the historical, political, and socioeconomic context rather than on the instinctual biological drives that all men share.

The rapid political ascendancy of the NSDAP in the period from 1928 to 1933 was marked by particularly strong support from youth. Since this generation experienced childhood deprivation in World War I, the argument becomes a psychoanalytical one of taking seriously the developments of infancy and childhood and their effect on behavior in adulthood. I wish to offer an added factor, one to be included as an explanation in addition to rather than instead of the other explanatory schemata of history. Both history and psychoanalysis subscribe to overdetermination in causation. It would be a poor historian who sought to attribute a war or a revolution to only a single cause. Similarly in psychoana-

"The Psychohistorical Origins of the Nazi Youth Cohort," *American Historical Review, 76*, 1971.
Copyright © by Peter Loewenberg, 1971.

lytic theory every symptom and symbol is psychically overdetermined and serves multiple functions. When the subject of study is a modern totalitarian mass movement it requires analysis utilizing all the tools for perceiving and conceptualizing irrational and affective behavior that the twentieth century has to offer, including psychoanalysis and dynamic psychology.

No genuine historical understanding is possible without the perspective of self-understanding from which the historian can then move forth to deal with historical materials. Likewise there can be no measure of historical understanding if we research what men said and did and fail to understand why they acted. The twentieth century has experienced the gross magnification of political and personal irrationality correlative to the exponential increment in the power of modern technology. No history will speak with relevance or accuracy to the contemporary human condition if it fails to assess realistically the profound capacity of the irrational to move men.

Psychoanalysts are concerned with many things that are relevant to the historical problem of what happens to children in a nation at war. They have studied the effects of separation from parents and have seen the long-term consequences of deprivation, material and emotional. They know the hows and whys of a child's identification with his parents. Above all, psychoanalysis as a clinical technique of investigation demonstrates that only the smallest part of human thought and conduct is rational. The world of disembodied minds acting in an emotional vacuum has no place in a psychoanalytically informed history. Too much of history is still written as though men had no feelings, no childhood, and no bodily senses. What is needed is a new kind of history, a history that tells us how men responded to and felt about the great political and economic events that shaped their lives, a history that gives due place to the irrational, the unconscious, and the emotions not only of men, but also of the child in the man. . . .

The concepts of fixation and regression may be best illustrated by an operational example taken from a clinical case. A German lady comes into psychoanalytic treatment because of intense marital discord and an acute telephone phobia that interferes with her work. She cannot speak on the telephone, breaks out into a cold sweat, becomes intensely anxious, and loses her voice. In 1943, when she was three years old, she experienced the bombing of Hamburg. She remembers the air raids, the burning and explosions. She was not evacuated. Her family lived near the city center. Her father was a fireman who was called to duty by a bell that rang on the wall of the house because the family had no telephone. The patient can recall being strafed by an airplane. She has no recollection, however, of any panic, fear, or rage. Her memories are affectless.

internal loss. She now, as an adult, re-experiences all of the emotions that were
They are clear but disassociated from any of the powerful emotions that must
have been present in the child. Now, in a current marital crisis, her feelings of
explosive destructive anger and fears of abandonment by a man who is important
to her cause a regression. The symptom of the telephone bell symbolizes an earlier point of fixation when she was traumatized by fears of external disaster and
internal loss. She now, as an adult, re-expriences all of the emotions that were
buried and repressed after the childhood trauma because the later, adult trauma
has mobilized the earlier point of fixation and caused a regression to the feelings
of the child.

Returning to the larger historical case of the German children of the
First World War, it is Germany's Great Depression, with its unemployment,
governmental chaos and impotence, and widespread anxiety about the future that
constituted precisely such an ''external disturbance'' as Freud describes. The
early point of fixation was the First World War, when the peoples of Central
Europe experienced prolonged hunger, war propaganda, the absence of fathers
and often both parents, and the bankruptcy of all political values and norms.

The psychological symptoms of regression to phases of ego functioning
''fixed'' by the traumata of a childhood in war included responding to internal
personal stress with externalized violence, projecting all negative antinational or
antisocial qualities onto foreign and ethnic individuals and groups, and meeting
frustrations that would otherwise be tolerated with patience and rationally
approached for solutions with a necessity for immediate gratification. The political expression of weakened egos and superegos that fostered regression was
manifest not only in turning to violence but most especially in the longing for a
glorified and idealized but distant father who is all-knowing and all-powerful,
who preaches the military virtues and permits his sons and daughters to identify
with him by wearing a uniform and joining combat in a national cause.

It is time to lay at rest the idea that psychoanalytical explanations are necessarily unicausal or that they are inherently incompatible with quantitative data
such as demographic, election, consumption, and health statistics. Indeed,
psychoanalysis can give these macrodata new coherence and meaning, thus
adding a vital qualitative dimension to history. Psychohistory uses dynamic
psychology to integrate political and economic explanations with past
experience, patterns of repetition, and the irrationality of conduct in times of
anxiety, deprivation, and stress. . . .

The demographic approach offers new categories of explanation and presents an advantage from the standpoint of evidence. Human motivation and
behavior is infinitely complex. Any choice of action by a single individual may

be attributed to a multiplicity of unique and idiosyncratic causes that could be clarified only after an extensive psychoanalysis. The appeal of a generational approach is that it deals with probabilities—with the law of averages on a macroscale—thus canceling out any of the many individual variables that determine conduct. Whereas it can always be said that in a particular case there are other variables that have been overlooked, such an objection does not hold when we deal with a demographic scale of events affecting a population. In the latter case we have responses of an entire society to events that, while they may be confirmed in many particular cases, are not limited in their general impact by the idosyncratic developments of a single life.

The seminal conceptual formulation of the generation as a force acting in history was established by Karl Mannheim in 1927 in his essay, "The Sociological Problem of Generations." . . .

Youth experiencing the same concrete historical problems may be said to be part of the same actual generation while those groups within the same actual generation which work up the material of their common experiences in different specific ways, constitute generation units. . . .
These are characterized by the fact that they do not merely involve a loose participation by a number of individuals in a pattern of events shared by all alike though interpreted by the different individuals differently, but an identity of responses, a certain affinity in the way in which all move with and are formed by their common experiences.

This means that those of a generation who experienced the same event, such as a world war, may respond to it differently. They were all decisively influenced by it but not in the same way. Some became pacifists, others embraced international Leninism, some longed to return to the prewar, conservative, monarchist social order, and the ones we are concerned with sought personal and national solutions in a violence-oriented movement subservient to the will of a total leader. What was politically significant in the early 1930s was the facility with which individuals of this generation moved from one allegiance to the other. Mannheim's point is that although the units of a generation do not respond to a formative crisis in the same way due to a multiplicity of variables, the overriding fact is their response to that particular event. Because of this they are oriented toward each other for the rest of their lives and constitute a generation.

An organization, such as a youth group, says Mannheim, may serve to mobilize latent opinion in a generation unit. It attracts to itself those individuals who share the formative experiences and impulses of the particular generation location, thus institutionalizing and realizing collectively the potentialities inherent in the historical and social situation.

Following the theoretical work of Mannheim, sociological demographers have developed the highly suggestive concept of the "cohort," a term whose Latin etymology significantly refers to a group of fighting men who made up one of the ten divisions of a legion in the Roman army. In the modern discipline of demography a cohort is the aggregate of individuals within a population who have shared a significant common experience of a personal or historical event at the same time. This is distinguished from the loose term "generation," by which historians usually mean a temporal unit of family kinship structure such as "the founding generation," or, more ambiguously, a broad and often unspecified age span during a particular institutional, political, or cultural epoch, such as "the generation of '48" or "the lost generation." An example of a cohort would be college graduates of the year 1929, who completed their education in prosperity and in their first months in the labor market experienced the onset of the great depression. This cohort is distinctively marked by the period-specific stimulus of the economic depression for their entire working years in the labor force so that they are to be distinguished from other cohorts, even thirty years later, by their common experience of having endured significant events simultaneously. The same may be said for those who served in the armed forces during World Wars I and II, or those who were children during a war. . . .

The concept of the birth cohort—that is, those born at the same time—implies common characteristics because of common formative experiences that condition later life. Character formation, the direction of primary drives, and the internalization of family and social values are determined in the years of infancy and childhood. Each cohort carries the impress of its specific encounter with history, be it war or revolution, defeat or national disaster, inflation or depression, throughout its life. Any given political, social, or economic event affects people of different ages in different ways. The impact of war, hunger, defeat, and revolution on a child will be of an entirely different order of magnitude than the impact on an adult. This commonplace fact suggests that the event specificity of history must be fused with the generational-age specificity of the cohort of sociological demography and the developmental-phase specificity of psychoanalysis and childhood socialization to understand historical change. In this sense history may be the syncretic catalyst of qualitative longitudinal life history and the quantitative date of sociological statistical analysis. . . .

The Great Depression hit Germany harder than any other country, with the possible exception of the United States. Germany's gross national income, which rose by 25 per cent between 1925 and 1928, sank 43 per cent from 71 billion RM in 1929 to 41 billion RM in 1932. The production index for industry in 1927–28 was halved by 1932–33. In the critical area of capital goods, production in 1933 was one-third of what it had been five years earlier. The very aspect of Nazi success at the polls in the elections of 1930 accelerated the withdrawal of foreign capital from Germany, thus deepening the financial crisis.

The greatest social impact of the economic crisis was in creating unemployment. By 1932 one of every three Germans in the labor market was without a job. This meant that even those who held jobs were insecure, for there were numerous workers available to take the place of every employee. The young people were, of course, the most vulnerable sector of the labor market. New jobs were nonexistent, and the young had the least seniority and experience with which to compete for employment. To this must be added that the number of apprenticeships was sharply diminishing for working-class youths. For example, apprenticeships in iron, steel, and metalworking declined from 132,000 in 1925 to 19,000 in 1932. University graduates had no better prospects for finding employment. They soon formed an underemployed intellectual proletariat that looked to National Socialism for relief and status.

The electoral ascendancy of the Nazi party in the four years between 1928 and 1932 constitutes one of the most dramatic increments of votes and political power in the history of electoral democracy. In the Reichstag elections of May 20, 1928, the National Socialists received 810,127 votes, constituting 2.6 per cent of the total vote and 12 Reichstag seats. In the communal elections of 1929 the Nazis made decisive gains. With this election Germany had its first Nazi minister in Thuringia in the person of Wilhelm Frick, a putschist of 1923. In the next Reichstag elections of September 14, 1930, the National Socialists obtained 6,379,672 votes, for 18.3 per cent of the total and 107 seats. At the election of July 31, 1932, the National Socialists became the largest party in the country and in the Reichstag with 13,765,781 votes, giving them 37.4 per cent of the total vote and 230 parliamentary seats.

This extremely rapid growth of Nazi power can be attributed to the participation in politics of previously inactive people and of those who were newly enfranchised because they had reached voting eligibility at 20 years of age. There were 5.7 million new voters in 1930. The participation of eligible voters in elections increased from 74.6 per cent in 1928 to 81.41 per cent in 1930, and 83.9 per cent in 1932. In the elections of March 5, 1933, there were 2.5 million new voters over the previous year and voting participation rose to 88.04 per cent of the electorate. . . .

In the elections of 1928, 3.5 million young voters who were eligible did not participate in the voting. "This," says Streifler, "is a reserve that could be mobilized to a much greater extent than the older nonvoters." He goes on to suggest that these young nonvoters were more likely to be mobilized by a radical party that appealed to passions and emotions than to reason.

The Nazis made a spectacular and highly successful appeal to German youth. An official slogan of the party ran "National Socialism is the organized will of youth" (*Nationalsozialismus ist organisierter Jugendwille*). Nazi propagandists like Gregor Strasser skillfully utilized the theme of the battle of the generations. "Step down, you old ones!" (*Macht Platz, ihr Alten!*) he shouted as he invoked the names of the senior political leaders from Left to Right and associated them with the disappointments of the generation of the fathers and the deprivations of war, defeat, and revolution. . . .

The Nazis developed a strong following among the students, making headway in the universities in advance of their general electoral successes. National Socialism made its first visible breakthrough into a mass sector of the German people with its conquest of academic youth. The student government (ASTA) elections of 1929 were called a "National Socialist storm of the universities" by the alarmed opposition press. The Nazi Student Organization (Nationalsozialistische Deutsche Studentenbund) received more than half the votes and dominated the student government in 1929 at the universities of Erlangen and Greifswald. In the 1930 student election it also captured absolute majorities in the universities of Breslau, Giessen, Rostock, Jena, Königsberg, and the Berlin Technische Hochschule. Both of these student elections preceded the Reichstag elections of 1930 in which the Nazis made their decisive breakthrough into the center of national political life. Developments toward National Socialism among the university students anticipated by four years the developments in German society at large.

The comparative age structure of the Nazi movement also tells a story of youthful preponderance on the extreme Right. According to the Reich's census of 1933, those 18 to 30 constituted 31.1 per cent of the German population. The proportion of National Socialist party members of this age group rose from 37.6 per cent in 1931 to 42.2 per cent a year later, on the eve of power. "The National Socialist party," says the sociologist Hans Gerth, "could truthfully boast of being a 'young party.'" By contrast, the Social Democratic party, second in size and the strongest democratic force in German politics, had only 19.3 per cent of its members in the 18 to 30 age group in 1931. In 1930 the Social Democrats reported that less than 8 per cent of their membership was under 25, and less than half was under 40. . . .

A number of scholars have interpreted the radicalization of newly enfranchised German youth in the years of the rise of National Socialism. The Nazification of the youth has also been variously attributed to the spirit of adventure and idealism, a lust for violence and military discipline, the appeal of an attack on age and established power, and the quest for emotional and material security. . . .

There is ample evidence that this generation of German youth was more inclined toward violent and aggressive, or what psychoanalysts call "acting-out," behavior than previous generations. At this point the explanations offered for this phenomenon are inadequate in their one-dimensionality. To say that the youth craved action or that they sought comfort in the immersion in a sheltering group is to beg the question of what made this generation of German youth different from all previous generations. What unique experiences did this group of people have in their developmental years that could induce regression to infantile attitudes in adulthood? One persuasive answer lies in fusing the knowledge we have of personality functioning from psychoanalysis—the most comprehensive and dynamic theory of personality available to the social and humanistic sciences today—with the cohort theory of generational change from historical demography and with the data on the leadership and structure of the Nazi party that we have from the researches of political scientists, historians, and sociologists.

In the half century prior to World War I Germany was transformed from an agricultural to an industrial economy, and her population grew from an agriculturally self-sufficient forty million to sixty-seven million by 1913. This mounting industrial population made her increasingly dependent on the importation of foreign foodstuffs. In the decade preceding World War I, five-sixths of Germany's vegetable fats, more than half of her dairy goods, and one-third of the eggs her people consumed were imported. This inability to be self-sufficient in foodstuffs made the German population particularly susceptible to the weapon of the blockade. The civilian population began to feel the pressure of severe shortages in 1916. The winter of 1916–17 is still known as the infamous "turnip winter," in which hunger and privation became widespread experiences in Germany. Getting something to eat was the foremost concern of most people. The official food rations for the summer of 1917 were 1,000 calories per day, whereas the health ministry estimated that 2,280 calories was a subsistence minimum. From 1914 to 1918 three-quarters of a million people died of starvation in Germany.

The armistice of November 11, 1918, did not bring the relief that the weary and hungry Germans anticipated. The ordeal of the previous three years was intensified into famine in the winter of 1918–19. The blockade was continued until the Germans turned over their merchant fleet to the Allies. The armistice blockade was extended by the victorious Allies to include the Baltic Sea, thus cutting off trade with Scandinavia and the Baltic states. Although the Allies undertook responsibility for the German food supply under Article 26 of the Armistice Agreement, the first food shipment was not unloaded in Hamburg until March 26, 1919. On July 11, 1919, the Allied Supreme Economic Council decided to terminate the blockade of Germany as of the next day, July 12. Unrestricted trade between the United States and Germany was resumed three days later, on July 15.

The degree of German suffering under the postwar Allied blockade is a matter on which contemporary opinions differed. Some Allied diplomats and journalists charged that the German government exaggerated the plight of her people in order to increase Allied food deliveries. Today the weight of the historical evidence is that there was widespread extreme hunger and malnutrition in the last three years of the war, which was intensified by the postwar blockade. We may concur with the evaluation of two American historians that "the suffering of the German children, women, and men, with the exception of farmers and rich hoarders, was greater under the continued blockade than prior to the Armistice."...

On the grossest level the figures show a decline in the number of live births from 1,353,714 in 1915 to 926,813 in 1918. The birth rate per 1,000 population, including stillbirths, declined from 28.25 in 1913 to 14.73 in 1918. The number of deaths among the civilian population over one year old rose from 729,000 in 1914 to 1,084,000 in 1918. While there was a decline in deaths from causes related to nutrition and caloric intake, such as diabetes mellitus, alcoholism, obesity, diseases of the gastrointestinal tract, as well as a decrease in suicides, the gross mortality of the German population increased due to malnutrition, lack of heating, and consequent weakened resistance to disease. Specific causes of death that increased sharply during the war were influenza, lung infections and pneumonia, tuberculosis, diseases of the circulatory system, diphtheria, typhus, dysentery, and diseases of the urinary and reproductive organs. All these diseases indicate a population whose biological ability to maintain health and to counter infection had been seriously undermined in the war years....

The evidence for deprivation is supported from Allied and neutral sources. The British war correspondent Henry W. Nevinson reported from Cologne in March 1919 that tuberculosis had more than doubled among women and children and that the death rate among girls between 6 and 16 years had tripled. Because the children were so weak, school hours were reduced from seven to two hours daily. He wrote, "Although I have seen many horrible things in the world, I have seen nothing so pitiful as these rows of babies feverish from want of food, exhausted by privation to the point that their little limbs were like slender wands, their expression hopeless, and their faces full of pain."

The British medical journal *Lancet* reported comparative figures derived from official German sources showing that the effect of food scarcity on the health of the German population was felt after mid-1916 but was stilled by skillful press censorship in wartime Germany. Among children from 1 to 5 years old the mortality was 50 per cent greater in 1917 than the norm of 1913. Among the children aged 5 to 15 mortality had risen 75 per cent. World War I was the first total war in history—it involved the labor and the commitment of full energies of its participant peoples as no previous war had. The men were in the armed services, but a modern war requires a major industrial plant and increased production of foodstuffs and supplies to support the armies. Yet the number of men working in industry in Germany dropped 24 per cent between 1913 and 1917. In the state of Prussia in 1917 the number of men working in plants employing over ten workers was 2,558,000 including foreigners and prisoners of war, while in 1913 the total of men employed had been 3,387,000.

In Germany this meant a shift of major proportions of women from the home and domestic occupations to war work. In the state of Prussia alone the number of women engaged in industrial labor rose by 76 per cent, from 788,100 in 1913 to 1,393,000 in 1917. For Germany as a whole 1.2 million women newly joined the labor force in medium- and large-sized plants during the war. The number of women workers in the armaments industry rose from 113,750 in 1913 to 702,100 in 1917, a gain of 500 per cent. The number of women laborers who were covered under compulsory insurance laws on October 1, 1917, was 6,750,000. The increase of adult female workers in Prussia in 1917 was 80.4 per cent over 1913. The number of women railroad workers in Prussia rose from 10,000 in 1914 to 100,000 in 1918, an increase of 1,000 per cent.

Another new factor in the labor force was the youthful workers. The number of adolescents aged 14 to 16 employed in chemical manufacturing increased 225 per cent between 1913 and 1917. For heavy industry the corresponding figure was 97 per cent. Many of these were young girls aged 16 to 21. This age group constituted 29 per cent of all working women.

That German women were massively engaged in war work was recognized as having resulted in the neglect of Germany's war children and damage to the health of the mothers. Reports came from government offices of increased injuries to children of ages 1 to 5 years due to lack of supervision. S. Rudolf Steinmetz evaluates the demoralization of youth between 1914 and 1918 as an indirect consequence of the war. He ascribes to "the absence of many fathers, the war work of many mothers" the damaged morals and morality of youth. . . .

Many of the war-related phenomena under discussion were not unique to the Central European countries. The factor of a chauvinistic atmosphere of war propaganda was certainly present in all belligerent countries. The absence of the parents in wartime service was also not unique to Germany or Austria. The children of other countries involved in the war too had absent parents and were often orphaned. French and British families undoubtedly experienced the sense of fatherlessness and desertion by the mother as much as did German and Austrian families. Two added factors, however, make the critical difference in the constellation of the child's view of the world: the absence of German and Austrian parents was coupled with extreme and persistent hunger bordering in the cities on starvation, and when the German or Austrian father returned he came in defeat and was unable to protect his family in the postwar period of unemployment and inflation. . . .

Today it is widely recognized that the emotional constellation of the childhood years is decisive for the future psychological health and normality of the adult. Modern war conditions, through the long-term breakup of family life, added in some cases to a lack of essential food and shelter, and a national atmosphere highly charged with unmitigated expressions of patriotism, hatred, and violence must inevitably distort the emotional and mental development of children, for imbalance in the fulfillment of essential psychic and bodily needs in childhood results in lasting psychological malformations.

It may be helpful to review briefly modern theories of phase-specific development and emotional growth from infancy to adulthood in order to point to the areas of greatest potential stress due to family or social trauma. What follows is necessarily no more than a theoretical model of development, an ideal typology of the psychodynamics of personality development that will be useful as a heuristic device against which to test empirical and cultural data. It does not presume to be a precise model of any single individual's development.

More is now known than ever before about the psychological processes and fantasies of children. There is a high level of agreement among child-guidance specialists that maternal deprivation of the child has long-ranging effects on the mental health and emotional strength of the adult. The first relationship a child forms is with his mother. His attitude to the object—in the first case, the mother—is a passive, receptive one; that is, the child is narcissistic and selfish, he wishes to be given pleasure and to have his discomforts removed. A number of British psychoanalysts of what has come to be known as the "English school" have stressed the quality of destructive oral rage that is normally present in all children. This cataclysmic world-destroying rage is, of course, intensified in cases of deprivation. . . .

A somewhat later and very great threat to a child's security is the trauma of separation. It is considered to be essential for sound personality development that the infant and young child should experience a warm, intimate, and continuous relationship with a mother or permanent mother figure, a relationship in which both infant and mother find gratification and pleasure. . . .

For the infant and child the mother is the supreme agent who can give gratification and assuage pain. "The absence of the mother," writes Margaret Mahler, "exposes the normal infant . . . to the danger of helplessness and longing, with consequent anxiety." The danger is particularly threatening to the child not only because of his utter dependence and helplessness but because of his own acute ambivalence. There is a great accumulation of aggression toward love objects during the oral-sadistic, anal-sadistic, and Oedipal phases of child development. The child must struggle with intense fears of loss of love due to his own hostility and aggression. He must preserve his love for the object (mother) despite his rage and fear. If the mother's love and acceptance of the child is not forthcoming, he reacts as if he has been rejected for his badness. There is a deficit in self-esteem. The child views himself as unlovable and worthless, as an evil creature who drives loved ones away. His healthy narcissistic balance is destroyed, and his ego is weakened. One way of coping with feelings of inner badness is to project these evil, asocial parts of the self out onto others. . . .

Children are traumatized by the horrors of war, by hearing reports and seeing actual pictures of killed and maimed fathers, mothers, and dead children. But it is a fantasy of the innocence of childhood and a misconception of the nature of children to believe that destruction and aggression are unknown to them. . . .

The young child experiences murderous death wishes toward all people who have disturbed, offended, or rejected him in fantasy or reality. The jealous desire to do away with an interfering sibling or rival is a universal commonplace. One of the most important social aims of education is to curb the unmitigated aggressiveness of children. At first direct action on destructive wishes is prohibited by outside authority. Later the child learns to inhibit these impulses in himself. They are defended against by reaction formations such as compassion and pity, and compulsive defenses such as scrupulous care and meticulousness. They may be repressed or sublimated into competitive and constructive activity. The child learns to criticize and overcome in himself his hostile, antisocial wishes, which is to say that he refuses them conscious expression. He accepts that it is bad to hurt, cripple, and kill. He believes that he has no further wish to do any of these violent and destructive things. He can only maintain this belief, however, if the outer social world is supportive of his struggle by likewise curbing its agression.

When a child who is struggling with his aggressive and destructive impulses finds himself in a society at war, the hatred and violence around him in the outer world meet the as yet untamed aggression raging in his inner world. At the very age when education is beginning to deal with the impulses in the inner environment the same wishes receive sanction and validation from a society at war. It is impossible to repress murderous and destructive wishes when fantasied and actual fighting, maiming, and killing are the preoccupation of all the people among whom the child lives. Instead of turning away from the horrors and atrocities of war, he turns toward them with primitive excitement. The very murderous and destructive impulses that he has been trying to bury in himself are now nourished by the official ideology and mass media of a country at war. . . .

Many political scientists and historians have pointed to the function of National Socialism as a defense against emotional insecurity. Harold Lasswell, in contrast to those who have interpreted Hitler as a father or a son symbol, develops precisely the theme of Hitler's maternal function for the German people, suggesting that nazism was a regressive attempt to compensate for mothering and family life that had been inadequate. . . . Similarly, research indicates that paternal deprivation in childhood, which assumes increasing importance in later years as the child approaches and works through his Oedipal conflict, also has a profound impact on the personality and ideas of youth concerning father images, political authority, and sources of power. In a study comparing father-separated from father-at-home elementary school children, George R. Bach found that "father separated children produce an idealistic fantasy picture of the father" that "seem[s] to indicate the existence of strong drives for paternal affection." In turn, then, "the severely deprivated [sic] drive for paternal affection provides strong instigation for the idealistic, wish-fulfilling fantasies." The absent father is idealized. This is in part a reaction formation—that is, a defense against hatred toward the father by replacing these repressed hostile feelings with their conscious opposite. . . .

The mentality of a state of war complements the child's most archaic psychic mechanisms for coping with himself and the world, the devices of splitting and projection. Splitting is what a people at war does by dividing the world into "good" and "bad" countries, those on our side who have only virtues and whom we love, and the enemy who is evil and whom we hate. We are thus enabled to get pleasure by gratifying our aggressive feelings. For the child, too, there are two kinds of men, one "good" and one "bad." In wartime the absent father-soldier is idealized. He is glorified and any hostile feelings toward him are projected onto the evil enemy on the other side.

Much of the recent emphasis in psychoanalytic research and clinical work, particularly in psychoanalytic ego psychology, has been on the importance of the years of adolescence for character formation and identity resolution. These are the years when the basic choices and commitments of a lifetime are made after much painful searching, testing, and doubt. What then happens when children who have been deprived become politically effective? How do they respond as adolescents to the frustrations of reality? There are many theoretical and empirical approaches to adolescent aggression. Albert Bandura and Richard H. Walters offer what is essentially a social-modeling or imitational view of adolescent aggression. For us their study is significant because it shows that aggressive boys come from families where they have experienced deprivation of affectional nurturance. The post-Oedipal child has to repress his sexual and hostile impulses in favor of affectionate attachments to his parents. In adolescence the biological maturation process leads to a temporary revival of the Oedipal strivings. But now the incestuous sexual and hostile wishes must be finally relinquished. The adolescent's affectionate ties to his parents must also be sufficiently loosened to guarantee his future freedom of object choice and a sound adjustment to social reality. His practical and emotional dependency on his parents must be definitely and finally abandoned. This detachment from parental authority is, said Sigmund Freud, "one of the most significant, but also one of the most painful, psychical achievements of the pubertal period."

In discussing the effects of childhood deprivation we have followed the phase-specific psychosexual development of the child. We saw, in order, the traumata of the oral phase, of separation-individuation from the mother, the struggles with aggression and control that constitute the anal phase, the Oedipal conflict, the latency years of grade-school political socialization, to the crisis of adolescence that precedes adulthood. Each phase has its special stresses and focuses of conflict. Each may become a point of fixation to be returned to at a later date if the turmoil has been too great or the storm too violent to permit the child passage unharmed. . . .

43. VANSINA: KINGDOMS OF THE SAVANNA

Ian Vansina (1929–   ) came to the United States from Belgium, where he obtained his doctorate from the University of Louvain in 1957. Presently Professor of History and Anthropology at the University of Wisconsin, he has done intensive field work in Zaire, the former Belgian Congo, where he has also taught. His research has been concentrated upon the cultural history and linguistics of Central Africa.

Kingdoms of the Savanna is an example of the new interest of contemporary historians in the history of nonliterate cultures outside the Western world and of the ways in which this history can be recovered. The sources and methods used by Vansina and other historians of regions where the keeping of formal written records is a recent development are a far cry from the traditional archival research of historians. Vansina, to be sure, used early Portuguese records of the Congo and Angola, extracting from these accounts of trade, diplomacy, warfare, and administration what could be gleaned about the nature and development of African societies in the interior. Beyond that, he had to rely on the oral traditions, both mythical-religious and historical, of the tribes themselves, and on the evidence of linguistics and archeology, both still underdeveloped in their applications to Tropical Africa. Further evidence can be developed from anthropological accounts of the cultural traits of societies: Kinship and authority patterns, the crops that are cultivated, the organization of economic activity and warfare, and the like.

There are limits to such reconstruction. We will never know much, for instance, about the individual characteristics and motivations of most ancient African rulers and builders of states, and even less about those of their subjects. Nevertheless, the broad outlines of the development and mutual relationships of civilizations can emerge, and vast blanks in our knowledge of the story of mankind are thus filled. Today this work of historical recovery is increasingly carried forward by non-Western historians, contributing to the uncovering of the roots of their peoples' cultural heritage.

The Birth of the Luba and Lunda Empires

Deep in the savanna of Central Africa—in the region west of the upper Lualaba and north of the Katanga lakes—a profound change in political structures took place during the sixteenth century. Invaders—the *balopwe*—occupied the area and founded a major kingdom, the Luba "empire." From there they went further west at a somewhat later date and established a kingdom in Lunda land. Groups of emigrants would leave this latter area for more than a century after 1600 and carry their political organization with them to the west, the south, and the east, so that by 1750 Luba/Lunda culture was spread from the Kwango River in the west to Lake Tanganyika in the east. This chapter describes the origins of the Luba kingdom and its further internal history and the origins and history of the Lunda empire, and the story of Lunda expansion in Angola, in northeastern Rhodesia, and in the area between the Kwango and Kasai. The history of the area is somewhat arbitrarily limited to 1700, before the expansions into the lands of the watershed between the Congo and Zambesi and into the lands later known as Kazembe.

The Birth of the Luba Kingdom

Around 1500 the area between Lake Tanganyika and the upper Kasai was organized into a multitude of smaller chiefdoms. In the western part these were ruled by the Bungo, the ancestors of the Lunda. In the central part, between the Bushimai River and the Katanga lakes, lived the ancestors of the Luba Katanga; here there were two bigger kingdoms, that of the Kaniok and the Bena Kalundwe. East of the Bushimai the chiefdoms were very small and the people who lived in them were called the Kalanga. Between the lakes and Tanganyika lived the ancestors of the Hemba and perhaps even then some Bemba-speaking groups. The degree of political organization which obtained there is unknown, but by 1500 a great immigrant named Kongolo appeared in the Kalanga lands and was to become the founder of what has been called the first Luba empire.

There is no unified tradition with regard to the origins or the coming of Kongolo and the versions that have been collected indicate only how badly we are in need of a general study of Luba oral traditions. The traditions which are extant tell that he was originally either from the northeast—from the area where the town of Kongolo stands now; or from the northwest—from the Bena Kalundwe of Mutombo Mukulu. In one version he was even said to be born near his later capital. Whatever his origin, he arrived in the country, subdued isolated villages and tiny chiefdoms en route, and built his capital at Mwibele near Lake Boya.

From Ian M. Vansina, *Kingdoms of the Savanna* (Madison: The University of Wisonsin Press; Copyright © 1966 by the Regents of the University of Wisconsin), pp. 70–78.

Some time after Kongolo had settled there, Ilunga Mbili, a hunter from somewhere east of the Lualaba, arrived with his party near the capital. He was well received by Kongolo and married the latter's two half sisters, Bulanda and Mabela, whereupon, apparently after a violent quarrel with Kongolo, he left again for his homeland. The quarrel seems to have occurred because Ilunga Mbili tried to teach the uncouth Kongolo the manners and niceties of behavior fitting for a chief; he obviously came from a well-organized chiefdom, but its location is practically unknown. After he had left, Bulanda bore Kalala Ilunga, and Mabela bore Kisulu Mabele.

Kalala Ilunga proved to be a marvelous warrior as a young man and helped Kongolo to subdue the whole southern part of the kingdom—which shows that the conquest of the kingdom was a process which took at least twenty years and probably more. But Kongolo, becoming suspicious of the successful Kalala, tried to kill him, and Kalala fled to his fatherland and came back with an army. Without making a stand, Kongolo fled to the caves of the river Lwembe near Kai, where he was betrayed by his own sisters and captured and killed. Kalala took the kingdom and built his capital at Munza, a few miles away from Mwibele. This was the beginning of what has been called the second Luba empire, but in fact it was the same kingdom. The story of Kongolo and Kalala Ilunga has become the national Luba epic.

After his accession, Kalala made further wars to enlarge his domains, conquering a number of chiefdoms on the western banks of the Lualaba just north of Lake Kisale and others on the boundary of the Kalundwe. One tradition collected by van der Noot has it that when he built his capital he had to fight the Bena Munza, the inhabitants of the place. If true, it shows how weak the kingdom still was. At Kalala's death, however, the kingdom seems to have achieved its basic organization.

Very little is known about its political organization and further research by a trained anthropologist is sorely needed. Only a very rough sketch of this organization can be given. The central Luba are organized in corporate patrilineages, which do not seem to fit into any segmentary system. . . . Every lineage was comprised of clients linked by contract to the lineage and linked by domestic slaves. One or several lineages would make up a village, and the village was directed by a headman, undoubtedly chosen from the main lineage in the settlement but officially appointed by a superior chief, who could be the king himself. The headman was assisted by a council of all the heads of the lineages existing in the village. Several villages together formed a chiefdom (these chiefdoms may have preceded the kingdom), and the chiefdom was headed by a *Kilolo,* a territorial chief. Several chiefdoms formed a province with a provincial chief, and all the provinces together made up the kingdom. The territorial hierarchy, however, was not that regular. Several chiefdoms depended directly on the king, and this was even true for some villages. A number of chiefdoms seem to have been hereditary—undoubtedly those of the "owners of the land"—while others were governed by chiefs appointed by their immediate superiors and confirmed in their appointment by the king. All the chiefs, with the exception of "owners of the land," were *balopwe* [members of the lineages of Kongolo or Kalala Ilunga]. Some chiefdoms were given out for life, others only for a period of four years. In all cases the king could depose a chief. The king ruled his capital [the *kitenta*], and every king founded a new capital. . . .

The central government consisted of the king and his titleholders. Titles were ranked and various functions accrued to different titles. The most important were: the *twite,* the war leader and the head of an officer corps—the only standing police force in the kingdom; the *inabanza,* keeper of the sacred emblems and the most important provincial chief; and the third main chief, the *sungu.* Other titles varied from chiefdom to chiefdom, but important ones were the *nsikala,* or ruler during an interregnum, the *kioni,* and the *mpesi.* Many titles were expressly set aside for close relatives of the kings. Many—indeed most of the other titles—were held by his relatives, especially by members of his mother's patrilineage. Titleholders resigned at the death of the king who had appointed them and were then either replaced or reconfirmed in office. A new titleholder had to pay a heavy amount in the form of presents to the king in order to secure his nomination; thus, in many cases titles were in fact bought. Although many titles were not hereditary, close kinsmen would often succeed each other in titled positions. . . .

This sketch applies to the organization of the central area of the kingdom only, to that part of it which was inhabited by the Luba. When non-Luba groups, east or far south of the Lualaba, were conquered later, the chiefdoms would be left to their original chiefs and controlled by one or two Luba villages with a supervisor chief from the central area.

The organization as described seems to be very similar in all other Luba kingdoms, such as those of Kalundwe, Kaniok, and Kikonja. (It differs in some important aspects from the Lunda organization, which will be described later.) There is no general agreement about the succession of the *balopwe* following Kalala Ilunga. Five findings, giving the source, are summarized in Chart II, and it is clear that the situation requires intensive fieldwork and, especially for the early part of the list, that no single source can be preferred over any other.

Kalala's son Ilunga waLwefu—or Liu—is known mainly as the brother of Cibinda Ilunga (who left the kingdom to found the Lunda empire around or shortly before 1600). He was succeeded by Kasongo Mwine Kibanza, a paternal grandson of Kalala, who was challenged by all of his five healthy sons. He defeated them all and conquered new lands. Ngoi Sanza, another king, is reknowned because he decentralized the kingdom by creating numerous autonomous chiefdoms. Among his successors, Kasongo Bonswe had to fight his uncles, who had been by-passed in the succession and who were backed by their maternal clans. With his son, Mwine Kombe Dai, a first period in Luba history seems to come to an end. There are no reports about conquests after Kasongo Mwine Kibanza, and the references to internal struggles do not mention campaigns between brothers for the kingship. Conquests and fraternal struggles are the two foremost features of the next period, which begins with King Kadilo, Mwine Kombe's son. The scanty data for this first century and a half of Luba history point once again to the necessity of further studies in depth.

44. CURTIN: THE ATLANTIC SLAVE TRADE: A CENSUS

Philip D. Curtin was born in Philadelphia in 1922. After undergraduate study at Swarthmore College, he obtained his Ph.D. from Harvard University in 1953, and taught at Swarthmore and the University of Wisconsin, where he is presently Professor of History and African Languages and Literature. Active in numerous professional societies, Professor Curtin has published extensively on topics in the history of Africa and the Caribbean.

In *The Atlantic Slave Trade* Curtin demonstrates that we really know very little about the actual dimensions of one of the greatest population movements in history, which had a profound impact on the history of three continents. The numbers frequently mentioned in connection with the slave trade are shown to be based on nothing more than unthinking repetition, in one account after another, of some very general 18th- and early 19th-century "guesstimates". Professor Curtin, after carefully evaluating all the available evidence, establishes a revised figure for the total number of Africans brought to the New World.

The interest in quantification of historical data is of relatively recent origin, further evidence of the influence of the methodology of the social sciences upon historians. While numbers have little bearing upon some of their more traditional interests, such as diplomacy and the abstract history of ideas, quantification can add major dimensions to social and economic history, and to our understanding of the dynamics of politics in democratic societies.

In our example, the question whether eight or forty millions of Africans were transported to the New World—with all that differential implies about the impact of the slave trade upon the societies of Africa and America, about conditions of slavery (mortality rates, etc.) and about European economic activity and development—is surely a matter worthy of Professor Curtin's painstaking investigation. Here, as in all worthwhile applications of the quantitative method, the question "how much?" is asked not for its own sake or because of the fascination of numbers and computers, but to help answer the broader question, how events really happened in the past.

Slave Imports into Spanish America

Spanish America poses another set of problems, and a small error could be important, simply because this trade was a larger part of the whole. During most of the long centuries of the slave trade, Spain carried few slaves under her own flag. After trying unsuccessfully in the sixteenth century to break the Portuguese hold on the Africa trade, she reverted to a system of licenses or *asientos,* issued mainly to foreign firms. An asiento gave the foreign shipper permission to infringe the Spanish national monopoly over the trade of the American viceroyalties, in return for an obligation to carry a stipulated number of slaves to specified destinations over the period of the contract. One source for calculating imports into Spanish America is therefore the series of asientos, which appear to be completely recorded from 1595 to 1773, even though all asientos were not equally precise in the terms they laid down.

Furthermore, an asiento's stipulations cannot be accepted literally. The asiento was considered a great commercial prize, but not for the sake of profits to be made on the slave trade. Quality standards and duty payments required by the Spanish government were too stiff to allow a high profit on slaves alone. The *asientista* counted far more on the opportunity for illicit sales of other goods to Spanish America in return for silver. Richard Pares, one of the most authoritative economic historians of the Caribbean, has doubted that any of the series of asientistas actually made a profit from the slave trade. Few, if any, actually fulfilled the delivery stipulations of the contract. Their economic advantage was in pretending to carry more slaves than they actually did, leaving room to fill out the cargo with other goods. For this reason, delivery figures are likely to be inflated through the corruption of American customs-house officers, even though the official returns (where they exist) show that deliveries were not up to the contract stipulation. A calculation of Spanish American slave imports based on a simple addition of the quantities mentioned by each asiento in turn would therefore give a greatly inflated figure.

On the other hand, certain factors work in the oppostie direction. Most asiento contracts gave the quantities to be delivered in *piezas de India,* not individual slaves. A pieza de India was a measure of potential labor, not of individuals. For a slave to qualify as a pieza, he had to be a young adult male meeting certain specifications as to size, physical condition, and health. The very young, the old, and females were defined for commercial purposes as fractional

From Philip D. Curtin, *The Atlantic Slave Trade* (Madison: The University of Wisconsin Press; copyright © 1969 by the Regents of the University of Wisconsin), pp. 21–30.

parts of a pieza de India. This measure was convenient for Spanish imperial economic planning, where the need was a given amount of labor power, not a given number of individuals. For the historian, however, it means that the number of individuals delivered will always be greater than the number of piezas recorded. Market conditions in Africa made it impossible to buy only the prime slaves and leave all the rest, but the extent of the difference varied greatly with time and place. The definition of a pieza and its fractional values also changed. The asiento of the Portuguese Cacheu Company in 1693, for example, provided for an annual delivery in Spanish America of 4,000 slaves, so distributed in sex, age, and condition as to make up 2,500 piezas de India. This implied the expectation that the number of individuals was 60 per cent greater than the number of piezas. In this case, though, it made little difference: the company failed to meet either standard of delivery. At other times, the relationship between piezas and individuals was much closer. One cargo brought into Cartagena by the South Sea Company in 1715, for example, contained 174 individuals, assessed as 166¾ piezas, the number of individuals exceeding the number of piezas by only 4.3 per cent.

A second cause for overestimation in using asiento data is the known existence of a considerable smuggling trade. While it was to the advantage of the official asientista to deliver fewer slaves than required, the unfilled demand created a market for smuggled slaves that met no quality standards and paid no duties. This part of the slave trade to Spanish America was apparently very profitable in most periods, but extremely difficult to estimate.

In spite of these uncertainties, the asiento figures have a considerable value, not as a record of the number of slaves delivered but as a rationally conceived estimate of manpower requirements. In this sense, they are not unlike the production targets in a modern planned economy. If the Spanish officials were correct (and they had access to information that is now lost), their estimates of demand might not be far from the actual imports, though chronic complaints of a labor shortage suggest that the demand estimated in piezas de India was likely to have been met only in terms of individual slaves delivered, if that. The total contractual obligations in piezas de India can therefore be accepted as a rough estimate of individuals actually delivered in the Americas. One recent authority calculated the number of slaves allowed by the asientos from 1595 to 1640 at 132,574, and a second gives a total of 516,114 for 1641–1773. The contracts from 1595 to 1773 therefore come to 648,688 slaves, or an annual average of 2,882 for 1595–1640 and 3,880 for 1641–1773.

The husband-and-wife team of Pierre and Hugette Chaunu found in their monumental study of the Seville trade that licenses were issued for 263 ships between 1551 and 1595, with an average allowance of 138 piezas per ship. To this recorded total of 36,294 piezas for 1551–95 (810 annual average), it might be appropriate to add 500 slaves a year for the period 1521–50—the total of 15,000 being intentionally large in order to account for the trickle that entered the Spanish American possessions before 1521, and for some between 1551 and 1595 that might have escaped the Chaunu net. We are therefore left with the figures in Table 5, representing the Spanish American slave imports between 1521 and 1773. (The double set of estimates for 1595 is unavoidable in the data as found in the literature, but the degree of error introduced is not significant.)

This total of 700,000 is notably higher than Deerr's estimate of 450,000 for the slave trade to Spanish America in the asiento period—and Deerr considers that period to extend up to 1789, presumably because certain aspects of the Spanish slave trade were still controlled during the latter part of the eighteenth century. The figure may, indeed, be a little on the high side, since its origin is an administrative estimate of demand; and that demand may not have been filled at certain periods. It is accepted nevertheless as the best approximation available.

TABLE 5

ESTIMATES OF SPANISH-AMERICAN SLAVE
IMPORTS, 1521–1773

	No.	Annual average
1521–50	15,000	500
1551–95	36,300	810
1595–1640	132,600	2,880
1641–1773	516,100	3,880
Total	700,000	2,770

45. PALMER: THE AGE OF THE DEMOCRATIC REVOLUTION

Robert R. Palmer, born in Chicago in 1909, was educated at the University of Chicago and at Cornell (Ph.D. 1934). Most of his distinguished academic career, devoted to teaching and writing about the history of the 18th century and the French Revolution, was spent at Princeton University. Presently R. R. Palmer is Professor of History at Yale University. In his two volumes on *The Age of the Democratic Revolution,* from the first of which, *The Challenge,* the following passage is taken, Professor Palmer describes developments that occurred in the last third of the 18th century in large parts of Europe as well as in America. He perceives them as part of one great revolutionary movement, born out of the spread of the ideas of the Enlightenment and the growing inadequacy of the Old Regime in the face of social changes common to the whole Western world. The work exemplifies the widening of perspectives among contemporary Western historians beyond national boundaries and a new vindication of the view that the Atlantic civilizations share a common heritage.

In Western Civilization, in the middle of the eighteenth century, there was no novelty in discussions of liberty, or human equality, or law, or limited government, or constitutional rights, or the sovereignty of the people. Greek and medieval philosophy, Roman law, Christian theology, and baronial rebellions had all made contributions to one such idea or another. A marked democratic movement had expressed itself in the English revolution during the 1640's, and the history of many European towns was full of clashes between populace and patricians. Such popular movements, however, had been local, sporadic, and unsuccessful; and of general ideas, such as ultimate human equality, or government with the consent of the governed, it is well known that the more general such ideas are the more variegated and contradictory may be the actual practices with which men learn to live. Actual practice, about 1750, was such that certain old ideas, or old words and phrases, took on a new application and a wider and more urgent meaning.

From Volume I, "The Challenge," by R. R. Palmer, *The Age of the Democratic Revolution: A Political History of Europe and America, 1769-1800* (copyright © 1959 by Princeton University Press; Princeton Paperback, 1969), pp. 20-24. Reprinted by permission of Princeton University Press.

If we say that a revolutionary era began about 1760, it is not because any persons or any organizations intended or worked in advance for a revolution. The modern conception of a revolutionary movement is the result, not the cause, of the revolutionary era that we are discussing. "Revolution" was a familiar word, but it usually meant no more than the revolving fortunes of governments, without great impersonal causes or any long-run direction; one might speak of Chancellor Maupeou's "revolution" in France in 1770, or the King of Sweden's "revolution" of 1772. The situation that began to develop about 1760 was revolutionary in a deeper way.

By a revolutionary situation is here meant one in which confidence in the justice or reasonableness of existing authority is undermined; where old loyalties fade, obligations are felt as impositions, law seems arbitrary, and respect for superiors is felt as a form of humiliation; where existing sources of prestige seem undeserved, hitherto accepted forms of wealth and income seem ill-gained, and government is sensed as distant, apart from the governed and not really "representing" them. In such a situation the sense of community is lost, and the bond between social classes turns to jealousy and frustration. People of a kind formerly integrated begin to feel as outsiders, or those who have never been integrated begin to feel left out. As a group of Sheffield workingmen demanded in 1794: "What is the constitution to us if we are nothing to it?"

No community can flourish if such negative attitudes are widespread or long-lasting. The crisis is a crisis of community itself, political, economic, sociological, personal, psychological, and moral at the same time. Actual revolution need not follow, but it is in such situations that actual revolution does arise. Something must happen, if continuing deterioration is to be avoided; some new kind or basis of community must be formed.

What we shall see in the following chapters is a groping toward a new kind of community. With it went the struggles of opposed ideas and interests. It has often been said, on the authority of no less a person than Alexis de Tocqueville, that the French Revolution was over before it began, that it was the work of men's minds before they made it the work of their hands. This idea can be misleading, for with it one may miss the whole reality of struggle. The Revolution was not merely the attempt to realize in practice ideas which had already conquered in the realm of thought. No ideas had "conquered"; there was no "climate of opinion" of any specific social or political content. The Revolution was a conflict between incompatible conceptions of what the community ought to be, and it carried out with violence a conflict that had already come into being. There is no reason to suppose (if we put aside historical metaphysics) that one side in this conflict was moribund, the other abounding with vigor; one, old and doomed in any case to extinction, the other, new and already riding upon the wave of the future. It is sufficiently enlightening to see it simply as a conflict, in which either antagonist would prevail at the expense of the other. It is hoped that readers of this book, whichever way their own sympathies may lie, may at least agree, upon finishing it, on the reality of the conflict.

In the absence of better words, and not wishing to invent more colorless sociological terms, we think of the parties to this essential conflict, so far as they may be reduced simply to two sides, as the proponents of "aristocratic" and "democratic" forms of the community, emotionally overcharged or semantically ambiguous though these words may be. It is held that both democratic and aristocratic forces were gaining strength after about 1760, that revolution came because both were rising, and that they took the form of revolution and counterrevolution at the close of the century, and of democratically and conservatively oriented philosophies thereafter. It follows that conservatism and counterrevolution were no mere "reactions" against revolution, but eighteenth-century forces against which revolution was itself a reaction. This idea is not the invention of the present author: recent works on the American Revolution emphasize the growing conservatism in British Parliamentary circles before 1775; Professor Valjavec insists that conservatism in Germany antedated the agitation of the 1790's; French historians stress the "aristocratic resurgence" preceding the eruption of 1789.

The next chapter sets up one of the guiding conceptions of the book, that of certain "constituted bodies," in Europe and America, most of them predominantly aristocratic in 1760, and including parliaments, councils, assemblies, and magistracies of various kinds. A continuing and universal theme of the period is the attempts of these constituted bodies to defend their corporate liberties and their independence, against either superior authorities on the one hand or popular pressures on the other. Resisting superior authorities, these bodies could be liberal and even revolutionary. The democratic revolutionary movement, however, came into play when persons systematically excluded from these bodies, and not content merely with the independence of these bodies as already constituted, attempted to open up their membership, change the basis of authority and representation, reconstitute the constituted bodies, or obtain a wholly new constitution of the state itself. The third chapter deals further with the philosophy and the problems which institutionalized aristocracy brought into existence. Chapter IV traces the conflicts of the aristocratic constituted bodies with kings in the 1760's and 1770's in France, Sweden, and the Hapsburg empire. Chapter V explores the clash of a similar body at the town of Geneva with its own citizens.

With Chapter VI begins the treatment of the English-speaking world, involving the structure of Parliament, the British constitution, and the American Revolution. Chapters VII and VIII consider the American Revolution, and the sense in which I believe it to have been truly revolutionary. It is shown in Chapter IX that the American Revolution, whatever its true nature, greatly added to the democratic and revolutionary spirit in Europe, to the desire, that is, for a reconstitution of government and society.

But while this spirit was rising, actual events followed the course of an aristocratic resurgence, traced in Chapters X to XIV. The parliamentary class in the 1780's in Britain and Ireland stopped the moves for democratization. Dutch, Belgian, and Swiss patricians put down the democrats in their respective countries. Whether an American upper class blocked the growth of democracy in the new United States federal constitution of 1787 is also considered. The privileged classes of the Hapsburg empire obstructed the equalizing reforms of the Hapsburg rulers. The Polish revolution failed. For a time it even seemed that the French Revolution might reinforce the privileged classes. But in the events of 1789, as explained in Chapter XV, the French revolutionaries laid down the principles of a more democratic form of state. The book closes with further comments on the relationship of the French and American revolutions. The story is brought, for all countries, to about the year 1791, to the eve of the great war in which all these national and social developments were to be gathered together into one tremendous struggle.

SOURCE NOTES

1. From Erwin Iserloh, *The Theses Were Not Posted* (Boston: Beacon Press, 1968). German text copyright © by Aschendorff, Münster. English translation and notes copyright © by Jared Wicks, S.J. Pp. 18-19, 19-20, 23, 46, 48-49, 50-51, 62-67, 108-110 reprinted by permission by Beacon Press.
2. From Charles A. Beard, *Economic Origins of Jeffersonian Democracy* (New York: 1915), pp. 1-7.
3. From Pierre Goubert, *Louis XIV and Twenty Million Frenchmen* (New York: Random House, 1970). Vintage Books edition. Copyright © 1966 by Librairie Arthème Fayard. Translation